Thinking Through Blake

ALSO BY HAZARD ADAMS

*William Blake on His Poetry and Painting:
A Study of* A Descriptive Catalogue, *Other Prose
Writings and* Jerusalem (McFarland, 2011)

*Blake's Margins: An Interpretive Study
of the Annotations* (McFarland, 2009)

Academic Child: A Memoir (McFarland, 2008)

Thinking Through Blake

Essays in Literary Contrariety

HAZARD ADAMS

McFarland & Company, Inc., Publishers
Jefferson, North Carolina

LIBRARY OF CONGRESS CATALOGUING-IN-PUBLICATION DATA

Adams, Hazard, 1926–
    Thinking through Blake : essays in literary contrariety / Hazard Adams.
        p.   cm.
    Includes bibliographical references and index.

    ISBN 978-0-7864-7958-0 (softcover : acid free paper) ∞
    ISBN 978-1-4766-1573-8 (ebook)

    1. Blake, William, 1757–1827—Criticism and interpretation. I. Title.

PR4147.A627 2014
821'.7—dc23   2014005175

BRITISH LIBRARY CATALOGUING DATA ARE AVAILABLE

© 2014 Hazard Adams. All rights reserved

No part of this book may be reproduced or transmitted in any form or by any means, electronic or mechanical, including photocopying or recording, or by any information storage and retrieval system, without permission in writing from the publisher.

On the cover: *The Complaint and the Consolation* print by William Blake, ca. 1797 (Yale Center for British Art, Paul Mellon Collection)

Manufactured in the United States of America

McFarland & Company, Inc., Publishers
  Box 611, Jefferson, North Carolina 28640
    www.mcfarlandpub.com

In memory of
Diana Violet White Adams
July 10, 1924–September 6, 2013

Contents

Notes on the Text	viii
Introduction, Which Could Be a Conclusion	1
Blake, *Jerusalem*, and Symbolic Form (1975)	17
Contemporary Ideas of Literature: Terrible Beauty or Rough Beast? (1977)	40
Essay on Frye (1991)	65
Reynolds, Vico, *Blackwell*, Blake: The Fate of Allegory (1993)	70
The World-View of William Blake in Relation to Cultural Policy (1993)	86
Conference 2: Chinese and Japanese-American Literary Relations (1994)	98
Is (Was) There No Tradition of Defense of Poetry in Chinese Culture? Why Has There Had to Be One in the West? (1995)	108
Four Problems (Among Many) for Humanistic Thought (1995)	122
"Literature" and the Visionary Tradition (1995)	127
"Literature" into "Ecriture"? (1995)	131
"An Antithetical Turn" (1996)	134
Ekphrasis Revisited, or Antitheticality Reconstructed (2000)	148
Quest and Cycle (2005)	161
Origin(ality) (2007)	165
The Marriage of Imagination and Intellect (2013)	171
Chapter Notes	183
Index	191

Notes on the Text

Essays in this book that have been published before appear as they originally did with the exception of a few small corrections and a few changes in wording. Brief prefaces written for all the essays in this book appear in brackets. Some comments and a few new footnotes that appear in the text in brackets have been added to the previously published essays. Identifications of original publication appear in the prefaces. All footnoted references to quotations from the writings of William Blake refer to *The Complete Poetry and Prose of William Blake*, ed. David V. Erdman (New York: Anchor Books, 1988) and are marked with E.

In some of these quotations I have inserted bracketed punctuation marks not in Blake's original text.

Introduction, Which Could Be a Conclusion

I

This book contains, in chronological order, a selection of essays I have written between 1975 and 2013, some previously published, some not. Each was written to stand alone, but taken together in chronological order, they reflect the development of literary thought as I have observed it since about 1965. Taken together, they chart also the development of what I have come to call my own neo–Blakean literary thought, which I regard as an effort to seek a proper ground for the practice of literary criticism, not a method but a philosophical base. It implies for both poetry (in the larger sense of imaginative literature) and criticism particular cultural roles, which I call, stealing from William Blake, "contrariety." Even Essays Six and Seven, which deal with the relation of Chinese literary thought to that of the West and may at first strike the reader as a curious interlude, bear obliquely on my neo–Blakean interests. Two essays address the work of other critics, the first (Essay Three) is about the great Blakean Northrop Frye, who with his *Fearful Symmetry: A Study of William* Blake (1947) had much to do with bringing Blake to prominence in the latter half of the twentieth century. The second (Essay Twelve) discusses the work of my late colleague Murray Krieger. The final essay ranges into the cultural and academic situation of the humanities, especially literary study, and discusses the relevant connection Blake expressed between intellect and imagination. In several of the essays, I either concentrate on Blake's work or turn to the notion of contrariety, derived from his writings.

The rest of this introduction could well serve as a concluding summary essay setting forth as succinctly as I can the neo–Blakean position at which I arrived and the intellectual moments that led me to it. Some critics may claim that I have distorted Blake to my own purposes. In what may be a hope-

Introduction

less effort to placate, I remind readers that my position is neo–Blakean, not Blakean.

II

My movement toward a neo–Blakean literary theory began innocently enough with *Blake and Yeats: The Contrary Vision*, published in 1955.[1] It grew toward *Philosophy of the Literary Symbolic* (1983) and then *The Offense of Poetry* (2007),[2] published, I regret to say, to virtual silence. In 1969, I had written an essay titled "Blake and the Postmodern," in which I tried to show that Blake had become a major influence in literature and literary criticism as the latter had moved beyond the New Criticism.[3] The dominant movement of the time was quickly to become Deconstruction, introduced to America in a lecture presented by Jacques Derrida at Johns Hopkins University in 1966 and published in English in 1970.[4] That lecture subjected to critique the treatment of language in the anthropological structuralism of Claude Levi-Strauss.

Structuralism had been popular in France and had invaded literary and other thought through the work of Roland Barthes and others. However, mainly because of Derrida's critique, it had a very short life in America. As the New Criticism had been in the 1930s and 1940s, Deconstruction was centered at Yale University. There, in addition to Derrida's presence, Paul de Man offered his own version with a strong influence of existentialism. J. Hillis Miller was won over from what had first been a commitment to the New Criticism and later phenomenological criticism, principally that of Georges Poulet. At Yale, Geoffrey Hartman wrote about Deconstruction.

The first edition of my anthology *Critical Theory Since Plato* (1971) did not include Derrida or any mention of Deconstruction. The penultimate essay in it was Murray Krieger's "The Existential Basis of Contextual Criticism," an effort to bring the New Criticism in line with Krieger's tendency toward the existential.[5] This matter arises again here in Essay Twelve, where I discuss Krieger's differences with and similarities to Paul de Man's form of Deconstruction.

Literary criticism was dominated by Deconstruction, despite the fact that Derrida wrote mainly about philosophical texts. As the twentieth century wore on, it gave way (despite leaving significant traces) to various political interests. Feminist criticism and scholarship brought to attention the work

Introduction, Which Could Be a Conclusion

of many women writers of the past, and the emerging gender studies had compelling interests other than literary criticism's interest in language, which had been dominant for some time. The later writings of Edward Said addressed issues of colonialism. Michel Foucault's work focussed on "power relations." The New Historicism often displayed connections to Marxist political thought, which had something of a resurgence. There arose questions of what belonged in the so-called literary canon and whether the whole idea of a canon was not merely a result of the manipulation of political power (including patriarchal power). These developments did not reflect the linguistic emphasis that had dominated philosophy since the late nineteenth century.

In previous writings I have, with deliberate simplification, divided the history of Western literary thought into four phases: The ontological, the epistemological, the linguistic, and the politically moralistic. Perhaps the most interesting thing about these phases is that each of them flourished for a shorter time than its predecessor. The ontological was dominant from before Plato into the Renaissance and never completely died out. The epistemological flourished from the seventeenth century well into the nineteenth and remains important. The linguistic came to real prominence in the twentieth century. In literary thought, Deconstruction was part of this, the last part, before political morality in its variety of forms became the principal characteristic of literary criticism.

Along with the growth and sudden ubiquity of information, generated by the digital revolution, discourses of all kinds have spread over the globe. As the anthropologist Clifford Geertz observed in 1980, the recognized genres in all disciplines were now "blurred."[6] Indeed, the word "literature" itself became blurred. Is there such a thing? Is there only "writing?"

The early and continuing influence of Blake on my work caused me to depart from the popular line of criticism and theory I have just discussed. One way to describe the difference is to recall the once famous argument between two prominent twentieth-century philosophers. I had early been attracted to Cassirer's work, which as a student I came upon in my father's study: Cassirer's *An Essay on Man* (1944) and the translation of two earlier works in one volume, *Substance and Function* (1910) and *Einstein's Theory of Relativity* (1921).[7] Heidegger I came to far later through his critique of Kant, *Being and Time*, and his literary essays.

Cassirer, influenced predominantly by Kant, held to the unknowability of the thing in itself (*ding an sich*) and developed the notion that knowledge

Introduction

was created within the symbolic forms of human creation: language, myth, art, science, history, and religion. With respect to language and its related form, myth, Cassirer was influenced by Giambattista Vico and Wilhelm von Humboldt:

> Man cannot escape from his own achievement. He cannot but adopt the conditions of his own life. No longer in a merely physical universe, man lives in a symbolic universe. Language, myth, art, and religion are parts of this universe. They are the varied threads which weave the symbolic net, the tangled web of human experience.... No longer can man confront reality immediately.[8]

This was anathema to Heidegger, who saw Cassirer's position, in spite of the inclusion of religion among the symbolic forms, as cut off from any real sense of the divine, or of reality. Heidegger's hatred of technology was in line with his rejection of Cassirer's symbolic forms. Heidegger's existential phenomenology clashed with Cassirer's neo-Kantianism.

An irony appears with respect to the two opposed lines of thought that Cassirer and Heidegger represented. Both in their own ways imprisoned human beings, one in the symbolic forms, the other in differential language (if we presume that Derrida proceeds from the Heidegger line).

My experience with Cassirer was followed by a reading of Vico's *New Science*. This remarkable book grounded primitive human experience and thought in what he called "poetic logic," which produced not abstract universals, of which primitive man was not capable, but "imaginative universals," to which an image is always fundamental: Pomona for all fruits, for example.[9]

The connection of all of this to Blake lies finally in Blake's emphasis on imagination. Most important, Blake connected imagination to intellect. I shall discuss this matter in Essay Fifteen. More radical than either Cassirer or Heidegger, Blake thought that reality was created by human imagination, infused by deity. W. B. Yeats called Blake a "too literal realist of the imagination." He certainly was a realist in that sense, but the addition of "too" contributed to the many suggestions that Blake was a mystic. It is true that Blake did not think, as Cassirer did, that human beings were trapped in their own creations. However, he did not assume the existence of a reality beyond the power of human imagination. He believed that perception needed improvement and that human beings were capable of improving it. The access to the real was art and science. Unlike Heidegger, he was not suspicious of what he called, in the last line of *The Four Zoas*, "sweet science." Indeed, despite his complaints about an epistemology based on the division of subject from object, he had an interest in science.[10]

An independent line of literary thought, with the important exception of the influence of Northrop Frye's *Anatomy of Criticism* (1957), did not develop at about the same time as Deconstruction or later. My work seems to have become its solitary representative in spite of much important scholarly and interpretive work on Blake.

III

"Criticism" has always been a problematic word. In one sense, it has implied negative judgment, in another an allegedly objective judgment, in still another interpretation and analysis. With respect to literature, or poetry in the larger sense, the last meaning became dominant, but in practice it has often been mixed with the others. What today most people call "critical theory," in a few cases associated strictly with commentary on literature, grew out of a European movement transferred in the mid-twentieth century to the United States by Max Horkheimer and Theodor W. Adorno, among others. It was sociological and political at its base and not limited or even mainly limited to the treatment of literature. Many American academics in college English and foreign language departments came to practice "theory" with an ideological emphasis. In time, all movements decay, and they flourish and come to decay far more rapidly than a century ago and before. The "theory" movement decayed into "cultural studies," in which "literary theory" in its old sense of a philosophical inquiry into the nature of literature effectively disappeared.

Given what has happened, I have adopted, as you have noticed by now, Stephen Owen's "literary thought," which I found in the title of his *Readings in Chinese Literary Thought* (1992). I introduce "criticism" at the beginning here partly to recall Alexander Pope's "An Essay on Criticism" and to offer "literary thought" as a philosophical ground for the activity of criticism. It is a "contrary" (about which I'll have more to say) to Pope's support of the externally imposed rules of "nature methodized." But Pope, I am happy to note, also wrote, "Some beauties yet no precept can declare" and "license is a rule." Rules, of course, have an historically instructive value; they rise and fall over time and in any age are part of a language describing what poets and critics have done, do, or are trying to do. The imposition of any set of rules or notions of taste, political or otherwise, becomes in time decadent and mostly irrelevant when its period of fashion has ended, though it remains of historical interest. Still, it can remind us to oppose an anarchy of attitude that would wholly reject a tradition of poetic utterance and the cultural role of poetry. Poems belong to poetry and its history, whether their authors know it or not.

IV

The history of literary thought can be written as a history of oppositions either between what poetry is and what it is not, or between two or more different ideas of what poetry is and does. The first of these oppositions seems to have been the Platonic one of the alleged irrationality of poetry and poets on the one hand and the rationality represented par excellence by mathematics on the other. The latter, of course, is identified with a claimed knowledge of reality against a claimed distortion of it perpetrated by poets. The literary views of Plato's Socrates are, however, more curious and varied than histories have sometimes acknowledged, for Socrates, who is not Plato, also declares that poets are possessed by a divine madness, which can hardly be all bad. He must admit that the possession might be demonic and there would be no way to tell whether it should be trusted to offer truth. Given the erratic behavior of the all-too-human gods of Greek mythology, the demonic might seem a distinct possibility. In addition, Plato's Socrates was a strong admirer of Homer and other poets.

The language of literary thought and criticism changes, but traces of the Platonic opposition linger in various guises. "Subjectivity," for example, succeeded irrationality and divine madness. "Objectivity" succeeded Platonic rationality. John Locke's distinction between primary and secondary qualities of experience lurks behind these terms. In his view, only the objective and primary qualities—the measurable—reflected reality.

On quasi–Platonic grounds, poetry would continue to be defended as utterance beyond the purview of rationality alone. Sometimes it was connected to religious mysticism, but at the same time mystical experience was often declared to be beyond words. In another version of defense, poetry was said to rise to allegorical expression of forms or ideas. In still another, poetic subjectivity made possible the expression of sentiment and feeling not accomplishable by rationality.

Introduction, Which Could Be a Conclusion

In all of these cases, an opposition, growing out of Plato, has been sustained by enmity toward or denigration of the role of poetry in human culture. Defenders of poetry were driven, and are still driven, into a position where it seems necessary to accept and work within an opposition that denigrates poetry even in cases where subjectivity is declared to be of value. Among these oppositions are

1. rationality and reason   irrationality
2. mathematics   poetry
3. object   subject
4. externality   internality
5. rules   anarchy
6. judgment   feeling
7. allegory   symbolism

The first four on this list are generally regarded as philosophical in nature, the latter three applicable to literature and adopted by criticism, though number five, of course, has moral, religious, and political sources.

Immanuel Kant reworked number four into a distinction between the "internal purposiveness" (sometimes "purposiveness without purpose") of the aesthetic object and the external purposiveness of science. The difficulty of doing this is revealed in the probably unintentional irony of a purposiveness without purpose. These words remain captured by an opposition that has traditionally favored one side, even as Kant attempted to overcome it. For that matter, "internal purposiveness" is also similarly captured. Nevertheless, as an influence on thinking about poetry, Kant made a significant advance.

Kant had recognized, after writing his critiques of pure and practical reason, that he had neglected what he came to call the "aesthetic," a term borrowed from the philosopher and psychologist Alexander Baumgarten, who published in 1750 a book called *Aesthetics*. Kant made possible a means of thinking about art as having an order or formal nature of its own. Of course, "form" is trapped in an opposition in which its opponent "content" is privileged. The opposition suggests the later distinction between allegory and symbolism, in which on the allegorical side the allegorical meaning is thought to be a poem's proper content and all else decoration. The symbolist movement can be seen as, among other things, an effort to oppose this notion.

The idea of art as not subject to judgment on an external principle was filtered into the revolutionary, and sometimes hysterical, pronouncements of artists themselves, as in the Pre-Raphaelites, Decadents, Surrealists, and

Dadaists. All remained captured by the oppositions inside of which they struggled to defend their arts.

V

William Blake's poetry is grounded on oppositions that he early called "contraries." This term persists from its first utterance in *The Marriage of Heaven and Hell* into his long poems *Milton* and *Jerusalem*. The significance expands as his work develops. Blake's statement in which "contraries" first occurs may be the most quoted one in all of his prose. The notion comes to provide an opposition to the oppositions I have mentioned and many others as well:

> Without Contraries is no progression. Attraction and Repulsion, Reason and Energy, Love and Hate, are necessary to human existence.
> From these contraries spring what the religious call Good & Evil. Good is the passive that obeys Reason [.] Evil is the active springing from Energy [E34].

This passage implies that some things are attractive, but also that it is necessary for some things to be repelled; some things should be loved, some things hated. Reason is fixed in its methods; energy is expansive. Reason analyzes; energy makes. In human history and culture, energy precedes reason, which systematizes and uses what energy has created.

Good and evil are ideas that proceeded from those contraries, which tend over time to decay into what Blake has both his character Los (E162) and his Milton call "negations," employed by the powerful to their own ends (E142). The idea is already present, though not named, in Plate 11 of *The Marriage*, where we are told that the naming power of the "ancient poets" eventually became corrupted by the powerful into a system of tyranny and one side of a contrary came to dominate (negate) the other.

> Till a system was formed, which some took advantage of & enslav'd the vulgar by attempting to realize or abstract the mental deities from their objects: thus began Priesthood.
> Choosing forms of worship from poetic tales.
> And at length they pronounced that the Gods had orderd such things.
> Thus men forgot that All deities reside in the human breast [E38].

The idea appears even earlier in *All Religions Are One*, where Blake introduces "Poetic Genius" as the creative energy fundamental to human identity. "Sects of Philosophy" are derived from that genius, as are organized religions "adapted to the weaknesses of every individual" (E1). The Bible is poetry, an "original" derivation from that genius and not one corrupted by the process of negation, except by its interpreters. The threat from a reason that has become overbearing, recognized here, is expressed as follows:

> The bounded is loathed by its possessor. The same dull round even of a univer[s]e would soon become a mill with complicated wheels [E2].

The "possessor," the worker of energy into system and fixity, the owner of power, in this instance the reasoner, comes to despise those whom he has enslaved and even enslaves himself in the process:

> Those who restrain desire, do so because theirs is weak enough to be restrained; and the restrainer or reason usurps its place & governs the unwilling [E34].

Blake here seems to be saying two things: first, that those who restrain their own desire are weak; second, that people with weak desire restrain that of others. This passivity generates a tyranny of followers and results eventually in fear, revolt, and a repeatable cyclicity of oppression and violence. Organized religion is the result of the process of decay: "Choosing forms of worship from poetic tales" (E38). In *The Four Zoas*, the process is described as eventually "Petrifying all the Human Imagination into rock & sand" (2:25; E314). History is cyclical, imaginative energy inventing, reason appropriating. In *The Marriage*, this is described as the actions of two portions of being; one is the "prolific," and the other the "devouring." Contrariety descends into "negation," but the original opposition is necessary and requires renewal.

The second chapter of *Milton* begins with a description of a place where "Contrarieties are equally True" (30[33]: 1; E129). Here "no dispute can come." It is a place of repose and sleep. In waking life, this contrariety exists in tension, which is of two kinds—the prolific "war and hunting" (E135) of ideas, dialectical "conversation," and the negative war and hunting of physical strife. "Negations" are the illusions of reason's drive for power. Contraries are real until they collapse into negations. Blake's prophetic character Los is correct when he declares in *Jerusalem*,

> Negations are not Contraries: Contraries mutually Exist:
> But Negations Exist Not [1:17, 34; E162].

Illusions are real, but only *as* illusions. Although he may seem to give actual existence to negations, Blake's Milton is right to declare,

Introduction

> There is a Negation, & there is a Contrary
> The Negation must be destroyd to redeem the Contraries [2: 31–32; E142].

He sees negations as illusions. Illusions are real.

When the Four Zoas "conversed together" at the end of *Jerusalem*, they have been redeemed as contraries after having fallen into negation. This conversation is proper "war and hunting," and reason in the form of Urizen, which word can be pronounced as "your reason" or "you risen," depending on his state of mind, has been described as a confused and pathetic wanderer, but is among the contraries in the end redeemed. There is no negating of him by the others, for that would commit the error that Blake's great poems oppose:

> And they conversed together in Visionary forms dramatic which bright
> Redounded from their Tongues in thunderous majesty, in Visions
> In new Expanses, creating exemplars of Memory and of Intellect
> Creating Space, Creating Time according to the wonders Divine
> Of Human Imagination... [98: 28–32; E257–58].

VI

Blake's dramatization of the struggle of contraries against negations describes the imagination (energy, in *The Marriage*) creatively opposing the drive to contain: "The cistern contains: the fountain overflows" (E36). The fundamental Blakean trope is synecdoche, which declares the identity of part and whole and plays an important role in this drama. "Identity" contains a metaphor: it expresses sameness even as it expresses difference. Things, like twins and like the two sides of a metaphor, are identical, but each has its own unique identity. In the conclusion of *Jerusalem*, it is declared that "All Human Forms" are "identified" (99:1; E258). This means, if we recall the actions of Blake's "ancient poets," that everything gets its name and in that name an identity, "even Tree Metal Earth & Stone" (99:1; E258). These, too, are "human forms." They, like ourselves, being named, are "mental," products of human imagination. In identifying each form, naming gives identity in the sense of uniqueness, but it also identifies all things as related to each other, metaphorically the same.

Metaphor can be thought of as horizontal, synecdoche as vertical, the latter as follows:

Introduction, Which Could Be a Conclusion

> To see a World in a Grain of Sand
> And a Heaven in a Wild Flower
> Hold Infinity in the palm of your hand
> And Eternity in an hour [*Auguries of Innocence*, 1–4; E490].

The principle here is synecdoche, as in one of the "Proverbs of Hell" in *The Marriage*: "One thought. fills immensity" (E36). Is there a sameness of and difference between contraries? If we return to Socrates' opposition of mathematics to poetry, what do we find? Mathematics is applicable in some way to everything in nature, while at the same time it is enclosed in its own system of number. Numbers as words have no fixed denotation except in relation to each other, that is, brought into the containing form of mathematics. At the same time, number is potentially infinite in both directions. In addition to this, the fractal looks very much like, is perhaps identical to, the poetic trope of synecdoche. Are mathematics and poetry both infinite containers, both same and different? Words accrue new meanings and lose meaning over time; in time language is potentially infinite.

VII

The most influential literary criticism that found philosophical support in Kant's *Critique of Judgment* was the American New Criticism, which flourished in the thirties and forties of the twentieth century. It began as resistance to the dominance of historical literary scholarship, and found its ground in Kant's concept of "internal purposiveness." Its appearance can also be seen as parallel to a shift in western philosophy toward concern with language, a move that Kant did not make, but some of his followers did. Well-known in the New Criticism was a phrase invented by the scholar-critic Cleanth Brooks—"the heresy of paraphrase," which declared the impossibility of successfully substituting without loss an interpretation for the poem itself. For Brooks, a paraphrase was an abstraction that could never contain the poem's "meaning," though "being" is a better word for what Brooks had in mind. In other words, an interpretation could never "negate" the independence of a poem by translating it into reason's terms. The New Criticism insisted on internality of meaning. Northrop Frye, not really among the New Critics, but certainly a Blakean, declared that if Shakespeare had been asked what something in one of his plays meant, he would have had to answer that he meant it to be part of the play. The poem itself was the container of its meaning.

Introduction

The turn to language of the New Critics had connections with neo-Kantian developments in philosophy as represented by Cassirer's *Philosophy of Symbolic Forms*. The problem for poetry in Cassirer's system was that poetry belonged to the symbolic form of art but remained within the symbolic form of language, his attitude toward which didn't seem quite to include it. This raised a number of questions. Is language at its temporal source a poetical form, as Giambattista Vico argued in *The New Science*, and if Vico was right about its origin, was it born only to find its ideal, meaningful form in a positive logic, as seems too nearly suggested by Cassirer?

As there is infinity and the infinitesimal in mathematics is there a kind of infinity for a poem in its existence in and synecdochically as the form of poetry? We are able to recognize a poem from the past as poetry. Sometimes we have trouble recognizing a contemporary one as poetry, and we cannot declare what might be a poem in the future. Is language, itself, originally poetic? Is its dynamism connected to this? Is language itself a potentially infinite poem? It seems capable of producing an infinite number of words and a plethora of meaning. Once in a great while, someone consciously attempts to make clear that poetry has an infinite potentiality even as the poem created is a container. Blake's *Jerusalem* and Joyce's *Finnegans Wake* are examples. They are what Frye called "encyclopedic" works. Frye declared that the center of poetry is the poem you happen to be reading. This would be what Blake thought of as a "center" that expands potentially to a "circumference," a potentially infinite container. Synecdoche, in its greatest form as macrocosm and microcosm, is the fundamental trope of what Vico called "poetic logic." It is ironic that he had to call on "logic" to describe the original poetic form of language.

It is not surprising that with the move in philosophy to language in the last hundred years or more there were suddenly so many poems about poems, showing that poets were becoming almost obsessively concerned with what poems are or do. One might notice also that Jacques Derrida's Deconstruction, which created the major moment in literary thought of the latter half of the twentieth century, might seem to have risen out of, though it did not, Vico's "poetic logic." Many critics have claimed that Derrida destroyed meaning; but it would be far better to claim that he posed an infinite potentiality of meaning, which, more rigorously than Brooks, would have to deny the possibility of a paraphrase or a final interpretation. Derrida was, of course, usually writing about all language and philosophical

Introduction, Which Could Be a Conclusion

texts, not poetry. Vico's "poetic logic" is language prior to all other forms of it. Blake's "ancient poets," prior to "system," named the things of the world.

In all of Cassirer's "symbolic forms" except art, meaning is externalized; that is, each form posits something supposedly external to which its symbols point, and the criterion of judgment is accuracy, verifiability. Each seems to point outward but its capacity for meaning and description is contained in its form. The pointing out is a part of the "fiction" (in the sense of making) of its form. The content of these forms changes in time as their languages expand and contract. Blake wrote,

> Reason or the ratio of all things we have already known. is not the same that it shall be when we know more [*There Is No Natural Religion*, E2].

What we know are the fictions that our imaginations create. A problem arises when some fictions come to be believed to possess fixed truth, negating the imaginative fictions of other forms operating according to other internal "rules."

Symbolic systems that divide things into, for example, the seven oppositions that I have listed are useful. When those oppositions come to be believed *in* and fall into negations, they have overreached their own boundaries and become tools of the tyranny that Blake in "London" called "mind-forg'd manacles" (E27), negations, where the opposite is demonized and suppressed.

In *Milton*, the place where "contrarieties are equally true" is called Beulah. It is an ideal mental place in which contrariety is relaxed, but not destroyed, not the world of common consciousness where we spend most of our lives and where the strife of contraries, when not fallen into negations, makes "progression" possible. As I have indicated, in one sense negations are not contraries, but illusions. In another, they are fallen contraries that need to be redeemed for creative use. They must be "destroyd" as negations, as Blake's Milton says (40[46], 33; E142), and they must again become part of intellectual life and its "war and hunting."

The way to oppose negation is to introduce a third term, contrary to the negating opposition as such, yet redeeming it as a useful fiction. Most important, that term must recognize, as others often do not, its own fiction-making. This, it seems to me, is implicit, or at least potential, in Blake's notion of contraries and negations.

VIII

What, then, is literary criticism, if it still rarely exists in the often negating face of "theory" and "cultural studies" as these words are commonly used today? It is not poetry that is the hybrid it seems to have to be in Cassirer's *An Essay on Man*. The hybrid is criticism. Pope's "An Essay on Criticism" is a poem, and at the same time it is regularly reproduced in anthologies of the history of criticism. Though Pope's title declares it to be *about* criticism, as his poem has grown older it has been moved closer and closer to the purely poetical. Certainly written to lay down the laws of poetry and taste that critics should follow, the poem becomes more and more an utterance dramatizing its speaker as a certain kind of person in a certain age with certain ways of judging. It becomes a poetic fiction. We look into the poem for that drama. We look outward from it to grasp its historical and cultural significance.

Literary thought, as I employ it here, is concerned with a philosophical ground for thinking about poetry. Criticism is properly a way of speaking to a reader about poems and poetry. It properly judges by the attention it gives to a poem and its desire to mediate, not by its declaration that this is good or this is bad. It is properly a hybrid, different from Pope's poem. Criticism is usually written in prose and stands, when done well, in friendly contrariety both to poetry and to discourse directed toward other subjects. There has never been a "science" of criticism, though it is directed toward a kind of analysis and interpretation. It is always imperfect in that it cannot duplicate the meaning of a poem, if that is what people expect of it, and it should be in this sense imperfect. R. P. Blackmur once wrote that criticism is an unfortunate necessity, implying that a mediator between poem and reader is often needed. Why?

It is needed because of the negations in the culture that dominate the thought and language of readers, principally the one of objectivity and subjectivity. In order to communicate, criticism has to employ the thought and language of the culture but must oppose it at the same time. It cannot itself become a poem about a poem and lose the mediating position that is its only reason for being. Criticism is not a third term contrary to negations. That is poetry.

Literary thought must declare that criticism must be ironic about itself. The New Criticism made much of irony in poems, raising it almost to a defining principle, but the principal necessary irony is that of criticism, which stands in an ironic relation to poetry and to readers, and to itself. From the first, it must keep a respectful distance. To the reader, it must be a constant reminder of the importance of what Vico called "poetic logic," which is the true contrary to the previously mentioned negations. To itself, it must admit its unredeemable provisionality. It knows that negations can be useful but must be redeemed as belonging to forms of fiction of the imagination. It is in this knowledge that criticism finds its cultural and educational role. A reviewer of my book *Philosophy of the Literary Symbolic* (1983) complained that I left nothing for criticism to do. Nonsense. There is always more to be said. Criticism is always provisional. The best becomes a part of the history of criticism itself.

Blake, *Jerusalem*, and Symbolic Form (1975)

[The composition of this essay has a brief history. Part of it was offered at a meeting of the Modern Language Association of America in 1972. A later version, principally Part One, appeared in *New Literary History* in 1973. The discussion of *Jerusalem* was added for the whole essay's publication in *Blake Studies* (1975). My work on *Jerusalem* continued in "*Jerusalem's* Didactic and Mimetic-Narrative Experiment" in *Studies in Romanticism*, 32:4 (Winter 1973), 627–654.]

A critical tradition of some length and dignity has treated Blake as a symbolist, first with the proviso that he had to invent his own symbols, later with the argument that his symbols were archetypal, whether of Jungian or fundamentally literary shape.[1] Along with this appellation, Yeats's phrase describing Blake as a "too literal realist of the imagination" has tended to stick.[2] But Yeats's phrase has such variable meaning that unless carefully applied it obfuscates or misleads. Though he may be regarded at some very high level of abstraction as belonging to the same tradition as Baudelaire's, Blake is not a symbolist at all in the obvious sense implied by the famous sonnet "Correspondances," and his techniques have little in common with Mallarmé's or with those of any of the poets discussed by Arthur Symons in one of the first studies of the symbolists.[3] Yet Blake may be treated as a more complete symbolist than those who have gone under the "symboliste" banner, if one means by symbolist a poet who regards literature as a "symbolic form" of experience, in the sense that has become common since Cassirer.[4] The view of Blake's work as more complete in its implications for critical theory than that of any poet generally regarded as symbolist has not been asserted, though implied in Northrop Frye's pioneering *Fearful Symmetry* and exploited in Frye's own subsequent theoretical work.[5] If Blake had exercised only this influence on Frye he would belong to a history of theories of symbolism, but his importance in this respect is far greater and his influence far more pervasive. He has had a germinal influence on the theories of numerous modern writers and made the most complete utterance of a philosophy of literary symbolism in his time. I shall see Blake as providing a transition from purely neoclassical English views of language to those developing in the later nineteenth and earlier twentieth centuries.

I

In *The Marriage of Heaven and Hell,* Blake offers a brief explanation, quite similar in argument to an important passage from Vico, of how poetic vision became reduced to systems of moral code.[6] The passage, comprising Plate 11 of the work, has usually been treated as offering an explanation of the cyclical decline into Urizenic abstraction of an original visionary perception. It could also be regarded as a Blakean myth of "dissociation of sensibility," if one were to follow along lines suggested by Frank Kermode.[7] Here I intend to treat it as part of the expression of a whole view of language informing the so-called prophetic books and anticipating twentieth-century ideas of "symbolic form" and constitutive poetic language.

The passage is as follows:

> The ancient Poets animated all sensible objects with Gods or Geniuses, calling them by the names and adorning them with the properties of woods, rivers, mountains, lakes, cities, nations, and whatever their enlarged & numerous senses could percieve.
> And particularly they studied the genius of each city & country. placing it under its mental deity. Till a system was formed, which some took advantage of & enslav'd the vulgar by attempting to realize or abstract the mental deities from their objects; thus began Priesthood.
> Choosing forms of worship from poetic tales.
> And at length they pronounced that the Gods had orderd such things.
> Thus men forgot that All deities reside in the human breast [E38].

The last sentence offers a picture of the prelapsarian condition, for dissociation and Fall are identical in Blake: human consciousness was, or properly is, to use Blake's characteristic terms, the "circumference" of experience or reality rather than its "center." One human breast contained the Gods, who always should be, according to Blake, the servants of Man. The senses existed originally in an "enlarged" state and contained the world. This gath-

Blake, Jerusalem, and Symbolic Form (1975)

ering in of experience was not contradicted by the first poets when they came to compose. Indeed, their activity, which we take to have been the creation of language, was the means by which real consciousness, as we now understand it, was established. The statement about this at the beginning of the passage is put rather curiously, however; for it seems uttered from a point of view toward language opposed to that of the poets, while at the same time the total passage laments the passing away of the point of view of those poets. The question I raise here is: were the "sensible objects" existent previous to their animation by the poets? For the moment, let us answer "no"; let us provisionally accept the idea that Blake did not intend us to imagine men at that critical moment of the invention of language originally confronting real inanimate sensible objects (we shall return to this). Let us rather assume that he intended the poets by the power of language—namely metaphor—to have *created* those objects in the way a circumferential power gives life to objects—by anthropomorphizing them and rejecting the existence of a subject-object relationship. It is as if the poets' world is composed of Zoas, living beings that contain everything in their giant human forms, and they are assigned the properties of natural objects as their parts of microcosms. Thus, instead of thinking only of a Zoa inhabiting a river like a ghost in what Blake would regard as a debasement of vision, one must rather think of the river as inhabiting the Zoa or better, identical with Him, as part in behalf of the whole. Human form and natural form interpenetrate.

The means by which this occurs, if its occurrence is attributable to poets, must be language. It is in words that the "calling" and the "adorning" mentioned in *The Marriage* must take place. The enlargement of the senses and their increased number are sustained by these acts of "calling" and "adorning." The additional senses, now lost, can be described collectively as the power of constitutive metaphor, which term I use here to denote all tropological uses of language. As the poets built language, regarded as fundamentally metaphoric, the world became realizable in words and there grew into existence a mythology, or, we might call it, literature itself. In this sense literature is a world of words, or if you like (because our answer to the question of what came first—world or word—was merely provisional), the world *made into* words. Blake calls this a "system," but we should remember that he calls other things "systems," too.

Then came the dissociation, for, as Blake says, "some took advantage" of what the system provided. To take advantage of something is to externalize it (to make it an "it"), or in Blake's terms, to retreat to the "selfish" center from the circumference. This thrusts everything outside and turns the outside into inanimate or "sensible" objects, abstracted from their "mental deities," who, as long as they are truly "mental," remain inside the circle. But the mental deities are relegated at this point to subjective illusions by the dominating epistemology of subject-object, which thus dispenses with such deities altogether. Another way of regarding the matter is as follows: the objects, now relegated to the realm of dead Lockean matter, could no longer be imagined as one with their deities and at best could only stand as *visibilia* for these now purely abstracted, imperceptible and thus mysterious powers, now collectively metamorphosed into a hidden clock-maker God. To put it a third way, the poetic verbal universe that holds subject, deities, and object together is destroyed by a competing idea of language that claims for itself only the power to point outward toward *things* beyond which lies nothing; or the power to point outward toward *things* which stand for an order of mysterious beings or Platonic ideas disembodied behind the veil of those things. With language no longer containing reality in its unified form as mythology but only *pointing toward* a distant reality, a mediating or interpreting force is required, namely what Blake calls a "priesthood," to rationalize the mysteries of this separateness.

Now what we have here are two fundamentally opposed views of language. In that of the poets, metaphor is absolutely fundamental, not merely a collection of tropes or devices added on to an assertion that points outward from itself. Metaphor as device is all that is left of the synthetic and myth-making powers of language after it has been redefined by priestly practice.

The difference is that between what Blake calls "allegory address'd to the Intellectual powers" and allegory which is available to the "Corporeal Understanding" (Letter to Thomas Butts, 6 July 1803). Both are forms of language, the former that of the poets, the latter that of the priesthood. But it is important to notice that the priesthood came after the poets and chose "forms of worship from poetic tales." It is as if the original mode of language were poetic and the whole process of externalizing language were built upon that original mode. It is as if poetry and myth preceded religion, if one thinks of religion as a system of beliefs to which are attached codes of behavior. Inasmuch as Blake's archetypal priest Urizen is also his archetypal scientist, it would appear that for Blake poetic myth precedes science in the same way. But the main implication is that we are talking about language. To what extent is the world that Blake talks about a linguistic world of "symbolic form?"

Blake, Jerusalem, *and Symbolic Form (1975)*

Before proceeding to that question I return to a previous one answered arbitrarily and only provisionally for the sake of launching the inquiry: were the sensible objects Blake mentions in the passage existent previous to their animation by the poets? Or is Blake for the sake of rhetoric simply acceding to our deeply ingrained linguistic habits of externalization or *pointing to* in order to get *his* argument going? This is like asking what the original Edenic condition was in Blake's mythology. But more and more experience with that mythology makes one less and less satisfied with locating Eden simply at the beginning of some linear stretch of historic or externalized time. For one thing, the mythology is a mythology, and we should not choose forms of history from poetic tales. If, however, we stick as closely as possible to Blake's terms, we can avoid both the linear temporal trap and the suggestion that Blake had literally in mind a Kantian "manifold of sensation" that the ancient poets by mythic categories shaped into a verbal universe. I find no mention of a manifold as such in Blake, nor any mention of Kant, for that matter. We shall try to avoid choosing forms of philosophy from poetic tales at this stage of our inquiry, though we may *eventually* do so. There are in Blake some mental deities that may serve us instead. There is, for example, the story of the shapeless horrific body of Urizen that Los must in some way form; there is the sleeping body of the world-giant Albion, whose unorganized dreaming state is, as history, the substance that must be transformed into a living vision. Both of these figures seem to imply the potential existence of a living, human, unified world adornable with the "properties of woods, rivers, mountains, lakes, cities, nations"— in other words, subject to, indeed requiring, the process of poetic naming. These horrific and sleeping bodies in Blake are the potentiality of imaginative creation. As potentiality they are not in time and history; neither are they matter that is *there* for the poets to confront as such. They are sheer possibilities of the imagination. Existence can be said to have its beginning in their poetic apprehension.

Another part of *The Marriage of Heaven and Hell* throws some light upon this and suggests how language acts as a creative force and repository of reality. In one of his "Memorable Fancies" Blake describes a printing house in Hell where "Lions of flaming fire" melt metals into living fluid, passing the fluid to "Unnam'd forms" who cast the metals into the expanse, there to be received by men in the shape of books arranged in libraries (E40). This, according to Blake, is how knowledge is transmitted from generation to generation. The body of earth—the mass of potential reality—is turned to flux and then named and ordered linguistically. As a result, history becomes not simply an outward linear arrangement of events to which words refer but is embodied as the presentness of words. The past comes into the present—belongs to it—because the only place that we can find it is in its construction in words, present to our reading. This may clear up the apparent oddity of Blake's method of drawing the "visionary" heads of historical personages, for he declared that they were actually present to him as he drew them. Without resort to theories of ghosts or madness, one can argue that Blake believed he was bringing these people to presentness in his paintings—by painting them as he *sees* them according to their presentness in the words of history books.

The Marriage suggests an idea of culture as embodied in words and, perhaps, an idea of history as more real when located in or *as* a verbal structure than externalized as a past. Indeed, the latter is quite impossible without making a verbal structure indulging the fiction of pastness, which in turn becomes itself a presence. Blake's idea of verbal presence, the only real existence of the past, he no doubt took from his reading of the Bible. Blake interprets Jesus's second coming as his continual presence in the presence of the Book itself. Blake has nothing good to say about the historical or so-called past Jesus, who is the supreme form of Antichrist. He is "outward Ceremony," meaningless ritualized behavior that mindlessly copies or points out and backward to an historically lost and forgotten or only vaguely remembered event (*The Laocoon*, E273). The opposite of this would be a shaped imaginative form, living in the immediate present, like the Bible and what it contains.

But of course it would have to be shaped. When it is shaped we do it the honor of referring to its events in the present tense. We can say that Jesus *comes*. To treat the matter otherwise is to externalize the events from the words and tacitly admit that the words don't contain and shape but only point to—in this case point *back to*—a lost past. So we may argue that when we talk of a verbal universe made by the ancient poets there is no point in referring to a *before* external to it that they transformed into a presence. Blake, facing what he will later call the "stubborn structure of the Language," was acceding to our manner of speaking. However, the passage from *Jerusalem* in which he uses the phrase "stubborn structure" shows that there is another sense in which we can assume the existence of an external material that the poet faces and must reshape. For Blake has posited a cycle or a form of Heraclitan opposites. Inside the presentness of Blake's mythology there is a formless flux, a contrary that his heroic artist Los must shape. The phrase I have mentioned appears in Plate 36 [40] as a parenthetical statement by the author himself and suggests what Los's supreme task is:

> (I call them by their English names: English, the rough basement.
> Los built the stubborn structure of the Language, acting against
> Albions melancholy, who must else have been a Dumb despair) [E183].

By "them" Blake refers to the cities of England, who have become in the poem part of an elaborate parallel-identity with the places of Israel. Blake has already told us in *Milton* that he will not let his sword sleep in his hand until he has built Jerusalem in England, and his poem *Jerusalem* is that building—the establishment of linguistic or metaphorical identity in visionary time and space between holy Jerusalem and resurrected London. At this point in the poem he calls his cities by their English names; he shapes the Biblical vision into the English tongue. Language is the vehicle of the mythic mode of constituting reality, which stands like Los at the base of culture. Los is described here as the archetype of the ancient poets. It is he who actually makes language as a receptacle for culture. This act gives the sleeping giant Albion the power of speech, of awakening, of shaping his nightmare world of flux and disorder into a reality. No longer will he be surrounded like a dumb beast by a buzzing confusion, which he has allowed to grow by his inarticulateness, his poverty of metaphor, his delusion that his language only *points to* things, his succumbing to the powers of what I shall call the cultural "anti-myth" of subject and object.

This structure or creation of the ancient poet Los is "stubborn," and the word is harsh enough to make us query it. Freed as we now should be from the need to address ourselves to the problems of beginnings, we can see that in the myth, where to query beginnings is pointless, Los's activity is really continuous, ever-present, or eternal in the moment. The stubbornness of the structure is twofold: language has the capacity to resist the stasis reason desires and stubbornly frustrates those who—like Urizen, Satan, and the "priesthood"—would choose to abstract a single form of worship from it (try to reduce it to a system pointing outward only to that one form—the clock world of deism). This is its metaphoric, Los-like structure. On the other hand, language resists stasis only as a result of the struggle that Los has with its dangerous susceptibility to externalization and hardening. Its stubbornness, then, can point either way.

By now we can see that what Blake calls Golgonooza is, in one of its aspects and perhaps in its primary aspect, the city of verbal form, the "stubborn structure" itself. As it is built by Los, so does it also fall by dint of those who abstract forms of worship from it, continually exhausting its possibilities in externalization and use. As a result, Los has to be at work continually.

> Here on the banks of the Thames, Los built Golgonooza,
> Outside of the Gates of the Human Heart, beneath Beulah
> In the midst of the rocks of the Altars of Albion. In fears
> He built it, in rage & in fury. It is the Spiritual Fourfold
> London: continually building & continually decaying desolate!
> [E203].

The work is always accomplished in the midst of the ruins that are continually made of it. The rocks are matter or Lockean substance that is made from language by forms of verbal externalization. The altars are the forms of worship abstracted from mythology. The process is eternal—timeless because internalized and thus lifted from linear, measurable time, endless when seen in time because of the constant need to refurbish the mythicolinguistic structure as it is plundered by those who use it to their purposes. It is, as Blake tells us, a "terrible eternal labour."

The labor is the eternal recreation of the act that Blake attributes in *The Marriage* originally to the "ancient Poets." Since *The Marriage* is present to us, however, it is more appropriate to say that the act is not a *recreation of* but is *identical to* the act of the poets. Seen cyclically, Los's work as the builder of language is a "Striving with Systems to deliver Individuals from those Systems" (E154). As the system that was formed from language (a mythology) is taken advantage of and corrupted into externality, or, in other Blakean terms, becomes the spectre of its original self, Los's eternal act of building the "stubborn structure of the Language" can be seen as a struggle with a spectral or "allegorical" system grown like a "polypus" from his original system (original not in the historical sense but in the sense that his system represents the fundamental nature of language—its metaphorical nature). Thus, Los is engaged in a struggle with his spectre—language converted to a sort of anti-myth. Confronted by the deterioration or purposive plundering of his system into an opposing system, he

> ... stands in London building Golgonooza
> Compelling his Spectre to labours mighty; trembling in fear
> The Spectre weeps, but Los unmovd by tears or threats remains

> I must Create a System, or be enslav'd by another Mans
> I will not Reason & Compare: my business is to Create
> [E153].

Like those in *The Marriage* who work with molten metal to make books, Los, who is a blacksmith, uses ladles of ore, shaping potentiality into the spiritual sword.

I have argued against the idea that the "ancient Poets" confronted an originally spectral situation. Los, however, seems to be in a more embattled position. Thus, in spite of my argument from one point of view—the mythological—that the action of Los is not recreation in time but original creation, I must from another point of view—that of externality, and, sadly enough, of critical interpretation—admit that Los, as the creative spirit of time, the container and maker of significant time, does have to rebuild a stubborn structure that has turned by deterioration into its spectral negation. The spectral negative stubbornness of language is for Los and for Blake the tendency of language toward generalization, abstraction, and dead metaphor:

> ... it is the Reasoning Power
> An Abstract objecting power, that Negatives every thing
> This is the Spectre of Man ....
> [E153].

One of Los's duties is to try to turn a negative relationship into a true contrariety—to mythologize rather than to accede wholly to the subject-object relationship. What we have regarded as cyclical and yet without external temporal beginning we ought to consider ideally as a dialectical contrariety between opposed linguistic tendencies. One is the purely prolific tendency of the free mythmaking imagination and the other the devouring tendency of the externalizing, purposive object-making and thus also subject-making rationality: In *The Marriage* Blake speaks of prolific and devourer as follows:

> ... one portion of being, is the Prolific. the other, the Devouring: to the devourer it seems as if the producer was in his chains, but it is not so, he only takes portions of existence and fancies that the whole [E40].

The devourer attempts to ingest the mythmaking power of language. But, in the process, that power can only turn into its opposite, because the devourer is a machine for externalizing. For the devourer to take something inside is really for him to externalize it at once in the form of what I have called the anti-myth of subject and object, of matter or measurable substance. The devourer can never be at the circumference of his thought, but only at the center, no matter how much he devours, for devouring is using and to use is to externalize. Ultimately, however, the devourer is at the circumference of a myth of his own that insists on placing himself paradoxically at the center of experience and surrounding him with infinite space and time. If he does not appreciate the irony of this situation, he is in trouble. Thus the curious difficulties Urizen in *The Four Zoas* has in finding a place to stand and his inability to attain to an apparent circumference.

We must pause now in the argument to expand a point made in passing. In measurable or externalized time, Los would seem to be condemned to a Sisyphus-like existence, building language as myth only to see it deteriorate, and then building it again. This surely sounds as if it were Hell, and it would be Hell if Los really lived in the externalized time that is opposed to his vision. Instead, he lives in prolific work, where every moment is imaginative creation and total accomplishment. To put it more accurately, time and the unfallen counterpart of Hell are in him—the area of human energy out of which come Blake's famous proverbs. It is not too much to say that this energy is artistic shaping in a language, whether of words or lines or musical forms, that this unfallen Hell at the bottom of the world (the strong legs and feet of unfallen man) is an unremitting source of symbolic forms. The work done here—in the mines and at the forge—is not easy, for it is accomplished against the pressure of anti-myth that, from the mythic point of view, obfuscates *particular* reality with generality and abstract nothingness:

> Some Sons of Los surround the Passions with porches of iron & silver
> Creating form & beauty around the dark regions of sorrow,
> Giving to airy nothing a name and a habitation
> Delightful! with bounds to the Infinite putting off the Indefinite
> Into most holy forms of Thought: (such is the power of inspiration)
> They labour incessant; with many tears & afflictions:
> Creating the beautiful House for the piteous sufferer.
> [*Milton*, E125].

The porches are the forms taken by the metals of the "Memorable Fancy" we have already examined, mythicolinguistic shapings from crude potentiality. The "regions of sorrow" or fallen Hell—unshaped because symbolically uncontained and therefore rampant spectral anxieties—are made part of, enter into, a larger containing form. The House of Albion is a house of cultural myth that assigns value and meaning to his acts:

Blake, Jerusalem, and Symbolic Form (1975)

> Others; Cabinets richly fabricate of gold & ivory;
> For Doubts & fears unform'd & wretched & melancholy
> [*Milton*, E125].

The passage I have quoted from *Milton* ends with a description of the artist:

> Antamon takes them [the spectres] into his beautiful flexible hands,
> As the Sower takes the seed, or as the Artist his clay
> Or fine wax, to mould artful a model for golden ornaments.
> [E125].

Blake is very hard on anti-myth, for in his view his own age has come to be so dominated by it that people tend to think only in its terms, which are the terms of Bacon, Newton, and Locke. Its domination has tended to render myth trivial or material for psychoanalysis by accusing it of subjectivity while reserving objectivity for itself. When anti-myth negates myth in this way Blake is prone to call it simply error, the completion of the Fall in opacity and contraction—Newton's trumpet blast (*Europe,* E65). Everything is reduced to Lockean material substance. The anti-myth comes to be regarded as the source of the single vision of truth and reality, but Blake always insists that this vision is a human construction like myth; indeed, it is built like an anti-type or fallen analogy upon (or, to be consistent, underneath) the very same mythological structures that it relegates to subjectivity—poetry and the other arts.

Now both myth and anti-myth are, as I apply the terms to Blake, modes of imaginative construction that result in what may be called mythologies. The way of myth is synthesis and art, the way of anti-myth analysis and science. The anti-myth creates the mythology of the subject-object split and proceeds to divide everything by analysis into smaller and smaller units, thus draining substance of life, freedom, and will. Blake opposes the dominance of anti-myth in his time by giving myth the fictive historical primacy we noted in *The Marriage of Heaven and Hell.* He also gives it a formal primacy by considering it to be the fundamental mode of imaginative construction. It puts together, and anti-myth takes apart. Because both are *modes* of activity and not themselves copies of anything, the question of which has truth or correspondence to reality is not a possible question. Indeed, the question is merely a reflection of a category, to borrow Kant's term, of the anti-mythic mode, and is meaningful only within its terms.

This suggests that both myth and anti-myth create mythologies, which are products of their ways of seeing. Indeed so, but Blake's insistence on the historical and formal primacy of myth suggests that without myth anti-myth starves. In this sense, myth potentially contains anti-myth (as the seed does the plant): anti-myth can never contain myth, though it is engaged in a constant effort to devour it. Its own tendency to externalize everything prevents its self-completion and its victory.

Art, the creator of the mythology of myth and the prolific to the anti-myth's devourer, the seed of thought, becomes for Blake the contrary of everything that operates by generalization toward abstract law—not just science but religion and, to some extent history, when history rises up the scale of abstraction to form a deterministic outlook. But art, as the fundamental activity of making languages, is also the source upon which all of these modes feed, distorting the source and requiring its rebirth in the process.

II

The next task is to imagine *Jerusalem* for what it is—a Blakean poetic structure, an embodiment of mythic form, a mythology. If Blake is correct, all poetry embodies mythic form or is, in Cassirer's term, "symbolic form." But we may expect from Blake a degree of rigor in this matter that would lead him to construct a special sort of poem, one that self-consciously embodies the principles of poetic construction as its content or subject. The structure of *Jerusalem* has been a sargossa sea for more than one critic seeking to discover its scheme.[8] Let us try to regard it as an act of mythic form, a making of and in language. Let us also assume that it self-consciously parades its mythic categories against the immense pressure of anti-myth, to which Blake was so sensitive, perhaps more sensitive than any artist of his age, with the possible exception of those who actually lost their minds. In other words, let us try to give some rigor and clarity to what Yeats was driving at when he called Blake a "too literal realist of the imagination."

Myth and anti-myth are both modes or processes of mental construction. Let us imagine that *Jerusalem* is that process, that it is the act made continually present of creating the world in verbal form as a true mythic mythology in opposition to the externalizing tendencies of anti-myth. What kind of verbal structure would do this with the rigor Blake most assuredly would require? It would have to be a structure the content of which is its form; it would have

Blake, Jerusalem, and Symbolic Form (1975)

to be a structure that is about itself or is itself *being made*. It could not *point to* an action external to it that it copied. It could not have a plot easily extractable for discussion. It would have to deny a past as anything except that which it contains as a now or a presence. Otherwise it would be pointing outward and backward from itself, and as such it could not be prolific.

These requirements bring us to a point already noted: in building language Los finds that language is indeed a "stubborn structure" always tending toward anti-myth, always having to be wrenched imaginatively into freedom from the conventions of anti-myth. We cannot expect from *Jerusalem* a structure capturable by conventional analyses of narrative. We must proceed as critics bereft of our tools and armed only with our own capacities for paradox.

Can we, then, consider *Jerusalem* to possess a beginning? Not in the conventional sense. Instead let us say that we *begin* to read *Jerusalem*. We locate Blake making the poem or the poem in the eternality of its being made. The poem is this act. I do not refer here to the historical act of its composition, for that is lost in past time like the Jesus Blake would call Antichrist—the Jesus who, it is insisted, was back there, externalized from the language of the Bible and thus lost or at least sealed in a separate historical account. There is to be evaded here, for the time being, the considerable question of whether an historical account is not itself the maker of a presence. For our purposes it is sufficient to say that history consciously points *back to* events and things even though it is admitted that at a higher level of abstraction we can regard historical accounts also as *containing* events and things as a presence. One of the curiosities upon which critics have marveled is the great number of apparent intrusions into the poem made by its author—the poem's "Blake." The point is that if Blake *is*, he *is* in the act that is his poem, the poem gathering into itself the composer as part of its presence. Blake *was* an historical figure, but this past or external Blake can only be considered in Blake's terms to be the Antiblake. He never *is* but only *was*. The most stunning of these intrusions is the interesting assertion in Plate 15. Blake has been offering his own vision of the "Schools and Universities of Europe," of Los working at his anvil, and of Albion's sons, Reuben and Abraham. It appears that he has embarked on a discussion of the activities of Reuben, the natural man:

> While Reuben enroots his brethren in the narrow Canaanite
> From the Limit Noah to the Limit Abram in whose Loins
> Reuben in his Twelve-fold majesty & beauty shall take refuge

> As Abraham flees from Chaldea shaking his goary locks
> But first Albion must sleep, divided from the Nations
> [E159].

Something holds Blake back. Blake, now poet of his poem, is thinking, "I am getting ahead of myself here," and reminding himself as author of and as actor of the poem—and at the same time reminding the reader, who will be seeking explanations—that the sleep of Albion must take precedence over what the reader and Blake are now seeing. It is in this sense *first*. In the fall into history that the poem reports and yet transforms into a presence, Albion must sleep. Blake is warning that his consciousness and our consciousness of Albion sleeping must not disappear. Inevitably the linearity of reading requires Blake to put something first, but to put Albion falling to sleep on the first plate and simply to go on *from* it would have given too much status to a linearity that must be continually undercut in order that externalization or *pointing to* may be wholly avoided or at least avoided as much as the "stubborn structure of the Language" will allow.

But once we begin to regard the reminder to make Albion sleep as an intrusion we discover that more and more of the poem must be so regarded and that perhaps we have mistakenly turned things inside out. If Blake in the poem is an intrusion we had better call the occasional falling of the poem into narrative an "extrusion," for in one way or another Blake keeps intruding, making assertions about what he *now sees*.

If we recognize that the intrusions dominate the poem, the reminder that Albion must sleep should be seen as an intrusive admonition to create *within* a mythic mode of apprehension, where Blake is seeing things directly and now, a story or "extrusion" from time to time in order to deepen the texture of the dominating presentness of the vision in the form of an action or fable. This really goes on *inside* the presentness established by Blake's dominating and circumferential intrusiveness, so what I call "extrusion" is an illusion—as illusory as Urizen's idea that the object surrounds the subject, when he in fact has given it its presence. Why this is necessary we shall have to consider; the irony of the poet's task with language is involved. But first we must examine other aspects of Blake's structure by attempting an eccentric gloss of Chapter I. The first two lines of the poem are

> Of the Sleep of Ulro! and of the passage through
> Eternal Death! and of the awaking to Eternal Life.
> [E146].

Blake, Jerusalem, *and Symbolic Form (1975)*

They suggest a conventional beginning on the model of *Paradise Lost* and *Paradise Regained,* but *Paradise Lost* begins with an invocation of the muse that is longer and more detailed in describing the poem's aim. By comparison Blake's seems terse. There are two reasons: this is a beginning that is not to call attention to itself as a formal beginning of a linear structure. A bold quick stroke and passage directly into the process of the poem accentuates the nature of the structure and plays down the lines as introduction. At the same time the invocation turns out not to be limited to these lines but to be spread sporadically through several plates. There is more of it, for example, in Plate 5, where Blake beseeches the Savior for aid. Indeed, the invocation spreads into nearly the whole of the first chapter, for the chapter is virtually all Blake's intrusion, Blake speaking *now* of what he sees *now.* Rather than the poem moving from a statement of its subject and a request to the muse to provide the story, Blake states his theme tersely as present to him *now* and as part of the process of its making in words. Blake never recedes from his poem, and the poem thus resists turning into a narrative form with a linear temporal content. Even when the presentness of this process must be transposed into interludes of story it will not be for long, nor will Blake consistently employ a past tense. Indeed, he will mix present and past tenses with apparent disregard for temporal consistency. He will walk up and down in his time just as he describes Los walking up and down in history. He will stand, like Los, anywhere in the presence of the poem and judge past and future accordingly. Indeed, by Blake's paradoxical spatial logic, to walk up and down *in* time is really to become *a* circumference containing time. Obviously Blake is attempting to keep a strict control over the imagery of temporality in his poem so that time is never thrust rudely outside the poem as something the poem *points to.*

The theme is also stated tersely so that it too does not have an easy chance to grow into an outward-pointing verbal structure. Instead it is converted immediately into a presence:

> This theme calls me in sleep night after night, & ev'ry morn
> Awakes me at sun-rise, then I see the Saviour over me
> Spreading his beams of love, & dictating the words of this mild song
> [E146].

At once after this we have the Savior's words addressed to Albion as presently spoken and Albion's reply, and we have the vision present to Blake, who observes Albion's reaction:

> But the perturbed Man away turns down the valleys dark ...
> [E146].

When Albion's speech ends, Blake speaks in the past tense: "So spoke Albion," and we have glided into a fictional convention, but almost immediately we are drawn back into the presiding present consciousness of the poet in his process, as Blake observes the situation of life in London and looks out even further to Wales and Scotland, finally returning to continue the invocation from which these extrusions have taken place:

> Trembling I sit day and night, my friends are astonish'd at me.
> Yet they forgive my wanderings, I rest not from my great task!
> To open the Eternal Worlds, to open the immortal Eyes
> Of Man inwards into the Worlds of Thought: into Eternity
> Ever expanding in the Bosom of God. the Human Imagination
> O Saviour pour upon me thy Spirit of meekness & love:
> Annihilate the Selfhood in me, be thou all my life!
> Guide thou my hand which trembles exceedingly upon the rock of ages,
> While **I** write of the building of Golgonooza ...
> [E147].

This passage leads without break back to the subject seen as present and happening all around (but in Blake's terms within) him. There is no pause or shift in perspective as he begins to tell of it, and everything is in the present tense. Numerous characters are presented to us without explanation. Hand and Hyle, Kox and Bowen, the area of Entuthon-Benython, and the state of Beulah are simply there before us. To *explain* them would be to have relegated them to some outer lost pastness. They are really *here*—*in* the verbal structure—and their context and presence are their definition.

We now face the section in which we learn of the struggle between Los and the Spectre. Blake's direct vision of the lamenting Jerusalem and Vala is modulated to a "past":

> Los heard her lamentations in the deeps afar!
> [E148].

The struggle of Los and the Spectre is then recounted, mostly by dialogue, in the past tense. There are two interrelated explanations for this. First, it is a device to indicate the continuous nature of the struggle. The struggle is Los's work; it is the nature of his art. As I have already argued, Los's work is eternal, but not the labor of Sisyphus. The device of the past tense works here to give the sense of "terrible eternal labour" having taken place though we recognize that strictly speaking Blake wants us to have

Los and Spectre immediately in our presence. I have mentioned the irony of the poet's task with language and the necessity of deepening the texture of the poem with a story or fable. Here we find Blake as Los-poet doing just that—sacrificing the present to make the point of continuousness and eternality in the terms dictated by the "stubborn structure," yet not giving away too much. Indeed, to give way to the present tense entirely in telling a tale seems to result not in creating a presentness at all but paradoxically a stylistic distancing that has the very opposite effect from that sought. The best example of this is Joyce Cary's admitted failure, *A Fearful Joy,* in which the story is recounted totally in the present tense and the result is the reader's excessive consciousness of the tense as a device.

Blake may yet in some Protean way struggle free to preserve the presence of his vision as a whole despite his forced compromise with the present tense. Blake argues that "Vision or Imagination is a Representation of what Eternally Exists. Really & Unchangeably," and he suggests that allegory and fable can contain some vision (*A Vision of the Last Judgment,* E554). Properly speaking and consistent with his own view, we might suggest that vision can contain fable within itself, and perhaps must do so, not as a courtly and obeisant gesture to the "stubborn structure of the Language," but as part of the eternal struggle of the artist to use the language, even granting it some of its own terms, countering its stubbornness with the resourcefulness of the imagination.

Second, then, the story of Los and his Spectre is a fable, an "extrusion," to perpetuate our barbaric term. As a fable it illustrates something; its aim is to display the Spectre to us in its horrible entirety. And, more important, it is the struggle of Blake with his medium. It is the making of the poem. The story as fable ultimately gives way to its summation, Blake's vision, in Blake's present, of total spectrality:

> And this is the manner of the Sons of Albion in their strength
> They take the Two Contraries which are called Qualities, with which
> Every Substance is clothed, they name them Good & Evil
> From them they make an Abstract, which is a Negation
> Not only of the Substance from which it is derived
> A murderer of its own Body: but also a murderer
> Of every Divine Member: it is the Reasoning Power
> An Abstract objecting power, that Negatives every thing
> This is the Spectre of Man: the Holy Reasoning Power
> And in its Holiness is closed the Abomination of Desolation
> [E152–3].

The summary is made, the conclusion reached. Immediately we are told that all of this—the contention of Los and Spectre in the fabulous "past," the summary, and the final display of the Spectre in its total abstractness—is the reason that Los still works:

> Therefore Los stands in London building Golgonooza
> Compelling his Spectre to labours mighty ....
> [E153].

We return to a present we have never really left.

Characteristically, the passage just quoted that the fable illustrates comes neither at beginning nor end of the fable but is intruded somewhere near the middle, for after it and after the famous "I must Create a System" speech, we return to the dialogue with the Spectre, modulating from "Los cries" back into "the Spectre answer'd." In this way the presentness of these "past" events is preserved against the pastness of the verbs.

The work to which Los puts the Spectre in the rest of the fable is the perfecting of the Spaces of Erin. In the description of this act it is made clear that these labors contain time and space as the pulsations and extensions of the human body itself—time apprehended by the human heart rather than the human body spatialized and measured by external standards or "mathematical form." This is what Blake characterizes as a "Striving with Systems to deliver Individuals from those Systems." The vision of the completed spaces and of Golgonooza follows. Los "stood" before his furnaces, the artist viewing his completed vision, and saw Erin; at the same time—for Los viewing Erin is an internal microcosm of Blake viewing his poem—Blake speaks out amazed at how he has so far managed to transform things by means of the fable of Los; he proceeds to perform a kind of "anatomy" of that transformation itself, in which it is shown that the accomplishment he views—Golgonooza—is held together by words:

> And the screws & iron braces, are well wrought blandishments,
> And well contrived words, firm fixing, never forgotten ...
> [E155].

Blake then "sees" Golgonooza directly in a long and detailed description which delineates the "interiors" of the city and the "exterior" Ulro that is a vision of the dangers of externalization—"the Cave; the Rock; the Tree: the Lake of Udan Adan," etc.—referred to as "there" (E157). The "spatial" description of Golgonooza is paradoxical in that no map can be made that points outward to it. Golgonooza remains, then, form captured in words and only in words. It is, within the poem, the poem's microcosm. It is said to unfold from a microcosmic center like a flower, as the poem spreads forth from any moment in the process of its being.

In Blake's vision, which acts as a circumference for the fable of Los and the Spectre, Los "walks round the walls night and day," and in this way also Los's vision is a circumference like Blake's. Los in the poem contains the vision of Golgonooza in the way that Blake contains the process of the poem. In this way, too, time as a receding lost past is brought back inside as a presence:

> He views the City of Golgonooza, & its smaller Cities:
> The Looms & Mills & Prisons & Work-houses of Og & Anak:
> The Amalekite: the Canaanite: the Moabite: the Egyptian:
> And all that has existed in the space of six thousand years: Permanent,
> & not lost not lost nor vanishd ...
> [E157].

The City Los finally "beheld," that is, Los's vision, is that of completed hope. The making of the City does not complete work, which goes on eternally, as we have seen; but, something to be continually built, it can be treated as, in some sense, a continuous possibility in the artist's mind. As Los "beheld" this vision, Blake now clearly "sees" the present situation, which is really "the Past, Present & Future, existing all at once" (E159). Then comes the passage continuing the invocation to the Divine Spirit, the vision of the Schools and Universities and Reuben, to be followed by the "Albion must sleep" intrusion, already discussed.

These things should prepare us for a fable recounting events in Albion's sleep, such as we have received in some of the earlier prophecies; but in a constant dialectic between fable and presence Blake will provide the fable only sporadically, not only working this new fable of Albion in with the presence of the poem's process, but also weaving in the fable of Los again, so that now three things are going on at once—the two fables being sometimes in the present tense, sometimes in the past.

When Blake sees Albion, the fable is treated as a presence:

> I see Albion sitting upon his Rock in the first Winter
> And thence I see the Chaos of Satan & the World of Adam
> When the Divine Hand went forth on Albion ...
> [E159].

The fable of Albion is made present because Blake now sees the present historical state. Albion's sleep is modern history, and is being subjected always to Los's efforts to shape it into some acceptable form. The sleep of

Albion thus contains Los's activity of trying to bring visionary shape to England by identifying England's (Albion's) parts with the tribes of Israel. This work at the forge Blake reports as the creation of Los's bright sculptures, which appear to be the fundamental symbols of his art:

> All things acted on Earth are seen in the bright Sculptures of
> Los's Halls & every Age renews its powers from these Works
> With every pathetic story possible to happen...
> [E161].

And the sculptures are identified with the "Divine Written Law" and the "Holy Gospel," which suggest that for Blake the primary source of literary archetypes is the Bible.

In the remaining part of Chapter I another characteristic of Blake's structure is apparent. One fable grows into another, one set of images begets another. The fable of Los and the Spectre begets the story of Los and Enitharmon or the fable of the Emanation. Albion's sleep generates a parallel situation between Albion and Jerusalem. The logic of the appearance of these new situations is the logic of metaphor, not cause and effect, not plot. The fables, which are stories and dialogues, are poised against Blake's present vision of Albion sleeping. The fables are extrusions into story of Albion's sleep or his nightmare delusions, including his own speeches.

Albion's last speech ends with his succumbing to that death-sleep in which Blake has already seen him, or *sees* him, from the beginning. In defiance of a spatialized before and after, Blake's structure of present intrusion is balanced against "extrusions" into a fabulous "past." This makes the Fall occur always now and Los's redemptive acts eternal.

III

The structural principles I have outlined are also the principles of the remaining chapters of *Jerusalem,* though each chapter has a special governing aspect of its own. At the end of Chapter II Albion's fall is perceived under the aspect of fallen Albion as a Jehovah or lawgiver. Los is seen as the organizer of the senses of natural man and as a quester into the interior of Albion, even to the center, which is London. Albion's delusion or dream is here the moral law and the results of its application. Blake's vision extrudes fables in all the chapters. These fables grow metaphorically from

Blake, Jerusalem, and Symbolic Form (1975)

those already established (though in another arrangement they could conceivably generate the ones that precede them). Blake's intrusions are not as numerous in the later chapters, but after Chapter I the continual presence of Blake is well established and remains the principal element that governs the poem.

The principal uniqueness of Chapter IV is the conclusion of the poem, which has been called an apocalypse, but should be examined closely to determine just what it contains and implies. In Plate 94 Blake views Albion lying on his rock in miserable death-sleep; after an extended description in the present tense, Blake announces: "Time was Finished!" This is measurable time, of course—the external time of history. What replaces it is the vision of time as an artistic *presence.* Though the apocalypse announced is treated as a past, we recognize that it is really Blake's vision in the present converted to a past tense that does not in this case or any other Blakean case really signify an historical past at all: it is a vision of how work is accomplished, of the ultimate of desire, and as such is neither past nor future but present in the human mind as a tacit endorsement of its myth-making. When Albion "opened his eyelids," Blake himself remarks: "Ah! shall the Dead live again." When Albion "rose" and "walked" into heaven "clothed in flames," Blake reminds the reader that the reader himself sees this every day:

> ...Thou seest the Sun in heavy clouds
> Struggling to rise above the Mountains. in his burning hand
> He takes his Bow, then chooses out his arrows of flaming gold [E255].

We realize that "he" is literally both the sun and Albion, and every morning *is* by the power of metaphor a vision of completed desire. Following this comes Albion's hurling of his selfhood into the fiery furnaces, the call to Jerusalem, and a treatment of Albion as composed of the four Zoas in their proper relations. In Plate 98 the tenses are mixed, and the effect is of action in the "past" and completion in the "present," as if Blake wished a whole process to be completely prepared and realized in a single linguistic moment, act and meaning unified.

Finally the four Zoas who comprise Albion are described in what we must take to be the ultimate act of prolific work, the making of reality in the languages of man:

> And they conversed together in Visionary forms dramatic which bright
> Redounded from their Tongues in thunderous majesty, in Visions

> In new Expanses, creating exemplars of Memory and of Intellect
> Creating Space, Creating Time according to the wonders Divine
> Of Human Imagination, throughout all the Three Regions immense
> Of Childhood, Manhood & Old Age; and the all tremendous unfathomable Non Ens
> Of Death was seen in regenerations terrific or complacent varying
> According to the subject of discourse & every Word & Every Character
> Was Human...
> [E257–8].

We realize here that apocalypse is not the *completion* of work in any temporal sense but the doing of work under the right conditions. These conditions are those of true contrariety—the "war and hunting" of heaven—in which real work is the constant building of languages. Languages contain in themselves space, time, history, science, and art. These languages are the human forms or circumferences of reality.

One of the aspects of the Fall was that words became separated from their humanity, and the covenants of Jehovah became abstract, tyrannical moral codes. In the 98th plate this is rectified in vision, for Blake "saw"

> ... the Words of the Mutual Covenant Divine
> On Chariots of gold & jewels with Living Creatures starry & flaming
> With every Colour, Lion, Tyger, Horse, Elephant, Eagle Dove, Fly, Worm
> And the all wondrous Serpent clothed in gems & rich array Humanize
> In the Forgiveness of Sins...
> [E258].

As the poem ends Blake discovers the name of the Emanation of all human forms—the correct name of all that Man loves and desires, the *completion* in vision of all that man with language can do—the imaginable world named Jerusalem. Named, it becomes a possibility.

In a sense then, though Blake's poem ends, it contains not an end but returns to its beginning, and the poem as a whole is work being done. It shows us the "reprobate" contrary quality of language, seeking to refurbish the system that according to *The Marriage of Heaven and Hell* "some took advantage of." Blake's poem is the prolific that provides food for the twentieth-century literary theorist to devour in order to externalize the critical doctrine of symbolic forms and constitutive symbols, by which he then interprets Blake.

Blake's view suggests that we create symbolic worlds, and that these are for all practical purposes the only worlds we have. What we have made them makes us what we are. We can only make a world with a language,

Blake, Jerusalem, and Symbolic Form (1975)

indeed in a language. There is nothing imaginable independent of a medium to imagine in. Our languages constantly die into use and must be reborn. Further, each language has its own limits and requires its opposite. Blake's vision of language was that myth precedes science and reason, that the latter feeds on the former. But he also believed that in his time the devourer's language had so dominated reality in the form of "Single vision & Newton's sleep" that civilization itself was in danger unless the contrary mythic language of poetry and art rose to the challenge of spiritual warfare. Linear, anti-metaphorical language is the contrary that must be reshaped back into its opposite, but only in order that the devourer may consume its contrary in prolific use. This is the "fitness and order" Blake sought; the vision of it leads to his remark: "What is the Life of Man but Art and Science?"

Contemporary Ideas of Literature: Terrible Beauty or Rough Beast? (1977)

[In the following essay, I attempted to address the developments in criticism and theory that had arisen in America since about 1965. The essay was a contribution to *Directions for Criticism: Structuralism and Its Alternatives*, eds. Murray Krieger and L. S. Dembo (Madison: University of Wisconsin Press, 1977). Contributors were all among the first senior fellows of the School of Criticism and Theory, founded by Krieger and me at the University of California, Irvine, in 1976 (since moved to Northwestern and thence to Cornell University). They were, in the order in which the essays appeared in the book, Murray Krieger (introduction), Edward W. Said, myself, Hayden White, René Girard, and Ralph Freedman. The essayists were provided with six recent anthologies: *In Search of Literary Theory; European Literary Theory and Practice: From Existential Phenomenology to Structuralism; The Languages of Criticism and the Sciences of Man: The Structuralist Controversy; Velocities of Change: Critical Essays from MLN; Issues in Contemporary Literary* Criticism; and *Modern French Criticism: From Proust and Valéry to Structuralism*.

The essayists were asked not to review the anthologies or even respond to narrow issues that the anthologies seemed to raise. Rather, they were to respond, as Krieger indicated in his introduction, in ways that might "contribute to ... awareness and ... understanding of questions currently seeking gestures from those helping to shape where criticism is going."

Krieger's commentary in his introduction contrasted Edward W. Said's essay to mine. Said attacked the New Criticism and Structuralism for "forfeiting an active situation in the world." Krieger saw my essay as clearly opposed to Said's. I didn't see it as Krieger saw it. He wrote of a position opposite to Said's in which literature is, as he said, "privileged" over other discourse, but I did not and do not think literature is in any way privileged over other symbolic forms. I thought it different in its linguistic emphases, intentions, and imaginative function from, say, natural science, which I regarded as an imaginative form with its own modes and processes. I was arguing for self-consciousness in criticism, the tempering of one's prejudices, and a sense of the critical medium's limits when one is addressing a literary text.]

Anthologies of things "modern" or "contemporary" have short lives. As soon as they appear they are out of date. This is most obvious with books produced on the crest of new movements or designed to introduce relatively unfamiliar material. The books under discussion all ride a crest, with the exception of *In Search of Literary Theory,* which has an air of familiarity.[1] This crest is the movement into the American ken of certain modem continental modes of criticism and that mixture of them known in France as the *nouvelle critique.*

It is a difficult task for the anthologists to make the necessary introductions when the movements themselves are still subject to dynamic revision and inner strife and at a point when positions are still being worked out or asserted, rather than analyzed. Though Saussure's linguistics, certain phenomenological approaches, and the work of prominent figures like Jakobson and Bachelard have been around for a long time, there is no history of continental critical developments. There has been much debate and invective, but the sort of analysis that Murray Krieger so ably performed for the American New Criticism as early as 1956[2] is only now beginning to appear, the most formidable example being Jonathan Culler's *Structuralist Poetics.*[3] As a result there has not yet been a satisfactory sifting down in these or any other volumes, and there has been some difficulty in finding quite the representative texts. Barthes's "The Structuralist Activity" appears twice in these books (and I admit to using it in my own *Critical Theory Since Plato*), but it is a weak essay and gives little idea of Barthes's work.[4] Jakobson on metonymy is an important essay, and Poulet's "Phenomenology of Reading" is perhaps an obvious choice. One of the books before me has Heidegger on Holderlin; another does not. Derrida and Lacan appear only in the Johns Hopkins symposium and there rather unsatisfactorily.[5] Of course, they are not strictly literary theorists, but neither were Plato and Kant.

The problem with the anthological presentation of criticism is often the failure to get at the intellectual presuppositions of those not necessarily—at the moment—focusing on literary texts or even on literature, if literature exists, which is one of the ideas that the *nouvelle critique* calls into doubt.[6] Anthologies often leave theoretical questions unplumbed in the welter of discourse that they offer. One senses in these books a babble of tongues and in many cases, worse, a jangling of jargon unapproached even in the early days of the American New Criticism. This in spite of Barthes's idea, in "The Two Criticisms" that there are simply two types of critical approach—the academic and the new.[7] Barthes's essay, which was severely and notoriously attacked in France, appeared curiously provincial to an American when it was published in *MLN* in 1963. It seemed about twenty years out of date. The struggle Barthes was describing against the positivism of the academy in France had had its parallel in America in the thirties and early forties, though on different grounds. Barthes *sounded* like the American New Critics:

"What [academic criticism] rejects is that this interpretation and this ideology may decide to work within an area purely internal to the work. In short, what is refused is *immanent analysis;* anything is acceptable so long as the work can be related to *something other* than itself, to something other than literature."[8]

As I have observed, even the concept "literature" is eventually called into question by the *nouvelle critique,* but up to this point Barthes's complaint appears very much like that of Blackmur in the well-known "A Critic's Job of Work" (1935), and the attack on positivism is familiar from the essays of Tate written about 1940.[9]

Yet there are very significant differences. Barthes concluded his essay by citing as among the "immanent" approaches rejected by the academic positivists the phenomenological, thematic, and structural. The first and third were virtually unknown when the American New Critics began to write, though they preached some aspects of both and certainly invented the second, which Barthes describes as a criticism that "reconstitutes the internal metaphors of a work."[10] Edward W. Said is surely correct when he regrets that the structuralists have been isolated from North American criticism.[11] He is also correct, I think, in stating, in spite of Barthes's simplifications, that structuralism is a kind of positivism in itself.[12]

I come away from a study of these contemporary movements with a sense that there are fundamental divisions among them not really conveyed by any of these anthologies. These differences are little understood, for they are coming to the surface here only slowly. Vernon Gras is helpful in this because he organizes his anthology in such a way as to separate "exis-

Contemporary Ideas of Literature (1977)

tential phenomenology" from "structuralism," the two movements being ideologically opposed when perceived in their purity. But there are mixtures in practice. Both structuralists and phenomenologists marvel sweetly over the mysteries of verbal mediation. Do we have as a result a "terrible beauty" being born? Or is it a "rough beast?"

What seems certain to me is that we are in danger of losing literature entirely in the so-called crisis of language that seems to have been created by our time. (The French literati do have a way of defining everything in crisis terms, don't they?) Criticism threatens to break down all boundaries and to rival (by obliteration) literature itself. There is something of the egotistical sublime in this that seems to render the structuralist critic, when terminally infected, incapable of getting outside the positivistic presuppositions of his own "ordinary" language. To call what he is doing the "science of man" does not hide the fact that the implicit attitudes toward language and art are those of the familiar *social* scientist. Some vestige of Keatsian empathy is lacking—the Keats who sought to peck around in the gravel with the sparrows.

At the other end of the scale is the phenomenological critic, whose godfather, Heidegger, seems sometimes to be the Germanic professor struggling in a curious no man's land between the dryness of metaphysical language and the language of the romantic poem. The French critic Poulet writes meditations or Mallarméan orations on poems. The American critic, Bloom, moves radically to obliterate distinctions and seeks miraculously to turn himself into a poet through criticism.

What is the old saying? First similarities, then differences? Or is it the other way around? No matter, both are necessary to communication, and the critic must balance them. This requires that he look at literature from its own point of view, even as he knows that he must maintain *his* point of view as well. I think the structuralists and phenomenologists fail in this, but at opposite extremes. The anthologies do not bring this problem to light, but perhaps some further study can. Rather than the compromise or mediation between them suggested by Gerald R. Bruns in a recent interesting book,[13] what is needed is an independent position aware of but free of the recent efforts of Gallic rationality. I do not think this position can be one arising out of Wittgensteinian language analysis, so well studied by M. H. Abrams.[14] Here, too, it seems to me that the attitude toward language does not escape the positivistic. The poem's own formal attitude toward itself is not given adequate play.

Both Giambattista Vico early in the eighteenth century and Ernst Cassirer early in the twentieth, speak of the difficulty and yet the necessity, for their endeavors, of trying to see something from its own point of view. In *The New Science,* Vico remarks of the difficulty of coming to understand the way human thinking arose in and as "poetic logic." He tells us that he expended twenty years in the effort to understand that development from inside itself: "We had to descend from these human and refined natures of ours to those quite wild and savage natures, which we cannot at all imagine and can comprehend only with great effort.[15] Cassirer observes, "We cannot reduce myth to certain fixed static elements; we must strive to grasp it in its inner life, in its mobility and diversity, in its dynamic principle."[16] The problem with respect to poetry is the same as that with myth: even the most careful of discursive approaches betrays an alien perspective. Cassirer himself is an example. Much as Cassirer insists on the empathetic principle, he proceeds from a treatment of myth to discussions of language and art, distinguishing between them while at the same time using the linguistic art of poetry among examples of art. His opposition between language and art is unwittingly contradicted by these examples, and poetry is left unaccounted for. Language for him, after all, is language as it has purged itself of myth and is purifying itself in the direction of mathematics. He does not fully rid himself of the tendency to see literary art strictly from the perspective of such ideal discourse, because for him language is to be defined from the point of view of its own state of ideal perfectibility—the end of a long development toward abstract purity. There is here a submerged eschatology that envisions perfectibility of a certain sort. This eschatology, which we can rightly call positivistic, wars with Cassirer's respect for myth, estranges language from art, and poetry, if it is to be regarded as an art, from language. It forces the very struggle that Cassirer wants to avoid.

Vico's struggle is with the received notion of tropes. In classical parlance, tropes are deviations from normal language, and the trace of this concept persists in Vico's description of the tropological nature of "poetic logic," even though Vico's point is that in his primitive "poetic logic," which is comparable to Cassirer's "mythical thought," tropes were not in any sense deviant but fundamental to the way language creates itself and its thought. This attitude toward tropes as deviant recurs in the language of contemporary structuralism and makes a perspective even partly from inside poetry theoretically difficult—almost, I think, impossible—for the structuralists.

Among them, too, Saussure's terminology of *signifiant* and *signifié*, which assumes in language a certain relation or disrelation between word and concept, requires when poetry is the subject, the fabrication of a terminology—difference, nothingness, etc.—to express the absence of a conventionally or substantially conceived *signifié*. Indeed, among some critics the idea of language as creative of such *signifié* as it has, or any concept of language as fundamentally "poetic," is dismissed as requiring "demystification" or reduction to terms compatible with a fundamentally classical or rationalistic norm of discourse. The problem of self-contradiction in Cassirer and what might be called terminological barbarism in the structuralists arises from unstated assumptions about language that may be described as positivistic and anti-artistic in spite of the interests and values professed on the surfaces of these discourses. But pursuit of this matter must be somewhat delayed at this point.

In the face of a dominant rationalism, particularly on the continent, generated by Descartes, there was a struggle waged by certain theorists, and it was dominated by defensive tactics from Baudelaire through Mallarmé to Valéry. They tried to make the case for poetry in a language dominated by the enemy. In employing that language in a straightforward way the literary theorist finds himself driven either to speak in paradoxes (such as the resort to "silence") or finally to hold extreme positions that impose severe limits on the cultural role of art. Most such efforts have failed somewhere—maybe have necessarily failed—because they do not sustain an almost impossible linguistic rigor and irony.

The position I would present is not now fashionable. Though it has some affinities with structuralism, it regards structuralism as captured by positivism. It has some sympathy with modern phenomenological criticism, but departs from its basic philosophical attitudes by recourse not to Heidegger but to a Cassirer purged of the contradictions I have mentioned. One of its own fundamental ideas is that, as Herder and von Humboldt concluded, language is constitutive of thought. Thought does not precede linguistic formulation but takes form in it, form being more than mere appearance, shape, or order, and not a term opposed to "content." Concepts are therefore linguistic. Von Humboldt says, "Languages are not really means for representing already known truths but are rather instruments for discovering previously unrecognized ones."[17] But language is not really an instrument to *look through;* it is radically creative and "no object is possible without it for the psyche."[18] One could go so far as to say that concepts inhere *in* and *as* language. They are not something that language copies or represents (for then they would precede language), nor are they properly regarded as separate from language once they have been created by, in, and as language. However, even though concepts are creations inside and as the very form of language, language hypostasizes concepts and fictionalizes an apartness for them. This is what I have called elsewhere the creation of "antimyth"—the fictive projection to an "outside" of something language really has inside itself, followed by the fiction that the outside preceded its containing substance.[19] It seems to me that von Humboldt was struggling toward some such idea when he wrote:

> The least advantageous influence on any sort of interesting treatment of linguistic studies is exerted by the narrow notion that language originated as a convention and that words are nothing but signs for things or concepts which are independent of them. This view up to a point is certainly correct but beyond this point it is deadly because as soon as it begins to predominate it kills all mental activity and exiles all life.[20]

I would declare that it cannot be said (except with the reservation that it can be said self-consciously as a fiction) that *signifiants* signify anything. The terminology of *signifiant* and *signifié* is, at this level, of value only inside the linguistic fiction that hypostasizes concept or meaning. The structuralists perhaps recognize this in their insistence that *signifiants* signify only difference between words, not concepts or what we normally think of as *signifiés*. Difference for them is the empty space or nothingness between words that ultimately makes no word adequate to the expression of a concept. Structuralism, bereft of a true *signifié*, finds it necessary to construct the fiction of this void between words, this nothingness, as a something because it is tied to the assumptions implicit in its original terms: a *signifiant* must have a *signifié*, if only a *signifié* declared to be an absence.

I hesitate to claim that structuralist theory here is merely sound and fury, but it does claim that signifiers signify nothing. Structuralist terminology always tends to turn terms we employ in common speech inside out. A long list could be created: signifiers do not signify, deconstruction is a new construction, demystification creates a new mystery, difference implies similarity, and so on. This is structuralism's own exhibition of irony and of a new and not always acknowledged mystery. It has always been the fate of criticism to say one thing and to mean another; the question is whether or not structuralist ironies and mysteries are the best we can expect or whether they are not examples of a polysemous perversity from which we shall all, after the first great wave, require deliverance. I observe here only that such acrobatics reflect, for me, at least, the inability of language, when pure abstraction and logical purity in the guise of ordinariness is regarded as its norm, to cope with its own linguistic art.

The reason this occurs is that structuralist discussion of poetry proceeds—as so much discussion of poetry has traditionally proceeded—from deeply ingrained assumptions that words copy things and if, as in Plato, things themselves are copies, then words copy ideas, or words copy their meanings. It is amazing how thoroughly this point of view dominates the discourses even of those structuralists who profess not to believe it. In apparently trying to get at this point, von Humboldt distinguished poetry from prose, but ever so tentatively:

> The characteristic difference between poetry and prose ... is that prose declares by its form that it wishes to accompany and serve. Poetry cannot do without at least appearing to control thought or actually bringing it forth.[21]

The prose-poetry distinction seems inadequate to us today, some prose having declared its alliance with the poem, but there are two important attitudes implicit in von Humboldt's description. The endless play of the possible relation or disrelation of *signifiant* and *signifié* that we find in the work of Jacques Derrida and his coining of the term *différance,* where the *signifié* becomes only the result of the process of interpretation, comes at the whole problem of poetry from the point of view of what von Humboldt above calls prose. This play is perhaps more than what Kenneth Burke calls "good showmanship," but it never breaks out of itself into real engagement with literature. Derrida does not, of course, pretend that it does, but his influence spreads to those who would have it do so if it could, or they would abolish "literature." Whether there is any way to produce any other result from this insistent prosaicism and Gallic rationality is uncertain.

But what if it is possible, taking Vico's lead, to begin with the idea that "poetic logic," if not historically prior, is logically prior to other logics built upon it, or, in a terminology I shall use, projected outward from it? Historical priority is claimed by Vico for his "poetic logic" and by Cassirer for his primordial unity of language and myth, "myth, language and art being as a concrete, undivided unity, which is only gradually resolved into a triad of individual modes of spiritual creativity."[22] But Cassirer's assertion, like so many modern assertions, draws a line at some unspecified historical point in every culture. Before, all is one. Afterward, language, myth, and art are forever separated. This has led to efforts to rescue literary art from language, in Cassirer's ideal, eschatological sense of the term. We are well aware of the many theories of absolute opposition between literature and ordinary language, between "depth language" and "steno language" (as in Philip Wheelwright),[23] and so on.

I wish to accept the logical priority of "poetic logic" and something I shall provisionally call "poetic language," but I am not prepared to proclaim an absolute fissure between poetic language and any such language as might be set up in opposition to it. Instead I wish to admit the possibility of a continuum of language from a poetic center outward. At the end of his *Anatomy of Criticism,* Northrop Frye speculates about the relation of poetry to mathematics, though it is clear that in fundamental respects they hold radically different places on such a continuum.[24] Yet paradoxically they meet, too. The continuum I propose is an unmeasurable one running from a poetic center, with all the priority that implies, outward through the zone of ordinary language, if it exists, through the area of Wheelwright's "steno language" to mathematical symbolism, which marks the outer circumference of symbolic creativity. We may, as we proceed, have reason to believe that William Blake's ultimate identification of true centers with circumferences may apply here; that is, the center really contains all the possibilities implicit in the totality.

It should be clear that this priority of the poetic center absolutely reverses the assumptions about language upon which modern social science bases its methods, since modern social science with its quantitative assumptions places mathematics at the center, building abstract models of human behavior outward from it. Before most structuralist criticism has begun, it has made assumptions about the language of poetry that are diametrically opposed to placement of such a thing as a "poetic logic" at a center.

If we are to make the effort to adopt or even acknowledge (since adoption may finally be impossible) the point of view of the centrality of "poetic logic," from which all things proceed (and to which they return?), we must rethink what can appropriately be said about poetry. For example, we can hardly declare tropes to be deviations from some norm. From this point of view, the idea of discourse, which eliminates all tropes in asserting a norm that is really an ideal of pure mathematic abstraction, is the real deviation, or, to put it better, the movement outward from the center of language. Metaphor, metonymy, and the rest are not, at the center, merely devices to lend vividness to argument or to entertain. The ideal of such purification toward the bare bones of logic, culminating in mathematics, is, of course, derived from assumptions about how the mind works. Rather than computers being made to copy the mind, the mind is declared to be a copy of a computer. The concept of "ordinary language," so popular among analytical philosophers, becomes confused with the ideal abstract mathematic concept of language.

The point that there is no ordinary language has been cleverly made by Stanley Fish, who attacks the distinction between ordinary and literary language by declaring the nonexistence of both.[25] My commentary here has proceeded along somewhat different lines from his, but it acknowledges that the radical distinction between something called literary and other language has been a millstone around the neck of criticism, though it seems that it was one that for a time—as a defensive measure—had to be worn. The construction of a fictive concept of literary language as special or privileged (par excellence in the theorizing of Paul Valéry) was a defensive maneuver against an oppressive cultural force, but it has played into the hands of the positivistic opponent by adopting the same sense of normality as is everywhere in positivism. Ordinary language seems to me a misleading fiction useless to criticism as long as it is employed to declare poetry in some way deviant. To insist on deviance in this situation is to establish an unmoving center. It is a dead center like Dante's Satan and devours poetry by varieties of reduction.

Fish argues that the distinction has forced criticism to claim that poetry is either more than language (message plus, or the "surplus" of the structuralists), which leads to a concept of decorative form, or less than language (message minus), which eliminates content and gives us theories of "pure poetry." This situation does exist as long as we define the center of language as conveyance of a message, not creation of thought that is one with itself. But Fish's analysis does not focus finally on the issue that is fundamental for my purposes. That is, whether language is creative or only imitative, formative of thought or only representative of it. To Vico's "poetic logic" I want to add the characteristic of symbolic formation. I am not content with a poetic logic that claims the mythic (as in Cassirer's mythical thought) identity of word and thing or with the transparency (as in Michel Foucault's Renaissance thought) of words, leading to things.[26]

With poetic logic as the center, tropes are no longer tropes in the classical sense. In the classical view there must always be a gap between word and concept. There is always a possible improvement by substitution. Language is never quite adequate to what it wants to represent. This classical idea of the relation or disrelation of word to concept is what led the romantic period to generate a special derogatory meaning for "allegory." On the other hand, if we regard a word as generating in itself a concept, the concept is not an otherness, and the word does not "signify" in the ordinary sense of this term. The structuralists attempt to make the term "signify" ironic by claiming the signification to be of nothing or difference.

According to my view, language projected along the continuum from center to mathematic circumference came to create the verbal fiction of the nonverbal concept or pure idea. But this fiction, apart from language, has no more substance than the Kantian thing-in-itself, for it is always created *from* and *in* words. We cannot as critics (without totally abandoning respect for the point of view of the poem) drive language outward into a situation where it is merely approximating a preceding nonverbal idea.

Instead of the problem of words and concepts, which has been the domain of the structuralists, what about words and things? Phenomenologists tell us we must get back to things and free ourselves of the tyrannical abstractness of words and ideas. But this, too, presumes the existence of the norm of language far out from the poetic center. On the contrary, we must affirm that things are not simply just "as they are" but that the imagination has a hand in constructing them and that this construction is with and in language. From this point of view the imagination is linguistic (or symbolic, to include other "languages"), and one may well ask, What are things apart from the form which man gives to them via his symbolizing? They are merely a pure potentiality. This is to say that a world prior to the human fiat lacks full reality or is unfinished, and that the real is something we *proceed to make* rather than *refer back or outward toward*. The reality we claim to reach out to beyond our forms is, from this point of view, a will-o'-the-wisp, a nightmare caused, as Blake insists, by our looking in the wrong direction. To have created the "antimyth" of the abstract otherness or objectivity of the world as the exclusive reality is to have created a symbolic structure that projects such a world and ignores all else. This is exactly what Blake's Urizen does, and in doing it he creates hell and becomes Satan himself.

I choose, borrowing from Vico and Cassirer, to seek a theory of radical creativity in language that gives priority to the poetic. In this attempt I adopt the term "symbolic" roughly in Cassirer's sense. But the term "symbol" presents something of the same problem for me as *signifiant* does for the structuralist. Benedetto Croce was quite right to ask what a symbol, used in this sense, symbolizes.[27] Rather than re-creating the distance between *signifiant* and *signifié,* I employ symbolization to indicate an act of linguistic creativity with and in language. For the symbol, there is no symbolized, only the realm of the potential to be worked up into the symbol. In Croce's terms, this, of course, involves the identity of intuition and expression. Being is not prior to, but the result of, language.

I give to man the creation of language in the manner of Blake's "ancient poets," whom Blake declares to have confronted a pure potentiality and set about making by naming the world. Today each of us grows up in a language that, like Blake's eternal London, is constantly decaying even as it is being built. True, as continental criticism likes to tell us, we cannot recapture purity. We have the endless task of retrieving language from its own tendency toward ruin. But if *creation* does not go on as decay takes place, the world of human culture, which is the real world, decays and becomes hell. Hell is the diminishment of culture, the result of human passivity.

My view directs us radically toward the future, not toward the individual death that is the one reality of the existentialists, but toward the continuing act of linguistic creation, toward a passing along of the cultural role. It restores the literal root meaning of "poet." However, it connects the maker not merely with the poet as conventionally conceived but with all who symbolize, including those makers who seem to be taking apart but actually are constructing antimyth. It becomes clear, from this point of view, for example, that history, which seems directed toward an outward past, is the act of creating that past, a symbolic past, which is the only past we have. We are always thus on the threshold of history in an entirely different sense from the common one. We are always making it.

The difference between *signifiant* and *signifié* is itself a fictive creation in language as it operates at a distance from the poetic center, beyond that unlocatable point where poetic logic has turned into antimyth. To look back from this vantage to the poem is to submit it to a mode of thought that appears to be the poem's contrary, where the poem is declared to require interpretation and to hide a *meaning,* where the poem is, in romantic terms, an allegory. But these are all characterizations finally not of the poem but of the limitations of this point of view toward the poem. This point of view, somewhere outward from the center toward mathematics, is in the area of the positivistic, where language itself invents the dislocations that we, when we stand *there,* thrust back upon poems.

As I have said, this area appears to be purely the opposite of the poetic and locked in an endless contrariety with it. Cassirer at the end of *An Essay on Man* found it so.[28] I myself have so treated it, and in a sense it is true[29]; but such treatment erects a too hard-and-fast opposition, declares an absolutely and simply located point of difference on the continuum, thrusts us back into an awkward distinction between ordinary and literary, steno and depth language, and overspatializes and quantifies the unmeasurable continuum between center and circumference.

I propose that this whole continuum is radically creative, but that as we pass further and further outward, what we create is the fiction or antimyth of externality—until we reach mathematics, where something very strange happens, for mathematics proceeds to assert its power to contain, claims that the world is mathematical rather than that mathematics represents the world. In any case, we see that our continuum defies measurement and that we cannot even say where poetry ceases and another form of language begins, where antimyth replaces myth, though we do know by our own declarations when it is that we face a poem.

The adoption of the terms *signifiant* and *signifié* as applicable to the whole continuum of language is, from the point of view of the center, a betrayal of poetry. It is a reduction of everything to a positivistic perspective. From the center, poetry is not an aspect of language, but language is a constant growing out from poetry, though still tied to it. This is why William Blake claimed that the sort of center I have been discussing is the real circumference—an expanding center—a container of all possibility. If the perspective shifts outward, then poetry becomes escapist fantasy or decorated messages, or lamentation over the failure of language to overcome difference or to get back to things.

It is true, of course, that if we are to talk about poetry, criticism must, because it projects itself farther out on the radius than any poem it treats, employ the categories of analysis and reduction. Criticism, increasingly aware of its situation, tends in our own time to find its own predicament as interesting as—sometimes more interesting than—poetry itself. It tends, as in some recent continental work, to project itself inward from itself and treat its own activity as a poem to be interpreted. A certain amount of this is to be expected and is valuable as a built-in check against irresponsibility, but it has its serious dangers—the possibility of infinite regress, the tendency, as one projects one's critical stance farther and farther out, to deaden analysis into more and more reductive quantitative procedures, or the loss of the poem in the narcissism of the critical act. Criticism is most effective when its analytic procedures are observed with a certain skepticism and the irony of its place is fully acknowledged. From the point of view of the poetic center, it is criticism that is ironic, not the poem. The old opposition of art and science catches criticism in the middle of the continuum, that unmeasurable area where neither term seems quite to fit. From this odd perch, irony is one of the things criticism projects back into poetry when criticism's own language cannot hold the poem together in any other way. We as critics project the discontinuities of allegory into poems because these fissures are *our* condition. It should be no surprise that the self-regarding activity of continental criticism should valorize allegory. To do so is for it to justify itself. But this takes us back to a conclusion already reached that criticism is finally, like all symbolic forms, a *making* of its own. It makes an antimyth of bifurcations even when professing to seek out a unity in the poem. It is involved in a both-and situation like the dream as Freud imagined it. The danger to criticism is to lose its own sense of irony; to fail to remember that the poem has a point of view.

It is necessary here to state that the theory of radical creativity, though it refuses to draw a line *measuring off* poetry from other forms of discourse and argues for the creativity of all language, does not quarrel with our needs as critics to create an ironic fictive opposition where a continuum is the reality. Nor does it, in claiming the radical creativity of language, deny that language projects the antimyth of human passivity and automatism—the undesirable floor of things (against which we warn ourselves in language)—old chaos and ancient night. Even antimyth—the world of linguistic bondage and frustration, of subject and object—is a necessary projection if only to impel us toward renewed creativity. Blake called it the "starry floor" beneath which, through God's mercy, man could not fall. Much language is in the process of dying, and much language that is thought to be near the poetic center in one age is found to be dead by another. But the source of even our automatic language and the language we perceive being slaughtered around us was and is the poetic center. This is not to deny that many distinctions must be made—though ironically made—along the continuum, lest the term "literature" disappear in my system as it threatens to in structuralism, all discourse swallowed by poetry rather than all poetry swallowed by discourse. This is the problem Murray Krieger saw clearly some years ago in a neo–Kantian theory.[30]

I take seriously, then, the effort that emerges in romanticism to establish the idea of the symbol, no matter how halting, lacking in rigor, and full of lost opportunities and dead ends individual efforts to develop a theory of poetry out of it may have been. The distinction between allegory and symbolism marks the first step toward a wrenching of these terms from their tropological meanings or their references to devices in a poem (their classical context) and toward reference to poems as wholes in the light of the creative powers of language as it operates at its own center. The distinction was therefore the first step toward a theory of symbolic forms, and it was one of the first toward a theory of fictions. Rather than regarding the distinction as mystification, I regard it as a positive effort in theory, even though it certainly did arise in part as a desperate defensive maneuver against dominant materialist orientations.

To trace the development of the theory of symbolism[31] along these lines would be to seek an appropriate description of literature's cultural role. I believe that role was inadequately stated in the New Criticism and has been obfuscated in modern continental criticism. Anglo-American criticism has never been very patient with the search for philosophical foundations. Modern continental criticism has been so concerned with philosophy—laboring for the most part in the immense shadow of Descartes—that it has often remained satisfied with its own self-regarding philosophical activity at the expense of the poem. (It is not surprising that it is from this tradition that the death of literature is proclaimed.) Of course, there have been exceptions on both sides, but I believe this characterization is helpful as a beginning. Anglo-American criticism has been a mixture of skepticism and pragmatism floating atop the influence of Kant. These tendencies have frequently been noted by commentators, but less often by the dominant critics themselves. (John Crowe Ransom did write on Kant, though somewhat eccentrically.) But Anglo-American criticism has not wanted to philosophize past a certain point, struggling as a matter of principle to maintain theoretical independence. Thus Kenneth Burke declares himself willing to employ any insight that will help him on the way, and Northrop Frye deliberately draws back at the end of his *Anatomy of Criticism* from engaging fully the philosophical questions his speculations seem to raise. There is a reason for this that requires at least a measure of respect. It is that Anglo-American critics tend to maintain a reticence about any criticism beginning from an abstract philosophical position and demanding judgment from that point of view. It is a reticence expressing profound respect for that unmeasurable distance between criticism and the poem.

Yet I am not satisfied with its hesitation to explore its own assumptions, and I do not rest easily with its pragmatism.

On the other hand, modern continental criticism has been Cartesian and subjectivist in its orientation, and existential in its play with *angst*. It has assumed a philosophical situation that it requires literature and those who write about it (or about themselves thinking about it) to endorse, all else—including the theory of symbolism—being mystification. The critic seems tempted to compete with his texts, to surpass them, and in his most ebullient moods, as I have noted, to deny the existence of literature entirely.

Among work written in English attacking the concept of the symbol, as it was developed out of romanticism, that of Paul de Man is perhaps best known. "Literary History and Literary Modernity" reveals his position *visa vis* language:

> The writer's language is to some degree the product of his own action; he is both the historian and the agent of his own language. The ambivalence of writing is such that it can be considered both an act and an interpretive process that follows after an act with which it cannot coincide.[32]

However, of these two concepts of writing, it is the latter that dominates his work and continental criticism at this time. In another essay, both ingenious and influential, called "The Rhetoric of Temporality," he regards the concept of the symbol as a "mystification" that threw the romantics into irresolvable contradictions.[33] It is important to pay attention to this argument, since in the present ebullience of the continental spirit, it threatens to sweep all before it. Its emphasis is entirely different from that of the position I am taking. De Man declares that continental criticism "represents a methodologically motivated attack on the notion that a literary or poetic consciousness is in any way a privileged consciousness, whose use of language can pretend to escape, to some degree, from the duplicity, the confusion, the untruth that we take for granted in the everyday use of language." For de Man "unmediated expression" is a "philosophical impossibility."[34]

Lurking beneath both statements is the classical attitude that language is best described as a copier of a preceding reality and is best definable in terms of its use as conveyor of a message. The emphasis is *not* laid upon language as a maker and container of thought. For de Man, language stands between man and a hidden meaning that it can never fully express. From the point of view that I am taking, this meaning is a creation of language, which hypostasizes it, though in truth such meaning continues to inhere in language, and self-consciously so when language operates at its poetic center. The further out from that center language operates, the further outside of itself it tends to appear to thrust its so-called meaning. At the center it declares its meaning to be itself or interchanges the concept of meaning for that of being. But for de Man, there is no poetic center; language is a system of signs radically cut off from meaning:

> It is the distinct privilege of language to be able to hide meaning behind a misleading sign, as when we hide rage or hatred behind a smile. But it is the distinctive curse of all language, as soon as any kind of interpersonal relation is involved, that it is forced to act this way.

Here the problem of *communication* is essential. I, on the other hand, take the possibility of *creation* as so. This is a critical difference in perspective that has epistemological implications and from which all our subsequent differences proceed. There is no doubt in my mind that communication is faulty, but it does not necessarily follow that language is inevitably a faulty means of conceptualization as making. De Man holds that the actual expression always fails to "coincide with what has to be expressed,"[35] while I claim that a poem is first of all a making, not a copying or representation. Indeed, de Man goes so far as to reverse entirely this notion, proclaiming that in the word "fiction" is an admission or self-conscious awareness of the fact that no expression fully reveals meaning. My own view is that the term "fiction" emphasizes that something has been made rather than faultily copied. But de Man argues:

> That sign and meaning can never coincide, is what is precisely taken for granted in the kind of language we call literary. Literature, unlike everyday language, begins on the far side of this knowledge; it is the only form of language free from the fallacy of unmediated expression. All of us know this, although we know it in the misleading way of wishful assertion of the opposite. Yet the truth emerges in the foreknowledge we possess of the true nature of literature when we refer to it as *fiction*.[36]

Several remarks are pertinent here. It is curious for de Man to insist that we seem only to declare this to be true by stating the opposite. It is interesting that the word "fiction" has spread its influence into areas other than literature—physics, for example, where it clearly is identified with creation or making of a thought. But the fundamental observation I want to make here is that the passage says that language vainly attempts to communicate a fully preexistent meaning, that language and thought do not create, and that a "fiction" is a deviation from an established reality or meaning (though how this is possible if we cannot ever arrive at meaning is unclear). De Man's and my emphases may appear merely logically independent, but there is a fundamental disagreement between us about the role of language in thought, the nature of the imagination, and, indeed, the human condition.

I deal with de Man's position at some length because it is a common one in contemporary criticism influenced by structuralism and phenomenology, even when skeptically held. (Witness de Man's colleague, Geoffrey H. Hartman, who calls tropes "imaginative substitution" while worrying similar problems of mediation, tiptoe gingerly around de Man's position in an interesting but finally inconclusive review of *Blindness and Insight.*)[37] The difference of orientation between continental criticism and the theory I would like to develop is well displayed, as I have implied, by contrasting the valorization of symbolism in my position and that of allegory in de Man's. In approaching this matter, de Man points out, "Hans-Georg Gadamer makes the valorization of symbol at the expense of allegory coincide with the growth of an aesthetic that refuses to distinguish between experience and the representation of this experience."[38] This is the common distinction and works well enough for the use of these terms in romanticism, but it does not do justice to modern developments in the tradition with which I am concerned, where the distinction that is obliterated or at least softened is one between experience and the verbal *formation,* not the *representation,* of it.

With Gadamer, de Man goes on to treat the symbol as something with indefiniteness of meaning. This is all right, except that priority in his analysis is given to a clear meaning. By the very way he puts the issue, the symbol is made to be a representation of a previously existent meaning, rather than the other way around, where the symbol forms its own meaning. Indefiniteness of meaning is for de Man always to be deplored. It is mystification, weak thought. It is, in fact, a debasement of allegory, which properly expresses the relation of sign to meaning. A symbol can only be, to use Fish's terms, "message minus." But what if this indefiniteness of meaning is really a sign in itself of the inevitable failure of a naive theory of interpretation to reach an assumed preexistent meaning that has never really existed—consequently a failure to reach the poem? The huge commentary in modern criticism about the impossibility of translation and the "heresy" of paraphrase argues in favor of this view.

The symbol in de Man, as in most of the *nouvelle critique,* is treated as a trope, and a very inadequate trope at that, for it can never deliver on its promises. Now there is considerable truth to this position if one examines much romantic *practice,* and I do not quarrel with this evidence; but I prefer to consider romantic *theory* of the symbol as a searching in the direction of a description of the poem as a whole, where the characteristics of the so-called trope "symbol" are ultimately seen as pertaining not to a device or element in the poem but to the poem as a whole. De Man's treatment of irony as a trope is in the same way completely different from that of the American New Critics who came to use the term as descriptive of whole poems rather than of parts of poems.[39]

By the same process the romantics made allegory a term that means "nonpoem." What de Man must see as supremely important—the *meaning* of the poem—is what the romantics called "allegory" and what to them and later critics became the hated paraphrase. The confusion that resulted was twofold: First, poems containing allegory as it was traditionally understood were routinely denigrated when disliked, even though it is difficult to find a major poem that does not contain allegory in this sense. Second, the term "symbol," on its way to becoming a term for a poem, kept slipping back to its usage as designating a special sort of trope with miraculous powers. This can be said to have led to much flying off into what T. E. Hulme called the "circumambient gas."[40] Insofar as de Man is complaining about this sort of miraculism in the so-called trope called the symbol, I am with him. It is another language in which to complain about romantic sentimentality. It is also regrettable that in making the term "allegory" mean nonpoem there was no term left available to criticism to describe, let alone do justice to, traditional allegorical usage, or what I call the hypostasization of meaning. But these are not the issues of concern. When de Man attacks romantic theorists, he attacks them for valorizing the symbol as *trope,* while I see them as struggling with the classical terminology of tropes against its fundamental assumptions about poetic wholes and toward a new theory of poetic wholes. As so often occurs in the history of language, romantic critics appropriated, or in Kenneth Burke's term "stole," the terms of the old rhetorical criticism, wrenching them for their own uses.[41] Ultimately they were struggling to move from the idea that a poem contains symbols (and for that reason is valuable) to the view that the whole of a poem is a symbolic form.

In de Man and continental criticism there exists a continuation of that profound disillusionment with language that is one dominant mood of romanticism. But there is another mood that continually seeks to formulate the full range of the possibilities of language. I do not believe it accurate to characterize this effort as "mystification." Rather than assuming, as de Man does, that Friedrich von Schlegel erred in substituting "symbol" for the term "allegory" in the later version of his "Gesprach uber die Poesie," I believe that he was on the track of something.[42] The word may be an "alien presence" in the later version (though I doubt it), but that may be because the essay as a whole does not catch up with romantic thought.

Certainly romanticism was incomplete and in many respects abortive. E. E. Bostetter is correct in so viewing it:

> What seems at first glance triumphant affirmation is revealed on close observation as a desperate struggle for affirmation against increasingly powerful obstacles. The ultimate impression left by the poetry is of gradual loss of vitality and confidence too easily won and precariously held; of diminishing faith in the power of man; of a growing gap between the material and the spiritual and deepening doubt; of affirmation hardening into an incantatory rhetoric sharply at odds with the perceptions and experience it conveys. Romantic poetry becomes in part the testing of a syntax that proved inadequate to the demands placed upon it.[43]

Romanticism failed in these ways because it asked too much of language and was not content with considering what it is that language *can* do. Part of the failure stems from continuing to treat the symbol as a trope in the old classic sense while at the same time struggling toward a concept of the poetic whole as a symbolic form.

The turn in Coleridge from Kant to Schelling is perhaps indicative of romanticism's yearning for an ultimate. Kant was content to admit that thought could never achieve the thing-in-itself. De Man connects this yearning with the romantic concept of the symbol, which would be a vehicle supposedly to achieve the ultimate—a form of language transcending language. He sees Wordsworth renouncing the "seductiveness and the poetical resources of a symbolical diction" and turning to allegory. This retreat he thinks inevitable to any right-thinking poet, the union of *signifiant* and *signifie*, subject and object, and so on, being impossible. Further, for de Man, allegory is fundamentally temporal, in that an allegorical sign refers always to a "previous sign with which it can never coincide" in the enclosure which is language. "It is the essence of this previous sign," he says, "to be pure anteriority."[44] Here de Man draws on the continental existential tradition, from which all he has to say follows: In a temporal system of allegorical signs there is, from the point of view of any given moment or word, only a regress back through an infinite series of escaping meanings. The present can never capture the ultimate meaning.

Martin Heidegger, whose influence on de Man and the whole movement is immense, seems to offer a fictive beginning for this otherwise infinite regress. In his *Introduction to Metaphysics* there is perhaps the best example of his characteristic etymologizing in search of true meaning.[45] Commentators on Heidegger have complained about this apparently pedantic etymologizing, but it is not merely a quirk of the professor. It is quite central to his whole approach, which is fundamentally theological. He presses words back to "origins," where it can be imagined that word and concept were one. With the modern word "being," he reaches back past Aquinas, Aristotle, and Plato all the way to Heraclitus and Parmenides, where he restores a unity of meaning to the original word, before it was, Osiris-like, torn apart. This modern Isis reconstructs its meaning by deconstructing its history. The myth behind all this is that of the single original word given by God to man, which broke up in the Babel of tongues. Language thus represents the condition of the Fall. Heidegger finds the primordial word to have been radically creative, but the fallen word is a mere sign:

> Naming does not come afterward, providing an already manifest essent with a designation and a hallmark known as a word; it is the other way around: originally an act of violence that discloses being, the word sinks from this height to become a mere sign, and this sign proceeds to thrust itself before the essent.[46]

For de Man, allegory faces up to the fact of the Fall and "designates primarily a distance in relation to its own origin, and, renouncing the nostalgia and the desire to coincide, it establishes its language in the void of this temporal difference." According to this view the authentic voice of romantic literature is not its optimistic voice but its ironic one, emphasizing failure to reach ultimate meaning.

The myth of past origin halting the infinite regress of meaning is balanced in the future, in the existentialist view, not by a myth of achievement but by the fact of death. This word, incidentally, is never uttered in de Man's account of romanticism, but it lurks unspoken. Indeed, this fact obliterates all other meaning. Every fallen word looms toward it—the one authenticity. Is it possible to find in romanticism some possibility besides the disillusionment attendant upon the desire to transcend earth and the fixation upon death? Perhaps such an effort will be called "mystification." But both extremes I have mentioned seem to me excessively centered upon what Blake called the "selfhood" and its attendant egoism. If the symbol could be purged of its connections with the effort at transcendence and if we could find in it a reasonably mundane creative principle—one that concerns itself concretely with human culture—perhaps what begins in romanticism could be declared to have outgrown the crises Bostetter sees in it.

The romantic period certainly did not invent the distrust of words that now dominates continental thought. Joyce Cary uttered a well-known truth when he declared that poets have complained about words for at least two thousand years.[47] The "dissociation of sensibility," which is in some versions a dissociation of word and thing, word and thought, word and meaning, has been located variously in time. T. S. Eliot located it in the seventeenth century, Heidegger (if I am right) in the very development of language, Blake in the appearance of a "priesthood" of interpreters, and recently Michel Foucault in modernism.[48] For Foucault, the Renaissance treated language as transparent identification with things; classicism (French neoclassicism) resolved the connection of language with things in the idea of representation, all language being discourse; modernism separates literature from discourse. Foucault's analysis disregards almost entirely the movement in England and America called romantic, where both transparency and representation begin to be treated as unsatisfactory, and language begins to be seen not merely as enclosure but as intimately involved with thought in cultural creation. Foucault is a Frenchman, and France had no Coleridge to deliver to it the news of Kant and the imagination. From the Anglo-American point of view, France went violently from the neoclassic to the modern. As a result there is classicism and then there is Mallarmé, the tradition of representation and discourse and then the withdrawal of literature from representation and signification into the aesthetic, where art is made deliberately to have no relation to things. In England, the intervening Romantic Movement struggled to assert for art an authority over things while at the same time trying to formulate the difference between art and neoclassical discourse.

English aestheticism is regarded in the Anglo-American tradition as a dead end. Its major product,. W. B. Yeats, outgrew it. The shades of a positive romanticism persist in him. Mallarmé fights his battle in isolation. For him, it is a choice between the old neoclassicism, still alive on Parnassus, and the dominant scientific positivism that has set the tone of modernism. Mallarmé chooses to practice a stately withdrawal and style of contempt. It is a brilliant tour de force, much to be admired, but finally it is an attempt to make something positive out of a negative act. Exercise of the modern French imagination has always required the acknowledgment of subjectivity. Exercise of the English imagination since Coleridge has always demanded a stirring toward encompassment of the objective. The presiding deity in the French situation is Descartes; that in the English is, through Coleridge, Kant.

But the romantic theory of imagination could not have developed and presaged its later forms without the special anxiety with which the question of words had come to be viewed. It took the threat of enclosure to raise the possibility of the specifically *linguistic* imagination. Though Bostetter rightly argues that romanticism for the most part failed through excessive claims, including claims for the imagination, it contained in itself the germ of a more modest cultural, rather than metaphysically transcendent, role for art. The French never had to fall from the dizzying heights of English romanticism, but neither did they ever rise to the achievement of a positive view of imaginative power directed toward a specifically human culture. It is only such an achievement—recognized as occurring in language—that can truly free us from both the old classicism and the old romanticism and the positivistic strain of modernism that has emerged from them.

Perhaps at this point the most useful example of the romantic distrust of language, created by one who claimed not to be a romantic and judged romantic art to be "sickly," is the attitude of Goethe's hero at the beginning of *Faust*. Faust's quarrel is with the apparent impossibility of attaining to ultimate knowledge. His resentment appears to be specifically against words and the paraphernalia of science. Faust is first seen sitting in the gloom of his cavernous study. He complains that his search for knowledge has been a mere "rummaging around with words."[49] The study with its books piled to the ceiling all around him has become an enclosure. Faust is stirred to escape from it, but wherever he turns he finds himself meditating on symbols that return him to himself.

The situation presented is crucially different from the Platonic myth of another enclosure in the *Republic,* where Socrates incites one to escape from the enclosure and its illusions through the reason. It is different, too, from the later locked-in personality deplored but accepted by Walter Pater, who, at the beginning of the English Aesthetic Movement, declares not merely the impossibility of ultimate knowledge but the imprisonment of man in a radical subjectivity that separates him totally from the world: "Experience, already reduced to a group of impressions, is ringed round for each one of us by that thick wall of personality through which no real voice has ever pierced...."[50] Goethe, whom Schiller "proved" to be a romantic after all,[51] takes Faust beyond this initial impasse to tragedy and in Part Two to accomplishment, returning him to the world, where he becomes a builder of culture. This conclusion reflects an element of vitality in Goethe, which he possessed even to the end of a long career and which has placed him beyond philosophical categorization. He is both classic and romantic or neither. In his various pronouncements there is one consistent thread, however, and that is the insistence on the poet's connection with the concrete and particular, with earth—the Virgin and Child are an excellent subject for art, not because of their religious significance, but because they are human. In *Faust,* he says, "It was .. . not in my line, as a poet to strive to embody anything *abstract...*"[52] There are many problems in Goethe's pronouncements, but Goethe does verge on asserting a positive cultural role for poetry, moving from the negative enclosure of the Faustian study to establishment of the poetic power, not of transcendence, but of building on earth, presumably in language.

One apprehends a similar effort in Shelley's *Defense of Poetry,* though immensely complicated (and vitiated) by an attempt to place this cultural role in a Platonic context (where it does not fit) and by the presence of poems in the Shelley canon that lament even more desperately than Faust the enclosure of words—"Epipsychidion" and "Hymn to Intellectual Beauty," for example. Shelley locates imagination at a center and declares reason to be an emanation from it. He thinks of language "in the infancy of society" as poetry itself. He claims every "original language" to be itself the "chaos of a cyclic poem."[53] But he does not resolve satisfactorily any of the issues he raises about the relation of language to thought and to things, and he dissolves his essay at a crucial point into an unconvincing panegyric. Nevertheless, this one side of Shelley connects the poet to earth and to culture, placing the poet's function *here* rather than turning poetry into a complaint about failure to transcend the world, the expression of unquenchable metaphysical thirst.

What is the possibility of following out this impulse to see whether it can lead us neither to poetic language as a prison-house, where Gerald

R. Bruns finds it displacing or arresting the function of signification, nor to poetic language as what he calls the "speech of the world," where the word destroys the antithesis of words and things by asserting transparence?[54] The line of pursuit I favor is the attempt to view the word as neither enclosure nor transparency revealing a preexisting thing or meaning, but as potentially creative of cultural reality, which is of the earth, but an earth of man's making and remaking in symbolic form.

As you can see, though many regard as a terrible beauty the mixture of neo-romanticism and positivistic structuralism that is modern continental criticism and the emerging critical fashion in the anthologies under discussion, I am not sure that it is not a rough beast. If so, to extend the Yeatsianism, it belongs to a primary dispensation. Such periods are all right for hunchbacks, saints, and fools, but not for poets.

Essay on Frye (1991)

[This essay was originally presented in Northrop Frye's presence at a Modern Language Association Meeting, in which there was a section devoted to the work of Frye. It is reprinted from *Visionary Poetics: Essays on Northrop Frye's Criticism*, eds. Robert D. Denham and Thomas Willard (New York: Peter Lang, 1991). The essay does not deal with Frye's work on Blake, but rather concentrates on his *Anatomy of Criticism: Four Essays*, published in 1957. I treat that remarkable work as a hybrid text straddling the difference between literature and other forms, as the word "Anatomy" in the title suggests. *Anatomy of Criticism* complicates efforts to fix some texts in predetermined categories, as does Blake's *Marriage of Heaven and Hell*. An example I offer of such a text is W. B. Yeats's *A Vision*, about which Frye once declared he had thought of writing a book. I published my study of it, *The Book of Yeats's Vision* (Madison: University of Wisconsin Press), in 1995.

The inclusion of this essay in the present collection recognizes the importance of Blake in Frye's later work. My reference to what I call the purely mythical and mathematical poles, the area in which all language lies, is based on an argument made in my *Philosophy of the Literary Symbolic* (1983).]

> When first bold Norrie with his bounding mind
> A work to honor William Blake designed,
> He seemed a heretic to canon law,
> Yet made the canon copy what he saw,
> And when we youngsters to the matter came,
> Will Blake and Norrie were, we found, the same.

That is the proem. I proceed now to the prose part of my anatomical poem. But I cannot pass to my real subject, which is how the science of Frye's *Anatomy* is also art, without pausing in true anatomical fashion to express my gratitude, among that of countless others, for Northrop Frye's first book, *Fearful Symmetry,* and the inspiration it gave us and still gives us after forty years.

Having said that—and it could be said about each of Frye's books as they have come out—I should like to concentrate on one point and try to clear up what I think has been a fairly widespread misunderstanding of his work, hard to eradicate because *Anatomy of Criticism* took a certain necessary shape. The misunderstanding comes from reading the polemical first chapter of the *Anatomy* and failing to notice two things: first, that as the work proceeds it turns itself outside in, appropriating a Blakean manner, the crucial point or vortex being where Frye discusses a literary form called the anatomy; second, that this turn is from declaring criticism to be a science to identifying criticism with other constitutive forms in such a way as to associate it finally with art and indeed to imply that the *Anatomy of Criticism* belongs to a literary genre that the book itself names and discusses. This move calls in question any simple difference (forgive me for introducing this word) between literature and science, raising the question of what criticism is among the human arts and sciences.

In an anatomically typical show of erudition, I should like to approach this matter via Blake. I quote first from *Jerusalem* (plate 27):

> Jerusalem the Emanation of the Giant Albion! Can it be? Is it a Truth that the Learned have explored? Was Britain the Primitive Seat of the Patriarchal Religion? If it is true, my title-page is also True, that Jerusalem was & is the Emanation of the Giant Albion. It is True and cannot be controverted.

And now from a rhetorically parallel passage in the conclusion of the *Anatomy*:

> Is literature like mathematics in being substantially useful, and not just incidentally so? That is, is it true that the verbal structures of psychology, anthropology, theology, history, law, and everything else built out of words have been informed or constructed by the same kind of myths and metaphors that we find, in their original hypothetical form, in literature?
> The possibility that seems to me suggested by the present discussion is as follows [352].

There is, of course, in Frye an important difference of gesture (within the same) appropriate to a scientific style of hypothesis-testing as against the stance of prophetic discovery in Blake. However, the informing myth is the same. In Blake, the primitive seat of religion is in Britain, that is, *here*; and Jerusalem in her externalized form is elsewhere or emanated from *here*. In Frye, the verbal forms of the human sciences emanate from myth and metaphor. Myth turns its inside outward to interpretive discourse. I quote from the conclusion of the *Anatomy*:

Essay on Frye (1991)

It looks now as though Freud's view of the Oedipus complex were a psychological conception that throws some light on literary criticism. Perhaps we shall eventually decide that we have got it the wrong way round: that what happened was that the myth of Oedipus informed and gave structure to some psychological investigations at this point [353].

One is tempted to observe that it may have looked as if Frye's notion of the archetype were a concept that throws some light on literary criticism. Perhaps we shall eventually decide that we have it the wrong way around: that what happened was that Blake's myth of Albion and Jerusalem informed and gave structure to Frye's critical investigations.

But the situation is more complicated than that. The parallel is inadequate. Freud's theory may have emanated from dream or myth, but keeps its distance, interprets, allegorizes, plays the role of Blake's great priest Urizen. It is lost from myth and claims freedom from it. Jerusalem has not just emanated from Albion, Jerusalem has changed and managed to dominate Albion by seeing him from her alien position. Frye's *Anatomy* starts out that way, sounding more like the Enion whom the pathetic Tharmas of *The Four Zoas* accuses of anatomizing him:

> Why wilt thou Examine every little fibre of my soul
> Spreading them out before the Sun like Stalks of flax to dry
> The infant joy is beautiful but its anatomy
> Horrible Ghast & Deadly naught shalt thou find in it
> But Death Despair & Everlasting brooding Melancholy
> Thou wilt go mad with horror if thou dost Examine thus
> Every moment of my secret hours [Night the First E302].

One must immediately observe, however, that just as Los's vision in *Jerusalem* would reintegrate Urizen, who is supreme analyst and dissecting anatomist, back into the condition of prolific contrariety, so does Frye's vision integrate and contain his own Urizenizing in his concluding, albeit tentative, apocalypse. He does this by taking the "outsideness" of criticism—its aspect of externalizing science—inside by identifying his own work as an anatomy, which is one of the genres that *Anatomy of Criticism* isolates for discussion.

This having been done, we may read the "Tentative Conclusion," the rhetoric of tentativeness being a lingering aspect of scientific process, as a continuing commentary, inside this particular anatomy, upon itself and upon criticism. But criticism is by now not seen externally as a process of dissection, but internally as a fictive or constitutive form. The speculation on mathematics and its similarities to literature in the conclusion is not there to show that literature is mathematical or mathematics literary, but that mathematics is an art playing the role for the natural sciences that myth and literature play for the human sciences—that is, they are different, but they are also both Albions that send forth their Jerusalems in abstracted forms.

But Frye's critical theory is not quite one of these human sciences after all. Rather it plays a more or less mediatory role, for it is an anatomy, which, having itself aspects of a literary genre, never declares itself free of myth in the way that Freud's psychoanalytic theory by implication did.

An anatomy, as the *Anatomy of Criticism* indicates, inhabits what appears to be a curious halfway position between purely mythical and purely mathematical poles. Or perhaps it is better characterized as curiously marginal. Yet a margin can, if grandiose enough, be a containing circumference, the thing exiled only to be proved central after all. A characteristic of the anatomy according to the *Anatomy of Criticism* is that of the containment of a variety of forms and genres. It may include verse, fictive and argumentative prose, colloquy, and epistle. Frye's glossary describes it thus:

> A form of prose fiction, traditionally known as the Menippean or Varronian satire and represented by Burton's *Anatomy of Melancholy,* characterized by a great variety of subject-matter and a strong interest in ideas. In shorter forms it often has a *cena* or symposium setting and verse interludes [365].

Modern anatomies have a definite tendency to foreground a metapoetical element, that is, to be fairly forthright about commenting on themselves and the constitutive form that they possess. Further, they have, as Frye points out, a cyclical form, which is, of course, characteristic of *Anatomy of Criticism* with its great wheel of phases.

In *Anatomy of Criticism,* Frye wakes the sleeping beauty of romance, restoring her, if not to her medieval preeminence, at least to the Fryean democracy of genres. At the same time, Frye invites into the castle a creature thought by past criticism more appropriate to the moat, the many-limbed monster of anatomy itself. It is a curious creature which by nature turns its inside out, its vital organs flapping in the breeze like Cuchulain in his battle rage. Or we can say that anatomy is a genre threatening to devour all other genres and spew them forth. But still another way to see the anatomy is as a questioner of the division analytics, including its own, makes between genres and between literature and other constitutive forms. Frye's *Anatomy of Criticism* anatomizes criticism into its parts with great strokes of erudition and wit. It hacks up the body but it leaves a very sparse meal for the vultures because as it divides it also constitutes. This devouring, to use Blake's terms, is also prolific. That is the paradox of the anatomy as a form, and that is why the *Anatomy of Criticism* turns itself from science to art and back again. It is like the great egg of the world that Michael Robartes mentions in another modern anatomy, Yeats's *A Vision*. It manages this without breaking its shell.

At the very moment that I penned this last sentence there was a tapping at my chamber door, and there stood an old Arab tribesman who declared that he had been sent to help me complete my analytics. I thought first, this is the ghost of Yeats playing some joke at last—revenge perhaps—but I was transfixed by the Arab's opening remark and soon forgot my resentment. He said, "You should not make the other mistake that Frye's critics have made, and you are on the verge of it when you turn the *Anatomy* into art. Don't you remember that this mistake caused Frank Kermode to call the *Anatomy of Criticism* 'useless' (I employ his exact word)?" Stung by and righteously indignant at his remark because I saw that he had spied an imprecision in my discourse, I first thought to slam the door in his face. But there, the spirit of William Blake entered through my metatarsal arch. I grasped the old Arab firmly by his beard with one hand, and holding a copy of *The Critical Path* in the other, I pushed off and ascended with him to a height where I could declare that the art of the *Anatomy* was not aesthetic in the narrowly formal sense implied by Kermode's metaphysics, but like all art worthy of the name it participated "in the vision of the goal of social effort, the idea of a complete and classless civilization" (348). Thereupon my comrade, metamorphosed suddenly into a raven, croaked "never mind"; and I saw him nevermore, but found myself sitting again quietly in my study visited by a lovely yet stern muse, who whispered, "You have spoken long enough." And so, the envoi:

> When Frye declared the critic scientist
> In horror aesthetes shouted "Positivist!"
> 'Tis True, his work starts out acidulous
> And threatens us who've failed at calculus.
> But hold, anatomy's a genre with a torso
> As literary as a poem, only more so:
> Encyclopedic, episodic, long, prolific,
> In fact artistic, huge, and quite terrific.
> Now, some say art is one thing, science a shame,
> But Frye has proved them different, yet the same.

Reynolds, Vico, *Blackwell,* Blake: The Fate of Allegory (1993)

[This essay was designed to show, through attention to four writers, how allegory diminished in importance as the eighteenth century drew to a close. Blake's movement from a description of two kinds of allegory to an assertion that "vision" was far superior seems to express allegory's fate. In a letter of 2003, Blake wrote of having written a "sublime allegory" (E730). Seven years later in the so-called *A Vision of the Last Judgment,* he declared, "Fable or Allegory are a totally distinct & inferior kind of Poetry" (E554). His attempt to get the right word for what he was doing was very important to him through the many years of his career.

The period in which Vico and Blackwell wrote had many autodidactic scholars interested in mythology and anthropology (as we might call it today), and allegorization was a mode of interpretation. Quite a few speculative books were produced, among them Jacob Bryant's *A New System, or an Analysis of Ancient Mythology* (1774) and Edward Davies' *Celtic Researches* (1804), both of which Blake read, but how carefully or fully is not clear. No doubt he paid attention to and appropriated what he might be able to use. I discuss these matters briefly in "Synecdoche and Method," reprinted in my *Antithetical Essays in Literary Criticism and Liberal Education* (Tallahassee: Florida State University Press, 1990), 38–41.

Quotations within this essay are taken from the following texts and are identified within the text by a letter code ("C") followed by a page number: David V. Erdman, ed., *The Complete Poetry and Prose of William Blake* (Garden City: Anchor Books 1982) ("B"); Hazard Adams, ed., *Critical Theory Since Plato* (New York: Harcourt Brace Jovanovich, 1971) ("C"); Thomas Blackwell *Enquiry into the Life and Writings of Homer* (London: 1735) ("E"); Thomas Blackwell, *Letters Concerning Mythology* (London: 1748) ("L"); Thomas Goddard Bergin and Max Harold Fisch, trs., *The New Science of Giambattista Vico* (Ithaca: Cornell University Press, revised translation of the Third Edition [1744], 1968) ("N").]

Reynolds, Vico, Blackwell, *Blake (1993)*

At the expense of oversimplification, we can consider allegory in two ways. The first way is to treat it strictly as a literary device of the sort we find in Spenser's *Faerie Queene*. As a device it was, of course, variously used: to protect the author against censorship and political revenge, to give density to a work by creating various levels of meaning, to delight the reader, who is amused and satisfied to come upon or unlock a hidden significance, and to join abstract ideas to particular images, thereby giving to such ideas a delightful intimacy, visible presence, and animation.

The second way is to treat allegory as a tendency of language over a broader range of usages, considering its role in theories of the origin of language, religion, and learning, with particular reference to its connection with mythology. It is this second way that concerns me here, though, of course, the two are intertwined; in most important ways the second precedes and includes the first. Consideration of myth, language, and allegory was almost an obsession with certain eighteenth-century intellectuals; and the turn that speculation about these things took is particularly important to, though often ignored by, the history of criticism. If "allegory" was a term used honorifically, or at least neutrally through much of the eighteenth century, it began to take on a pejorative sense late in the age, partly because of conflicts difficult to resolve in the implied theories of scholars of mythology. It is in this context that the work of Thomas Blackwell (1701–1757) has its major interest, for Blackwell, a shrewd and learned scholar, professor of Greek in Marischal College, Aberdeen, stands somewhere between the many conventional students of myth of his day and later theorists with radically different epistemological assumptions.

In the eighteenth century, the question of allegory in the second aspect I have mentioned was tied to questions about the origins of human beliefs and understanding, if not the nature and origin of wisdom itself. This connection was mediated by theories of mythology. We can look at most of the scholars of myth and archeology in this period as naive antiquarians who worked from inadequate principles of etymology and archeological evidence to false conclusions, theorists limited in perspective either by traditional religious assumptions based on a literal reading of the Bible or by deistic and rationalistic biases. Or we can read them as unintentional inventors of speculative mythological works, predecessors of later, much more self-conscious artists who produced their own so-called fictive "systems." William Blake was one of these, and it is with Blake that I shall end, though the story I begin to tell certainly does not end with him

In order to follow this story through the work of Blackwell, I shall look briefly at the position Henry Reynolds (fl. 1627–1632) took toward myth in his defense of the ancients a century before, and I shall proceed to imply a parallel and contrast between the theories of Giambattista Vico (1668–1744) in *The New Science* and those of Blackwell. Vico was known neither to Blackwell nor to Blake, and this was perhaps unfortunate for Blackwell in that Vico offered a theory that, even if it might not have been entirely satisfactory, could have been an indication to Blackwell that there were ways to escape from the contradictions he expresses in a theory of language and tropes. In *The Marriage of Heaven and Hell* (1792), completed forty-four years after publication of Blackwell's last book, Blake found a somewhat different intellectual climate in which to exhibit tendencies present in Vico and, under some stress, in Blackwell.

Henry Reynolds's "Mythomystes" (c. 1632) is an attack on the lack of learning and shallow writing of the moderns. Reynolds argues that the moderns are trivial and the ancients were profound. The latter expressed what we would now call occult wisdom in allegories that were deliberately hidden from vulgar minds. The allegorical truth hidden in a work was for Reynolds its body—a body of reason, while the exterior sense was but the external covering, clothing, or "bark" (C, 196). All matters of rhetoric, including of course tropes, are relegated to this surface, which hides from vulgar minds that are likely to corrupt the truth of the "real form and essence," or the message (C, 196). The truth so hidden is a holy "mystery." The first savants were "those old, wise Egyptian priests [who searched out] the mysteries of nature (which was at first the whole world's only divinity)" (C, 201). Their medium was the hieroglyph, their manner *dissimulanter,* and their matter "high and mystical matters" (C, 202). The dissimulation was to protect truth from vulgar interpretation by the "profane multitude" (C, 202). Presumably a pure language lay behind the protective device of allegory. It is not surprising that Reynolds identifies this language with number, as it is in Platonic thought. A true knowledge of number would "unlock and explain ... mystical meanings to us" (C, 203), because God "through his wisdom disposed all things as in weight and measure, so likewise in number" (C, 202). Following Josephus Picus, Reynolds regards the Mosaic law of the Pentateuch as a container of hidden meaning. He calls it an "interpretation," indicating that the truth lies originally behind the text to be recovered there. One has to suppose that it is ideally prior to language, as number is the source and meaning of nature, which emanates from it.

Reynolds, Vico, Blackwell, *Blake (1993)*

This original truth Reynolds seems to identify with Jupiter, the source of the "golden chain of Homer, that reaches from the foot of Jupiter's throne to the earth" (C, 209). The connection of the Greek chain of being with the Pauline movement from invisible truth to visible signature leads to a connection between Greek and Biblical myth, the Greek figures being at least parallels to Biblical personages, and Moses and the Greeks both having learned from the Egyptians, though Moses was "inspired so far above them with the immediate spirit of Almighty God" (C, 210). Since the days of these ancients the fables have been further and further corrupted, and so there must be an act of recovery.

Allegory, for Reynolds, begins with the priestly creation of fables to protect high truth from vulgar corruption. This truth is prior to language; it is number, which one might say the world of appearance copies. In the course of history the original fables holding a mystical connection to truth became degenerate, corrupted, and trivialized by modem writers and misunderstood by modern scholars.

Some of these not unusual views came down to Blackwell (the notion of the invention of allegory in Egypt, for example); but before I consider Blackwell's work, I want to look at Blackwell's contemporary Vico. From among the legions of occultists, euhemerists, deists, Anglicans, and rationalists of his time who studied myth, only Vico has emerged to command our attention and respect. His work came relatively early in the century, *The New Science* having first appeared in 1720. It was importantly revised in 1730 and 1744. Vico's book has been amazingly fertile for a number of reasons: it includes a theory of the origins of language and thought attractive today to poets and critics because it grounds language and myth in tropes (a nonground some would say today, but that is part of its interest); it offers a theory of history based on a *ricorso* of rise and fall again attractive to poets; it offers a secular theory, carefully independent of Church doctrine; and finally, it offers a provocative distinction between "imaginative" and "abstract" universals. I shall emphasize this last point, because Blackwell lacked such a theory; though obviously skeptical of the Reynoldsian sort of Platonism, which privileged the pure abstraction of mathematics (belonging to Vico's "abstract universal"), Blackwell could never quite develop a notion of tropes that would emancipate his views from the threat of the Platonic.

Like Reynolds, and like Blackwell, Vico believed that many fables have come down to us in corrupted and even obscure form, but he entirely rejects any piety of the sort we find in Reynolds. For him, the Egyptian hieroglyphics do not contain mystical truth, nor do the Greek myths contain high philosophical allegories out of which a priesthood can extract original revelation derived from Egypt. About the Bible he is deliberately silent. However, Egyptian antiquity did bequeath two "great remnants" to us: One of them is that the Egyptians reduced all preceding world time to three ages; namely, the age of gods, the age of heroes, and the age of men. The other is that during these three ages three languages had been spoken, corresponding in order to the three aforesaid ages: namely, the hieroglyphic or sacred language, the symbolic or figurative (which is the heroic) language, and the epistolary or vulgar language of men, employing conventional signs for communicating the common needs of their life. (N, 69)

But for Vico, none of these languages has the authority of mystical truth, nor does it hide such truth. All are strictly secular human creations. Indeed, the earliest is a direct product of primitive reaction to natural phenomena by crude and savage people who did not have the power of reason, that is, the power to form "abstract universals":

> The first men, the children, as it were, of the human race [we note that the farther back we go the younger the human race becomes, while for Reynolds the very opposite is the case], not being able to form intelligible class concepts of things, had a natural need to create poetic characters; that is, imaginative class concepts or universals, to which, as to certain models or ideal portraits, to reduce all the particular species which resembled them [N, 74].

This is the purely secular and strictly linguistic source, for Vico, of "poetic allegories, which gave the fables univocal, not analogical, meanings for various particulars comprised under their poetic genera" (N, 75). Mystical interpretations were impositions on these purely naturalistic expressions of "poetic logic," often corrupted in the passage of time and change of custom. Here there is no incursion of truth from some higher realm of being, no revelation—at least for the Gentile nations. Rather, these primitive people "imagined the causes of the things they felt and wondered at to be gods" (N, 116). Human beings begin with a "wholly corporeal imagination" (N, 117). Everything emanates from the body—all passions, all ideas of the gods. Vico attacks the idea of the superiority of the ancients, even though he argues that the ancients did produce poetry that has never been surpassed. It was not invented by a priesthood to protect wisdom from vulgar distortion. All later so-called discoveries of esoteric wisdom attributed to the ancients are false. It was vulgar wisdom generated as it was in the absence of reason.

Vico concludes further that poetry is imitation. Here he clearly means the expansion of particular images, taken from life, into imaginative universals rather than deduction of particulars from universal ideas as in the Aristotelian syllogism (N, 168). He offers as an example of an imaginative universal the figure of Homer. A real fable always enlarges the "ideas of particulars" (N, 312). Homer received the earliest fables, in distorted forms. But this does not imply an original, lost "literal" history—events transferred bodily into a perfectly representational language. The original form was itself a fabulous form, the expansion of tropes into fabulous stories. But then distortion set in. The figure of Homer himself is a product of tropological thought. There was no one Homer. Rather his works are the product of the Greek people, and he is an imaginative universal created by their poetic logic.

The story Vico tells combats explanation of mythology as an esoteric allegory deliberately hidden by ancient wisemen. It also argues against the notion that language has a rational source in pure ideas rather than a poetic source in vulgar images and things (Vico's "imitation"). It opposes the Platonic notion that all language has always aspired to the condition of mathematics, which in its perfect abstraction most closely reaches the idea. There is no suggestion that language fell from some Edenic condition of abstraction. In other words, Vico turns the rationalist conception of language inside out.

But in historicizing and secularizing language, Vico ended up privileging the abstract universal over poetic logic after all. He thought of the invention of the abstract universal as progress, even as he valued poetry for its sublimity. Perhaps this is because of his sense of distance from those early human beings who thought in poetic logic. In writing *The New Science* he says that he "had to descend from these human and refined natures of ours to those quite wild and savage natures, which we cannot at all imagine and can comprehend only with great effort" (N, 100). Or perhaps Vico thought that there was no need to defend poetry beyond remarks like the following about sublimity: "The most sublime labor of poetry is to give sense and passion to insensate things" (N, 71); or, "it was deficiency of human reasoning power that gave rise to poetry so sublime that the philosophies which came afterward, the arts of poetry and of criticism, have produced none equal or better, and have even prevented its production" (N,

120). Thus Vico sides with the ancients, but for reasons entirely different from those of Reynolds.

Vico's New Science is not a defense of poetry. Its interests are in the nature of history and culture. Later writers like Croce and Cassirer carried on some of Vico's ideas into theories of art with implied defenses. Thomas Blackwell was a defender of Homer and of Greek mythology. Heir to the kind of interpretation of myth represented by Reynolds, he brought a somewhat different perspective to the role of the ancients by secularizing their thought, as did Vico. Yet Blackwell, without Vico, proceeded without a theory of poetic language that might have given his discourses greater consistency. Still, we see in him the defense of poetry only latent in Vico. Blackwell's *Enquiry into the Life and Writings of Homer* (1735) is a work of literary criticism, that ranges broadly into the relation of Homer to his culture. His *Letters Concerning Mythology* (1748) states as its aim "to explain the religious opinions of the ANCIENTS and their consequent Practice" (L, A). He offers a theory that tries to avoid various reductionist interpretations or explanations of the source of myth.

The book on Homer can be fairly described as a work of historical and relativistic criticism. Blackwell, who apparently believed in the existence of a real individual named Homer, describes the poet as having had the good fortune to be born when and where he was. He saw and learned "the *Grecian* Manners at their true Pitch and happiest Temper for Verse: Had he been much sooner, he would have seen nothing but Nakedness and Barbarity: Had he come much later, he had fallen in the Times either of wide Policy and Peace, or of General Wars, when private Passions are buried in the Common Order, and established Discipline" (E, 35). Homer, therefore, escaped perpetrating the incongruity we feel in Virgil between Virgil's refined language and the events he portrays (E, 47) As a result of this and of Homer's ability to present homely detail, we come to believe that all he tells us is true (E, 290). Homer characteristically employs "natural" machinery; and except where he uses Egyptian and Orphic allegories, "which he usually puts in the Mouths of his Gods," he pretends to write in "the *prevailing Language* of the Country" (E, 46). Few people understand that the prevailing language at that time wore a "metaphorical habit," that Homer's language, as in Trojan times, "retained much of the *Eastern* cast; their Theology was a *Fable* and their moral Instruction an allegorical Tale" (E, 47).

Having said this, Blackwell sometimes does, sometimes does not presume that this theology, moral instruction, and allegorical presentation were originally esoteric wisdom deliberately expressed darkly so as to hide truth from the vulgar. On the one hand, he holds, as did Reynolds that "allegorical religion" originated among the Greek priesthood in secrecy. On the other, it became arcane only when a priesthood attempted to establish and maintain its authority, by hiding doctrine (E, 83–84). Fable was "the first Form in which Religion, Law, and Philosophy (united originally) appeared in the World" (L, A3). Myth developed from the boisterous speech of primitive peoples. The allegorical element of myth is coincident with its flowering. Allegory and fable were the learning of Homer's day as they were in Egypt (E, 100). Mythology became debased when it became intermixed with history and accounts of actual people (he agrees here with Vico), and was further distorted in superstition, which takes representations for things, in corrupted transmission, and in the adoption of abstruse symbolical mannerisms (L, 171–8). The meanings of ancient myths are not reachable by euhemerist methods, though presumably those methods might help to erase the corruptions. But he holds that there are few myths that we cannot understand at all (L, 189) and these principally because of corruption, priestly secrecy, or the disappearance of traditions that fostered understanding (I, 189). Most is recoverable because "Symbols carry natural Marks that strike a sagacious Mind, and lead it by degrees to their real Meaning" (L, 204). At the same time, he argues that to be "entertained with this allusive shadowy way of writing" and to "discover the Art of an ingenious fiction and truly judge of its Propriety and Elegance" requires a "peculiar Cast of Mind" (L, 213). Furthermore, there is a paradox in the obscurity of fable: "The Veil of *Fable ... magnifies* the objects which it covers; It shows them in a grander Light, and invites the Eye to contemplate them more eagerly than if they were open and undisguised" (E, 326), but vulgar eyes will not grasp the meaning. The image of the veil, like that of clothing and bark in Reynolds, tends to work against Blackwell's desire to treat allegory and fables as original and natural ways of language. His remark that the ancient Egyptians were a people "addicted to *Metaphor* and *Allusion*," however, leaves it unclear just how Blackwell felt about this, since addiction suggests something unnaturally compulsive. Still, the rest of the statement seems less concerned with the unnatural. "Their very *Method of Writing* or *Sacred Scripture* was a complete and standing System of *Natural Similes*" (E, 169). Hieroglyphic was for the Egyptians uniquely capable of merging abstract and concrete. Blackwell's desire to connect Homer closely with Egypt and even to call him an "*Egyptian* mythologist"

(E, 168) is closely related to his interest in the concrete quality of Egyptian expression. Here he edges up to the Vichean imaginative universal.

Like Vico, Blackwell grounds his discussion of myth on the trope. Of the various species of mythology he mentions, the fundamental one "flows from pure untaught Nature; a Similitude, a Metaphor, is an Allegory in Embryo, which extended and animated will become a perfect piece of full grown Mythology" (L, 70). Here he parallels Vico's notion of the trope as a "fable in brief" (N, 129). Both seem to imply a synecdochic relation between trope and fable. As did Vico, Blackwell anticipated the views of Rousseau on the fundamentally tropological nature of early poetry.

For Blackwell, fable is the "truest species" of poetry (L, 310). Knowledge in Homer's day was "wholly fabulous and allegorical" (E, 100). The Hellenes described everything by means of some analogy and resemblance to human actions, this being their science. Blackwell denies that allegory came on the scene late. Rather, it was, with trope and myth, the earliest mode of knowledge and expression, "understood and receiv'd from the Beginning" (L, 212).

Although Blackwell refers to "sacred scripture," whether of the Egyptians or others, he never attributes supernatural authority to it. Like Vico, he reads the gods of mythology as human creations meant to explain and domesticate the natural world. Mythology is for him, as for Vico, a mimetic art and has its source in nature (L, 69). Religious utterances seem in his view to be attempts to conceptualize the world. He privileges no particular position. The ancient poets made gods of the "Principles of Being" as they were able to express them tropologically (L, 180) from the parts composing the universe (L, 409). Poetry and philosophy were one; only later were they separated, at which point poetry began to descend to the level of mere entertainment.

This means that the ancient myths are in some way instructive, but at the same time they are expressive of passions. Vico identified passion with poetic logic because it meant for him absence of reason. Blackwell, no doubt, thought along these lines, but he never quite draws the line between reason and primitive thought, as did Vico. Instead he holds on to the notion that the ancients combined reason and passion in their fables. Thus there was still instruction, identified with reason, in them. It is apparently poetry now that is purely passionate (mere entertainment?). At the same time, Blackwell insists that the ancient myths are pliable to the interpreter, at least insofar as there may be a sophisticated and learned interpretation, an interpretation of common sense, and a vulgar one. These correspond to three classes of readers: the wise and knowing few, the middle sort of reader of good sense, and the unthinking multitude.

Before I examine this shift to a readerly perspective and admission of the possibility, nay the inevitability, of multiple meaning, it is worthwhile to note a distinction Blackwell makes between "cool" and "sudden and flashy" myth:

> *Mythology*, Taken in the largest Sense, must be distinguished into two sorts: the one *abstracted* and *cool;* the Result of great Search and Science: Being a Comparison of the Harmony and Discord, the Resemblance and Dissimilitude of the Powers and Parts of the *Universe*. It often consists of their finest *Proportions* and hidden *Aptitudes* set together and personated by a Being acting like a *Mortal*. The other, sudden and flashy; rapid Feelings and Starts of a Passion not in our Power. The first of these may be called *artificial,* and the second *natural* Mythology; the one is a Science [where obviously reason governs but does not suppress passion], and may be learn' d; the other is the Faculty that for the most part, if not always, invents and expresses it. This cannot be learned; but like other natural powers admits of *Culture* and *Improvement* [E, 161-2].

There is, for Blackwell, nothing occult or divine about this power; it is "natural." According to him, men acquired the first power and improved the second. It is the cool element that Blackwell tends to identify with allegory, though its source seems to be in the "sudden and flashy." His treatment of metaphor and simile follows the same division, one hot and one cool, or, better, cooled: "Metaphor is the Language of *Passion;* as Simile is the Effect of a *warm Imagination;* which when *cooled* and *regulated* explains itself in diffuse Fable and elaborate Allegory" (L, 71).

The distinction seems to suggest a temporal or historical movement, with "natural" metaphor regarded as the origin of both hieroglyphic and speech. It "cools," though paradoxically it expands into fable and allegory. When Blackwell comes to defend myth, he does so on the grounds of the virtues of the "cooled," for the criterion seems to be the traditional one of delightful instruction: "Mythology in general is *Instruction* conveyed in a Tale. A Fable or meer Legend without a Moral, or if you please without a Meaning, can with Little Propriety deserve the Name" (L, 70). The recourse to instruction and its identification with reason or something like reason is difficult to identify with Blackwell's theory of the ambiguity of metaphor and the pliability of mythic meaning. One would think that moral instruction required a single clear sense. The following two remarks are central:

1. "A Metaphor is a *general Pattern,* which may be applied to many Particulars: It is susceptible of an infinite number of *Meanings*; and reaches far because of its Ambiguity." (E, 317)
2. "But there is still another Conveniency in this Method of Instruction by *Fable* and *Allegory,* that must effectually prevent any Fallacy, or hazard of being deceived: I mean its *Condescension* and *Pliableness* to all sorts of Subjects, and Aptness to illustrate indifferently various or even opposite Opinions. For Mythology confines you to no Creed, nor pins you down to a Set of Principles, beyond which, you must either not take a step, or lose her Company. On the contrary, she permits, nay assists, you to contemplate at ease." (L, 120)

In (1) above, Blackwell describes metaphor as if it were a Vichian imaginative universal but then goes on to deny the univocality Vico gave to it. In (2) above, Blackwell means to extend the idea of "general pattern" to show that fable and allegory have numerous applications to particulars, again as in the imaginative universal; but the passage ends by describing a situation of instability. This problem surfaces elsewhere:

> Mythology leaves us at liberty to think and reason as we list; and therefore can lead us no further astray than we ourselves have a mind to follow. You have seen how variously it represents the Rise of Things, according to the different Opinions of the Sages concerning them; like a Mirror that reflects whatever Object is held before it, and in the Colours it wears, whether genuine or not [L, 130–131].

The pliability theory seems to lead toward a pure critical impressionism; Blackwell is aware of the difficulty: "You ask first, whether the Meanings we ascribe to ancient Fables be not for the most part *Conjectures* of the Moderns, who admire every thing that is ancient, merely because it is so, and torture their Brains to find out Meanings and Mysteries which the Authors or the Contemporaries never thought of?" (IL, 186).

On the other hand, Blackwell insists on meaning: "the old Sages imposed no particular Person or Character upon their primary Gods, nor interwove those Characters in a tale, without a meaning" (L, 93). The resolution for him lies in his distinguishing literal belief from apprehension of meaning. Writing of a myth of Venus and Cupid, he remarks,

> Cou'd any body, do you imagine, take it into his Head after reading this Allusion, That the Author of it actually believed the little fluttering Thing he has so exquisitely described to be a real divine Person, and wou'd worship him

accordingly as *a God?* One shou'd think *not:* Especially as this very Parable has been taken for an Argument of his Unbelief...Or, on the other hand, wou'd it not be as absurd to say, that it had *no meaning at all?* It must be a strange Turn of Mind that cou'd lead to either: For to believe it literally, or to condemn it for Want of Ingenuity, are equally preposterous" [L, 10].

Clearly here, what Blackwell comes around to attacking is a *literal* reading. For this literality he substitutes his notion of levels of understanding. After a discussion of a myth of Vesta, he remarks,

> The emblems are explained. What more is to be done? To moralize—and draw Inferences from the Explication—? No—but only to observe a strange sort of Likeness between ancient and modern Superstition.—A passion diffused thro' all Ages and Generations, and acting uniformly, however its Objects may be varied. The Circumstance of the preceding Allegories that makes me say so is this: The Gods of the Ancients, you see, appear in a Double Light; as the Parts and Powers of Nature to the Philosophers, as real Persons to the Vulgar... Has not the same thing happened in modern Religious Matters? [L, 62].

The range is from allegorical to literal. Also, because myths have come down to us frequently distorted, their surface literality often has no meaning, yet they "point at some latent Truth" (L, 119).

Blackwell strives, against its Reynoldsian implications, to hold on to the term "doctrine" in connection with allegory, no doubt thinking it a valuable counter in a defense of mythology. Here the idea of different classes of readers comes in, but now myths have different aspects appealing to these classes as if deliberately so intended. This is perhaps finally the extent of myths' pliability:

> They fall naturally into *three* Classes, and had Worshippers suited to them of *three* different Characters. I. The PARTS and natural POWERS of the Universe, called out of *Chaos,* said the Poets; formed in *Chaos,* said the Philosophers, by an all-wise MIND that first regulated and still keeps them in order. II. GENII, or spiritual abstract Substances, supposed to exist in, or preside over these Powers, and III. HUMAN creatures deified [L, 246].

As we move down this scale, interpretation becomes simpler but cruder. The idea moves us back to the old idea of myth as a conveyor of secret mystical doctrine, probably supralinguistic and Platonic, guarded by a priesthood.

To be consistent with his own bent of mind, Blackwell should not be talking about the pliability of myths or even classes of readers but about their evasiveness to any mind wishing to interpret them willfully, any mind desiring to discover abstract, not imaginative, universals *behind* them. Yet if he *does* do this, he must then call in question the instructive quality of myth (if, as his age insists, it must be identified with reason) and undo the defense he has mounted for it. At this point he has left to him only the formula *dulce et utile,* which too easily divides myth into instruction and decoration. So we see him undecided over whether myths are allegories of reason (particulars standing for abstract ideas), whether myths are so pliable as to have no meaning and therefore are usable to personal ends by anyone, or whether myths speak their own language, not really pliable to the interpreter, but challenging the reader with an inexhaustible meaning or the illusion of a meaning always beyond reach.

Blackwell wished to build a concept of mythological wisdom which was neither that of the science he knew nor that of occult Platonism. He wanted his theory to be secular. Fleeing from these obvious choices, choices that continue to be brought before us today under various new guises, he found himself unhappily reduced to that last refuge of critics, the *Je ne sais quoi:*

> If ever the *Je ne sais quoi* was rightly applied, it is to the *Powers* of Mythology, and the *Faculty* that produces them. To go about to describe it, would be like attempting to define *Inspiration,* or that *Glow of Fancy* and *Effusion of Soul,* which the poet feels while in his *Fit* [E, 151].

But we cannot leave him there, because he never quite stays there. He never provides literary criticism with a language derived from his equation of myth and poetry, though his work certainly implies that the greatest poetry—that which does not merely please but is identical with philosophy in the sense of its ancient practice—is mythological and allegorical. He seems to have been struggling through the terminology of eighteenth-century criticism to a secular idea of mythic and poetic expression as a mode with its own laws. In this, Vico's secular notion of poetic logic and the imaginative universal might have been of use to him. Anticipating in his distinction between fiery and cool allegory the distinction of Schiller between naive and sentimental poetry, Blackwell seems to have seen myth as a mode of expression of human sympathetic identification with nature. The tools his age gave him were inadequate. A more sophisticated theory of language, and especially of tropes, was necessary. He was given the concept of hidden meaning that had to be driven back to mathematical "truth" or to the abstract universal on the one hand or attributed to divine intervention and/or poetic madness on the other.

The problem is perhaps best symbolized by a remark Blackwell makes just after he has argued that language is fundamentally in its very nature metaphorical: "few People imagine that the *Ordinary* Language wore this metaphorical Habit at that time" (E, 47). Here, in typical rationalistic fashion (later, positivistic fashion), the trope is relegated to outer clothing, not to the body itself. The image combats the very point Blackwell tries to make. It is this split between language and metaphor (taken in the sense of tropes in general) that generated the revolt against the term "allegory" which began late in the century and continued even into modernism, for in this figure "Habit" connotes decoration and triviality. "Allegory" came to be identified with a prettying over of what Vico called abstract universals. This meant that poetry was merely the prettification of what was regarded as the essence of language—pure abstraction.

William Blake is one of the last in the century to employ "allegory" in an honorific sense, but it is significant that he finally came to use it, for the most part, pejoratively. It is pejorative usage that tended to win the day as the word "symbol" came to be opposed to "allegory" and favored by poets and critics from Goethe to Yeats. Blake, however, did not employ the term "symbol"; rather, he came to oppose allegory with the word "vision." It is possible that "symbol," with its suggestion of the concept of the eucharist, implying a miraculous embodiment of a bodiless mystery, was anathema to a painter who, though many thought his work unworldly, insisted, "I know that This World Is a World of Imagination & Vision. I see Everything I paint In This World, but Everybody does not see alike" (B, 702). For Blake, the miraculous symbol would be no different from allegory.

In 1792 in *The Marriage of Heaven and Hell,* Blake told his story of the making of language and like Vico attributed it to the "ancient poets," his own imaginative universal for the inventors of poetic logic:

> The ancient Poets animated all sensible objects with Gods or Geniuses, calling them by the names and adorning them with the properties of woods, rivers, mountains, lakes, cities, nations, and whatever their enlarged & numerous senses could percieve [B, 38].

But there set in a gradual abstraction of these "mental deities," that is, invented gods, from their natural objects. Priesthood began when those who sought to gain and maintain power created a mystery around these deifying words. Blake claims that thus "forms of worship" grew up out of "poetic tales" and men "forgot that All deities reside in the human breast." Religion became the worship of an abstract mystery behind the veil of language and appearance. This situation Blake came to identify with allegory, though first he divided allegory into two kinds, favoring an allegory addressed to intellect, which he tended to identify with a creative imagination, over one addressed to the understanding:

> Allegory addressed to the Intellectual powers while it is altogether hidden from the Corporeal Understanding is My Definition of the Most Sublime Poetry [Letter to Thomas Butts, July 6, 1803, B, 730].

Blake's definition here does not imply a priesthood of interpreters hiding meaning from a vulgar multitude. He is writing about two attitudes or sets of assumptions to be met by the work of art. It is the "corporeal understanding" that divides things into body and spirit, primary and secondary qualities of experience and then proceeds to reduce everything real to number and measurement. Blake employs "corporeal" in a way directly opposite to Vico's. For Blake corporeality is the notion of matter so abstracted from itself as to have no image. It is this that paradoxically creates a "reality" of pure abstraction behind a veil of "appearances." The intellectual powers, for Blake, do not make this separation but instead oppose it, as did Vico's "poetic logic."

Seven years later, Blake had changed his mind about the word "allegory." He now identified it totally with the "corporeal understanding." The contrary term had become "vision":

> The Last Judgment [he is describing his painting by that name] is not Fable or Allegory but Vision. Fable or Allegory are a totally distinct & inferior kind of Poetry. Vision or Imagination is a Representation of what Eternally Exists. Really and Unchangeably. Fable or Allegory is Formed by the Daughters of Memory. Imagination is surrounded by the daughters of Inspiration who in the aggregate are called Jerusalem. Fable is Allegory but what Critics call The Fable is Vision itself. The Hebrew Bible & the Gospel of Jesus are not Allegory but Eternal Vision or Imagination of All that Exists. Note here that Fable or Allegory is Seldom without some Vision Pilgrims Progress is full of it the Greek Poets the same but Allegory and vision ought to be known as Two Distinct Things [*A Vision of the Last Judgment,* 1810, B, 554].

Thus, in Vichean terms, "allegory" had slipped from a term identified in his own work and in Blackwell's with "imaginative universals" to a figure of speech in which an "abstract universal" is represented by an image. This practice is what Wordsworth inveighs against in his preface to the second edition of *Lyrical Ballads* (1800), calling the result "personification of abstract ideas," admissible occasionally, but "utterly rejected as an ordinary device to elevate the style, and raise it above prose" (C, 435). The century closes with the most important critical document of the time not merely eschewing allegory explicitly; it does not mention it at all.

The World-View of William Blake in Relation to Cultural Policy (1993)

[This essay was written specifically for and delivered at a conference on cultural policy sponsored by the University of Calgary. The occasion accounts for the cumbersomeness of the title. It was published in *Cultural Policy. Past, Present and Future*, eds. Evan Alderson, Robin Blaser, and Harold Coward (Calgary: Wilfrid Laurier University Press for the Calgary Institute for the Humanities, 1993).

Here I build on the Blakean notion of contraries and also appropriate a term I have stolen from W. B. Yeats's *A Vision*—"antitheticality." The word features prominently in most of what I have written since. I return to this matter in essays toward the end of this book.]

I. The Problem of the Title

Blake would have thought the subject I have been assigned quite odd. I am sure he would have seen no connection between his "world-view" and "cultural policy," since to him "cultural policy" would have suggested something made by a king, a prime minister or, perhaps worse, if that is possible, a committee or board of scholars. In other words, it would be an abstraction, and, for Blake, "to Generalize is to be an Idiot" (E641).[1] He remarks of Sir Joshua Reynolds, "Generalizing in Every thing the Man would soon be a Fool but a Cunning Fool" (E649). Furthermore, if Blake were to have reflected on the phrase "world-view" he would certainly have objected to it. For him, observation, or being a spectator, implied passivity of the imagination, and this attitude would have made him as suspicious of "views" as he was of landscape paintings and portraits. The point is not a trivial one, as I shall eventually try to show.

The World-View of William Blake in Relation to Cultural Policy (1993)

There is another more mundane problem to be gotten around. Blake was not in any of the usual senses a man of the world. Indeed, he seems to have had little experience of it except what he imagined (this was, of course, quite a lot) from his reading, especially the Bible and certain books of travel for which he made engravings. As far as we know, the longest trip he ever made was from Lambeth to Felpham on the southern English coast, a distance of some sixty miles. Except for the three years he spent there and a brief visit to a friend in Kent, he seems never to have left London. In most conventional ways he was isolated from the great world, impolitic, professionally unsuccessful, childless, and at least in his later years, quite poor. He did not live in a world of politicians, political activists, theorists or professors; and the concept of cultural policy had yet to be invented. In his day there were no ministers of health, education or welfare, no national endowments for the humanities or Canada Councils. Hardly anyone had yet committed a social science. Such bodies as might have been thought in his time to further cultural life—the Church, the Royal Academy, the Royal Family—Blake viewed with either suspicion, resentment or contempt, usually all three. He was in many ways an outsider, an embarrassment to a lady of class who had to sit beside him at a dinner, without formal education and regarded as an artisan rather than an artist by many in the artistic establishment. His political views bordered on treason, if they were not in fact technically treasonous at the time. He had to stand trial in 1803 on what may or may not have been a false charge. He approved of the American and French Revolutions and spoke and wrote often in the tone of radical dissent, both political and religious.

II. Antitheticality

Blake was, it is probably fair to say, the first consciously antithetical artist. By this I mean that he conceived of his work as opposed to the usual oppositions embedded in the language of the culture. Among these were subject/object, body/soul, and the concepts of good and evil arising from them, involving preservation of social, political, and cultural power in the patriarchal and class system of the time. The young W. B. Yeats, one of Blake's first consciously (but too often erring) interpreters, misunderstood Blake's antitheticality (a term I have actually taken from Yeats) and described him, in effect, as the first aesthetic artist, the first aesthete. But if aestheticism means a detached formalism, it is about as far as possible from Blake's conception of art. Nor was Blake's attitude anything like that of aesthetic subjectivism, represented later in its most extreme form by Walter Pater, another hero (at one time) of Yeats. Both the aesthete and the subjectivist would have been for Blake merely the other side of the coin from the objectivist. Blake's aim was to establish a position antithetical to this negation, in which each side exists by deploring the errors of its opposite. Thus they play roles familiar to readers of Blake's longer poems—the young, frustrated Orc and the old repressive Urizen. Their progress is but cyclical, that is, no progress at all.

Recently Tzvetan Todorov has observed, as have others, the curious embrace of or at least flirtation with tyrannical political systems by early twentieth-century intellectuals and their criticism of democracy:

> We like to see our societies as ones in which both individuals and the collectivity have the right to set their own standards. Given which, the critique of existing norms is a crucial social task, and intellectuals have come to identify themselves with performing it. It is because the majority has chosen the path of democracy that intellectuals feel compelled to call it into question.[2]

This phenomenon begins, I think, with Romanticism and the revolutionary fervour and disillusion that followed it. Blake was never compelled to call democracy into question. For him democracy, though he did not have the word and imagined a more thorough form of it than anyone has seen on earth, was the antithetical dream of a classless, free society in the process of endless creation. Anything that contributed to it, including personal acts of charity and love, was what he conceived of as art.

Today Blake would have been vociferous in his criticism of the so-called democracies, not embracing some totalitarian form as an alternative but relentlessly pointing out where totalitarianism still lurked in political and social practices. There is a sense, of course, in which Blake must have appeared, in his own time, reactionary. He liked little that had happened in the fine arts since Raphael, and in various ways he was out of step with the contemporary. He had no sympathy with modern philosophy or the associationist psychology that for a while captured Wordsworth and Coleridge. But there is very little nostalgia in Blake, almost a principled flight from it to the future. As a result, his work has the opposite effect of that of his closest followers, the young "ancients" who gathered around him late in his life, the Pre-Raphaelites, and the early Yeats, who later detected in his own apprentice poetry a "slight, sentimental sensuality which is disagreeable."³ Blake's complaints about the modernism of his own time were aimed at certain fundamental assumptions that to his eyes corrupted politics, religion, sexuality, and science. In spite of his own preferences in painting for Raphael and before, he did not seek a return to the past but sought a new future.

Almost all the modern intellectuals whom Todorov has in mind as reactionary critics of democracy imagined nostalgically some lost age or embraced (or at least admired for a time) some fascist or totalitarian idea or strong man. If Blake wished to return to something in the past (and he did, of course, speak of a golden age), it was the act of creation itself. And this was but to remind his readers that creation was in their power and not something imposed from above or beyond or the past by a distant god. Thus creation is, for Blake, actually removed from the past into potentiality and from surrounding space into the human mind.

Therefore, Blake's world-view, if that is what we are to call it, is always a projection outward of possibility rather than a "correspondence" to anything out there. This projection is an activity of what he calls imagination and is identical with his notion of religious activity, though he frequently uses the term "religious" in a derogatory sense to mean the very opposite—passive reception of the law of external authority paralleling the passive reception of sense data that he attacks in Locke's epistemology.

Blake's world-view can, therefore, be characterized as symbolical, though symbolizing nothing existent (that would be allegory in his language), but that which is yet to exist, desirable both individually and socially. This symbolized does not exist somewhere like a Platonic form or idea. Blake's symbols do not have objects to which they refer or previous ideas which they signify. They are radical possibilities *in themselves,* without attachment to things in themselves.⁴ In this sense, Blake's world-view is not a view but is itself a sort of world, a world of language and design which does not copy nature, he declares, but projects a "vision." Blake's illuminated works are for spectators who can transcend the spectatorial, which in Blake is the spectral, condition. In his description of his painting "The Last Judgment," Blake wrote

> If the Spectator could Enter into these Images in his Imagination approaching them on the Fiery Chariot of his Contemplative Thought if he could Enter into Noahs Rainbow or into his bosom or could make a Friend & Companion of one of these Images of wonder which always intreats him to leave mortal things as he must know then would he arise from his Grave then would he meet the Lord in the Air & then he would be happy [E560].

It is noteworthy that Blake called his designs "vision," not "fable" or "allegory." "Vision," emphasizing the painter's eye, means for Blake an active seeing of what is greater than nature or the object as it is opposed to the subject. In the passage I have quoted above, Blake hopes for an act of vision in the spectator that will make him more than a spectator, a visionary identifying himself with a world of possibility. That world is neither an epistemological object nor a phenomenological one. Rather it is an ethical projection, but not connected in any way with received moral law.

III. A Visionary World

The archetypes of Blake's visionary world have been much discussed in recent decades, most illuminatingly by Northrop Frye in his monumental *Fearful Symmetry* and several of his subsequent essays: "Blake's Treatment of the Archetype," "Notes for a Commentary on *Milton*," "The Road of Excess," and "The Keys to the Gates."[5] We know a great deal now about the inter-relations of Urthona, Tharmas, Luvah, and Urizen, their fallen forms, their emanations, and the mental states inhabited by the giant Albion. There is no need to go over ground so eloquently treated. It is possible, however, to emphasize here some of the more general characteristics of Blake's visionary world or, as some have called it, mythology in order to see what is implied there for thinking about cultural policy.

I have divided this subject into four parts, and because Blake's visionary world is not a landscape or an external portrait but an imagining of mental activity, I begin with the problem of knowledge as Blake saw it.

(a) *Against epistemology:* The term "epistemology" suggests the very thing Blake opposed most vehemently. It is a term that has come to be identified with the situational view of natural science established by Bacon, Newton, and Locke—an object situated *vis-a-vis* a subject or *vice versa*. The attitude of subject/object carried outside the realm of science, as Blake saw that it had been in his day, inevitably generated alienation of individuals from all that surrounded them, requiring measures to dominate that threatening other. Perhaps Blake's most powerful image of this figure is the hapless Urizen of *The Four Zoas,* who travels through such a universe and can find no foundation for it. Finally, he surrounds himself with books of arbitrary law as a fortress against chaos. This merely generates in that other outer world the repressed energy of Orc, who must be endlessly chained down or crucified in order to maintain control but whose moments of revolt establish a new negative force with its own pattern of alienation and fear—Urizen all over again. Blake's aim was to provide a contrary to this situation of negative opposition, which may be necessary to science as a fiction but which Blake nevertheless described in an unflattering way as a "cloven fiction."

(b) *Contrary antithetical vision:* Obviously the contrary must be something not cloven in this way. At the same time it must not negate, that is, suppress that cloven opposite. Otherwise the cycle of alienation will continue with new terms playing the old roles. It cannot be a monolithic, seamless oneness. Rather it must maintain oppositions while it recasts their roles so that neither side can negate the other. This is one difference between a true contrary and a negation. There can be no "progression" in a situation of negation alone because it results either in continued suppression or in the cyclicity of the Orc/Urizen opposition. If, however, the negation is opposed by a contrary it can cease to be a negation because involved now in what Blake describes at the end of *Jerusalem* as conversations in "visionary forms dramatic" (E257). Establishment of a contrary requires, then, a sort of friendly opposition, yet clearly an opposition and tension. The heroic worker-artist Los in *Jerusalem* firmly asserts,

> I must create a System, or be enslav'd by another Mans
> I will not Reason & Compare: my business is to Create [E153].

Los's idea of system opposing system is not as precise as the whole poem seems to be and suggests that at this point in the poem Los may still be in error to some extent. *Jerusalem* is more like an antisystem, that is, antithetical to system as such, a true contrary that provides what system lacks or lacks what system imposes. As such, it isn't just an alternative system but *the* contrary. It would take too much space to show how *Jerusalem* antisystemically frustrates systematic analysis, though it would be instructive at this point. It is, however, possible to show that this contrary employs language in a way contrary to the view of language implicit in systems based on scientific epistemology. One can characterize this use of language as taking metaphor (in the sense of all tropes) seriously, that is to say, literally or literarily.

(c) A *vision of language, a language of vision:* For Blake it is language or languages (since there is for Blake a language of design) that constitute culture. Therefore, our view of language, a clear and distinct outline of what it is and can do, is critical to human life and will affect how society shapes itself. Blake's vision of language he offered relatively early in his career in *The Marriage of Heaven and Hell,* defining it, as was characteristic of his time, by imagining its origin in a symbolical story. In the story, he describes not just the invention of names by poets but the eventual hardening of language into "system." The "ancient poets animated all sensible objects with Gods or Geniuses" (E38), but gradually these gods became abstracted from their objects and under domination of an interpreting priesthood became objects of worship external to man, when they had originally been his invention and immediately experienceable. These original acts of naming were obviously metaphorical, so for Blake metaphor is fundamental to language and not something secondary or decorative added on to a system that has as its ideal form the pure abstraction from objects achieved in mathematics, where the trope has completely disappeared. Blake tells the story of language as if it were the history of a fall. If we read *Jerusalem* carefully, we discover that the fall was not the invention of abstraction but the suppression of metaphor in system, that is, the culture's failure to maintain the prolific contrariety of abstraction and trope. Concurrent with this was the failure to maintain the arts of life, which require the metaphor. Without it the arts can but copy a nature assumed to be already out there, for it is in the metaphor that two things unlike in nature are brought into "identity," a term I shall discuss at greater length in Part IV. Without metaphor the arts must accept the cloven fiction of subject/object, identifying art with either one or the other, and cut themselves off from true making. In such a situation language cannot change. The world ceases to move, and we are all like Urizen or the frozen Satan of the *Divine Comedy,* the alien world of matter surrounding and imprisoning us. For Blake, the word "allegory," when he uses it in a derogatory way, means a language that has become abstracted from images so that it can no longer perform the metaphorical act of identifying things, cannot see the particular in a new way, but merely arbitrarily identifies words with phantasmal ideas as if the ideas had some power greater than and outside ourselves, but a distant power that can't really be given the body that the allegorical image pretends it has.

The World-View of William Blake in Relation to Cultural Policy (1993)

(d) *Visionary religion:* Although Blake often used the word "religious" to indicate a tyrannical moral code imposed on people, often by those whose "desire ... is weak enough to be restrained" (E34), he can be said to promulgate a visionary humanistic version of Christianity that is strongly dependent on his vision of language. In one of his late engraved works "The Laocoön," done at a time when he had become more explicit in his writings about the meaning of Jesus, he speaks of the gods of Greece and Egypt as "mathematical diagrams" and cites as evidence Plato's works. In such States, Blake asserts, "All Visionary men are accounted Mad" (E274). This implies that Jesus represents the antithetical contrary to such gods. He is human, and he is as much a projection or part of the human mind as the abstract gods of Greece and Egypt (for good measure Blake adds Babylon). But the abstract gods are allegorical and empty inhumanity and would negate as seditious the contrary Jesus, who is crucified, as is the dying figure Luvah in the prophetic books.

Perhaps the most startling thing Blake does in "The Laocoön" is to identify his Jesus and Christianity itself with art. When Jesus advises giving to Caesar what is Caesar's, Blake believes that the coin implies empire and natural religion as well as worldly wealth or, simply, money. In citing Virgil's *Aeneid* (vi, 848), where Anchises contrasts sculptors in bronze, pleaders of causes, and astronomers with the Romans, who are urged to guide the nations by their military authority, Blake identifies more than artists, as we think of them, with art and asserts that when art is degraded and imagination is denied war governs the nations. Clearly Blake was no admirer of Virgil, and he cites the *Aeneid* passage not only in "The Laocoön" but also in the little engraved essay "On Virgil," where art and war are explicitly opposed to each other. Art is, for Blake, creative activity of all kinds; creative activity can be symbolized by the metaphor, which puts things together that are normally (or passively) thought separate without violating individuality. This Blake describes in his poem on the poet Milton as "annihilation" of "selfhood." By the latter word he meant the radical separateness, aloneness, and consequent fear and desire to dominate the other that is the condition of the epistemological subject. Art is true charity. False charity is that which would not exist if there were "nobody poor." True charity searches for identity, which is the foundation of Blake's religious vision and the ethic that would be a ground for a Blakean cultural policy.

IV. Guiding Cultural Policy: A Blakean Ethics

Blake's poetry has as its fundamental contrariety the opposition of identity to the negation difference/indifference. Its fundamental trope is the synecdoche; the contrary and the trope are closely related. Blake does not actually use the terms "difference" and "indifference." Rather he uses "individuality" and "universality," which can stand politically for the extremes of anarchy and totalitarianism, which are caught in mutual negation. The contrary, "identity," is a word Blake employs tellingly at the end of *Jerusalem:*

> All Human Forms identified even Tree Metal Earth & Stone. all Human Forms identified... [E258].

It is a mistake to think that identity for Blake meant some mystical indifference as much as it is a mistake to think that a metaphor declares an utter indifference of two things. To say that a metaphor is merely a comparison according to the apprehension of some common characteristics is equally a mistake, merely the other side of the same coin and an example of a naive imitation theory of language and art. Identity embodies the antithetical notion, denying that we should make a choice. Since from the point of view of familiar logic and of science this seems absurd, we must either declare the idea mad or presume that it expresses not the "natural" view but some other equally as serious. I would describe that view as both artistic (in Blake's sense) and ethical. The ethical implication is that we are both individual and universal (and thus involved one in another) *at the same time,* which is what Blake meant by identity, modeled on the metaphor. In this sense, nature or at least ethical action should copy art, the basis of which is the metaphor. (Oscar Wilde's Vivian, though somewhat impertinently, had it right.) But this notion in Blake is not merely metaphorical, across entities; it is synecdochic, that is, it joins wholes and parts. Over and over in Blake we discover that part and whole are identical, with neither privileged.

A Blakean cultural policy would, first, have to take as its ground this notion as an ethical principle for individuals and a political ethic for States. It would have to be held in tension with its contrary, which tends, when not opposed, to move in the direction either of totalitarian indifference or anarchic individualism.

A second ground for a Blakean cultural policy would be the acceptance and maintenance of the contrariety of art and science. Contrariety means equality and creative opposition. If this existed, more would discover what many scientists already know, that the human artistic impulse toward making is what refurbishes the human scientific impulse toward understanding. Blake had terms for this; he called the first "prolific" and the second "devourer" and regarded them as necessary to human existence.

If the first ground is the ethical one for cultural policy, the second is the educational ground, and it appears to generate a principle for curriculum. At the base of such a curriculum would be study of the languages of man or what Ernst Cassirer called "symbolic forms." At one end of the base would be language as understood and practiced by Blake's mythic "ancient poets," the languages of myth and poetry in which tropes played their appropriate creative, identifying roles, not imitative ones. (In "The Laocoon" Blake wrote: "Israel delivered from Egypt is Art delivered from Nature & Imitation" [E274]). They would also include the non-discursive languages of non-imitative visual design and music, which create new forms from old matter.

At the other end of the base would be number, the language of science, which generates antimythical structures that from one point of view look like copies of nature but can be regarded in a Blakean way as makings of nature that fictionally pretend to be copies.

An understanding of these foundations and an appreciation of their creative potentialities, limitations, and inter-relations, both intellectual and political, is the Blakean ground for any workable cultural policy. Either alone creates an educational policy susceptible to tyranny. The hegemony of the antimythical creates the tyranny of technological alienation. The hegemony of myth creates the tyranny of superstition. Our age, as Blake prophesied, is an age of the former. The consequence is the alienation and perversion of myth, which has taken on the destructive paranoical forms, among others, of Naziism, soviet genetics, religious fundamentalism, and corrupt nostalgias of concern to Todorov. This has been a negating response to the abstraction and technological madness that has been ruling us. Blake responded to it with a vociferous antitheticality, a broad defense of art, but he kept in mind the contrary, and therefore wrote: "What is the Life of Man but Art & Science" (E232).

Postscript on "The Laocoon"

Blake's own works are models of the antitheticality he advocated. He observed early in his career that one of the aims of art is to "rouze the faculties to act," a phrase containing a nice ambiguity when it is applied to education. He was not afraid of obscurity because "what is not too Explicit is the fittest for Instruction" (E702). Despite his opposition to allegory, which is usually associated with the didactic, Blake was not loath to identify his own work as didactic, though with a difference, and that difference can be described as its challenging nature. His late engraving of the Laocoon group is only one of his works that raises all sorts of challenges, "rouzing the faculties to act." The questions are about its parts but also about how its parts go together, if they do, causing us to reconsider our senses of parts and wholes.

Note first that Blake does not treat the statue he has "copied" as Laocotin at all. Indeed, the natural event that is supposedly depicted, Laocoon's agony, Blake treats as a sort of copy of art; for Blake describes the design as Jah, for Jehovah and his two sons Satan & Adam as they were copied from the Cherubim of Solomons Temple by three Rhodians & applied to Natural Fact or History of Ilium" (E273). These words are placed on the plate beneath the design as if they were the title. History itself (natural fact) finds its shape in a copy of an artifact, rather than the other way around. The Rhodians, apparently chronicling an event, were copying art. On all sides of the central design, and woven around it are single words, phrases, and sentences, some of the words being in Hebrew. Some sentences are truncated as if urgently uttered; others seem added in as if suddenly generated by thinking on those already there, though temporal order either of composition or of reading is made impossible to determine. In his edition of Blake cited in note 1, David V. Erdman attempts to order these items thematically; there is nothing at all wrong with doing this, but it is as difficult to accomplish definitively as it is to detect conventional narrative pattern in the prophetic books. This is because Blake was determined to be, as Yeats called him, a "literal realist of the imagination" (actually Yeats said "too literal realist"). Blake took his conception of metaphor and synecdoche literally, so one discovers that one can begin with virtually any statement in "The Laocoon" and find, if one's faculties really are roused, that it leads to and implies, contains or is part of the others, and is a synecdoche of a whole that seems to be potentially limitless.[6] One can easily imagine an infinite accretion of elements that would threaten to burst the plate, the words flowing beyond its borders. It is as if the plate requires another dimension, which is perhaps the reason that there is an engraved figure (another art) and that the figure is based on a sculpture.

As for the choice of poor Laocoon and his two sons, Blake claims them to be copies of works of art in Solomon's Temple; these "biblical" works symbolizing for Blake the "originality" or shaping and visionary quality of art above history and natural fact. Art is the form, in the sense of activity, into which an episode in the history of Ilium is put. Symbolically the original figures of the temple were shown to have been caught in the coils of the serpent of this world, nature, which for Blake always means objectivity, which is always locked together with its negation, subjectivity. As presented by the three Rhodians, Jehovah, Satan, and Adam become Laocoon and his two sons. You will recall that Laocoon made the right prediction but one nobody wanted to hear uttered. He and his sons became victims of epic events. Blake didn't think much of epics and here identifies them with "nature." They were poems which wrote "natural fact" or history in the pay of empire, to which Laocoon and his sons were sacrificed; one had to read epics "infernally"[7] before they revealed their own errors, and this meant getting epics back to the sources of art, symbolized by Solomon's Temple. This is evidence in Blake of his own version of what we now call "deconstruction." Blake's deconstructions are unusual, however, and antithetical to deconstruction as it is usually presented because they are always toward making something. Though that something may never be quite fully accomplished, the act and the direction bear witness to an ethical effort that is always in process. So there is no external world in Blake to view, only finally a way of acting, not to be watched, but to be performed.

Conference 2: Chinese and Japanese-American Literary Relations (1995)

[This previously unpublished paper, more properly called a report, discusses papers offered at the second meeting of the Conference on Humanistic Discourse, which had been created in the early 1990s by Murray Krieger and me at the University of California, Irvine. Regular members included Jacques Derrida, Wolfgang Iser, Ching-hsien Wang, Pauline Wu, Krieger, and myself. There were invited participants at each meeting. The conference was meant to concentrate on international cultural issues affecting humanistic thought. This second meeting was devoted to the Far East, specifically China and Japan.

Reading the report today, I find that much of it remains germane to the present situation eighteen years later. The essay which follows this one was inspired by my attendance at the conference and my growing understanding of cross-cultural differences as they might affect a world-view, as for example the one I had proposed for William Blake in the essay preceding this report.]

The second meeting of the International Conference on Humanistic Discourse was held at the University of California, Irvine, in the spring of 1995 and was devoted to issues and problems that arise in negotiating differences between Eastern and Western cultures. Invited to present papers were Professors William Tay, Leo Ou-fan Lee, Lin Yaofu, Chiyuku Kumakura, and Kojin Karatani. The group also heard from two of its own members, Pauline Yu and Ching-hsien Wang. Though a variety of topics was presented the problem of language and translation frequently came up in the papers and in the discussion sessions. Unavoidable, too, were questions of nationalism, colonialism, and the postcolonial situation. There were papers discussing issues related to Hong Kong, Taiwan, China, Japan, and the teaching and scholarship devoted to China in the United States.

Conference 2 (1995)

Pauline Yu's "Disorientations: Chinese Literature in the American University" took up this last matter. She began with an account of the history of teaching and research about China in America, offered some cautions, and indicated future needs. She brought to light the unfortunately unquestioned Eurocentric methodological assumptions that dominated East Asian study until quite recently and that have not entirely died out.

Chinese studies outside of China began among Europeans, largely Italiam, French, and German missionaries. It began in the United States with professorial chairs endowed by a few philanthropists, received impetus after World War II with the return of many veterans trained in Chinese and Japanese while in the armed forces, and was further developed during the Cold War as part of the strategic study of China supported by the government.

Research was dominated by the methods and interests of the social sciences. The discipline of comparative literature gradually opened up its European orientation to East Asian studies. But in Yu's view the orientation remained Eurocentric, comparatists failing to examine tacit assumptions and procedures: "Asian literatures may find themselves accommodated within a grand narrative, but do they speak?" She called for continued and far more probing reflection on the bases of critical procedures instead of "mechanical application of models."

The discussion that followed emphasized the position of Chinese Asian studies in the American university today. It was observed that when schools of international study and area studies programs were developed, examination of modern and contemporary China was not at all emphasized, but this has changed with the recent emphasis on business, as has been the case with other foreign language teaching as well. Discussion moved to the general problem of the neglect of the humanities generated by these forces, and it was suggested that it was caused in part by a change in emphasis within science to technoscience.

Lin Yaofu's "Toward a Vision of China: The Taiwan Experience" was a presentation of the situation of Taiwan in its historical context, specifically that of the last one hundred years—the Japanese colonization from 1895 to 1945, the Kuomintang regime of the Chiangs from 1945–1988, and the subsequent rapid pace of Taiwanization under Lee. The picture of Taiwan, especially Taipei, that Lin drew was not a pleasant one, and the search for identity he regarded as close to "schizophrenic humbug." In the discussion that followed, he added that every emerging culture creates a myth of its originality even though it is largely a melange of foreign models. He held that the true cultural father of Taiwan is China, not the "erstwhile colonial master." The true Chinese heritage he identified with Confucian tradition, and he doubted, because of the prominence of China, that any truly indigenous literature was likely to emerge on Taiwan. This led to consideration of the complexities of the language problem, which was the main topic of the discussion from that point onward.

It was observed that there had been various proposals for a new written language or borrowings from others. These included at one extreme romanization and at the other adoption of Korean. Some topics explored were situations, as in Vietnam and Turkey, where forcible introduction of romanization cut many humanistic roots; the question of to what extent cultures are determined by language; to what extent it is culture's mission to achieve a distinct identity; the extent to which Taiwan is a typically island culture, whatever that implies; whether it faces conditions similar to those of other postcolonial cultures; the degree to which any indigenous identity is a construct; and the extent to which Taiwan is a useful example of what any culture undergoes in attempting to create itself definitively as such.

The situation of the practice of literature in Hong Kong prior to its return to China was the topic of William Tay's "Colonialism, the Cold War Era, and Marginal Space: The Existential Conditions of Four Decades of Hong Kong Literature." Tay noted that Hong Kong has no tradition of literary writing in English, Britain having had no reason to pursue linguistic colonization and several reasons not to. In 1972, in fact, Chinese was legalized as an official language. The presence of Chinese literature in Hong Kong has always been supported by newspaper literary supplements, magazines, and publishing houses. These last can be described, during the years of the Cold War, as falling into three groups: the ones with foreign economic and political influences, the ones formed by in-house writer groups that were relatively independent, and the commercial ones aimed strictly at profit. In this period, Taiwan and China sponsored literary magazines in Hong Kong, and several comprehensive ones were quietly supported by the United States. Literary work in Hong Kong appears in many magazines not mainly involved with literature. Long regarded as marginal, Hong Kong literature has been important because it has been beyond control of the mainland "center." Because of the growth of popular fiction, serious literature is more and more marginalized, yet serious writers still have a voice in newspaper columns. An irony of the historical situation is that Britain, having shown no interest in Hong Kong literature, included literature in the Hong Kong Arts Development Council before turning Hong Kong over to the People's Republic.

Discussion (carried on, of course, two years prior to the take over) centered on the uniqueness of the Hong Kong situation. Tay remarked of the difficulty of theorizing about Hong Kong with familiar Western concepts about colonialism and postcolonialism There was a unique mixture of Western technology, Chinese tradition, the current Hong Kong political structure, and the mainland communist system. Further, there was no precedent for analyzing the situation of the impending take-over. He further observed that Hong Kong had faced difficulty with the teaching of Chinese literature in that it seemed to be feared that too much would encourage nationalism and too little might diminish the chances for development of a writing independent of the communist literature of the mainland. It was possible to imagine that Hong Kong's hybrid popular culture might influence the mainland more than the other way around.

Two papers concerned themselves directly with the problem of translating terms. Wang Hui's "Humanism as the Theme of Chinese Modernity" showed clearly the difficulties of moving "humanism" and "humanistic discourse" into the Chinese language. All of the Chinese words used to translate "humanism" have histories that cannot be ignored, and these histories differ radically from those of the English words. Explanations of these differences employ more words, which likewise must be explained. This is not to say that the Chinese and English terms have grown up in entire isolation; there have been importations, as for example the humanism of Irving Babbitt and Marxist humanism.

Wang Hui pointed out that it is difficult to demarcate humanism from enlightenment in China, though enlightenment is not exclusively identified with the European historical movement. For Wang Hui it is important to grasp the distinctions between three terms "renwenzhuyi," "rendaozhuyi," and "renbenzhuyi." They do not correspond to three sorts of humanism in Europe. The terms are related to the ancient words "renwen," and "rendao." "Renwen" refers to human and heavenly culture, and "rendao" refers to ethical norms. "Renwenzhuyi" usually involved Chinese ancient culture and the classics and generally meant culture or learning. Chinese scholars consequently adopted it to refer to sixteenth-century Italian Renaissance culture. "Rendaozhuyi" refers to any system of thought with the human being at its center and concepts of social value such as liberty, equality, and fraternity. "Renbenzhuyi" is also human-oriented but employed more for scholarly researches of an anthropological bent. But it is also the term used to translate "humanism," though it is used far less often than the other two. From a Western point of view these terms seem unstable and sometimes inconsistently employed, but this is because of a desire to fix them according to notions of Western historical development.

After a brief tracing of the history of these terms, Wang Hui turned to the tangled relation of Chinese humanistic discourse and Marxism. He pointed out in remarks supplementary to his paper that the distinctions between science and the humanities and social sciences are blurred (from the Western point of view) in China, that the Chinese Academy of Social Sciences, which contains literature, was once a branch of the Academy of Sciences, and that before the twentieth century the Chinese did not have separate humanistic disciplines such as literature, history, and philosophy in the senses in which these terms are institutionalized in the West.

Leo Ou-fan Lee's "Some notes on 'Culture,' 'Humanism,' and the 'Humanities' in Modern Chinese Cultural Discourses" also addressed the problems of translation and talking about the Chinese terms in another language. Lee pointed out that it has been argued that Confucianism itself was a humanism, being centered on "ren" or "humanness." But this view, he held, must be historicized, since the whole matter has had a "zigzag course." Humanism in its Confucian connection has at one time been used against communism, and at another time it has been argued that Confucianism and Marxist humanism were compatible. Lee also took note of the source of "rendaozhuyi" in the nineteen-eighteen essay of Zhou Zouren, but observed also that "rendao" or "human way" was left there by Zhou without a clear signified, though "rendaozhuyi" came to be identified with humanitarianism and with a literary practice known as critical realism. It was another group of modern intellectuals, influenced by Irving Babbitt, who rendered "humanism" as "renwenzhuyi." This has been regarded as a conservative movement in defense of Chinese traditionalism. Lee remarked also of Mao Zedong's critique of humanism in his well-known speech of 1942, in which he attacked humanism on the ground that there was no human nature in the abstract beyond class identification. Mao was directly attacking "rendaozhuyi," but humanism of all sorts was taboo until Mao's death in 1976.

Although "rendaozhuyi," or "humanitarianism," had little to do with humanism in the West, nevertheless Chinese intellectuals who professed it identified it with Western humanism, and even with its official suppression it would appear in revolutionary discourses. Obviously humanism has carried different shades and sometimes opposed meanings, as it has in the West.

Lee also observed, as did Tay with respect to Hong Kong, that cultural discourses in Chinese developed in the public sphere. The modern school and university do not alone define Chinese culture. The print media play a major role, and the space for cultural discourse encompasses both academia and the popular press. Further, the professional disciplines in the humanities are, by Western standards, not clearly defined.

In the contemporary period, Western intellectual norms have been adopted along with the language and methods of Western humanities. Still, academics have not dominated the cultural sphere, and when they have participated it has been in public, so to speak. One result of this is that the essay still dominates as the principal medium and high theory does not.

Finally, Lee observed that although a visually dominant media culture has grown up, writing remains predominant. At the same time, Western cultural studies have been introduced and will inevitably contain audiovisual media. Through all of this, the use of the Chinese written character maintains an important cultural difference from phonetic systems.

Discussion revealed further the great divergence distinguishing Chinese and Western cultures in the areas of literature, criticism, and humanistic discourse generally. There seemed to be no clear definition of the last in China, partly, perhaps mainly, because it exists in the public sphere in a variety of forms. It was noticed that in the West the tendency was to globalize concepts and incorporate alien ones into larger forms, whereas the Chinese seemed to practice a sort of criss-crossing and negotiation of terms.

Ching-hsien, Wang, who writes as a poet under the pseudonym of Yang Mu, contributed to the conference a poem originally entitled "Cheng Hsuan Awakened from a Dream," but retitled for this presentation "Confucius at the Center of a Humanistic Discourse." In the poem the Confucian exegete Cheng Hsuan is awakened by the spirit of Confucius warning him of difficult years ahead. He reflects on the official position he once held. He seems never to have been able to settle differences before having to intervene in them; he is still a shameful public functionary. He recalls, with some irony, that he had developed some skill in each of the four parts of the Confucian curriculum: literary study (philology), virtue, government, and oratory. Now old, he thinks of his life as a timber beam; it has produced much, like the burst of spring outside his window, and his scholarship contains China's turbulent history. There is trouble ahead, and death.

The poem is a testament to a certain intellectual tradition that privileges the poet as scholar. It seems to oppose government, or at least bureaucracy and planning. It speaks for the virtue of literary study, which includes the writing of poetry, though with a certain wryness, suggesting that it, too, cannot bring its kind of litigation to closure except with the poet's death. In the context of the conference the poem seemed to be a sort of anti-paper, asserting the poetic art against humanistic discourse as technique. It raised the question of translation as well as the question of what role the poet or poems play in various cultures.

Discussion began with attention to problems of translation, the usual ones, but also the question of what happens to a poem when it is dragged by interpretation into humanistic discourse, thereby losing its untranslatable or uninterpretable element. Discussants then turned to the poem's various dimensions. Wang asserted in response to questions that his poem was political against politics, the poet needing to resist a terrible situation by having nothing to do with it: "In Confucius' day it was thought that if it's possible to contribute to government we do that, but if it's impossible we hide ourselves and cultivate inwardly to prepare ourselves in a better way for the day when the chance is right. Then we come out again. At the end of the Han dynasty it was a chaotic time, so to go to cultivate scholarship and plow the land was a more meaningful thing than just to preserve fame or wealth or whatever in the government." It was observed that to read the poem in a sealed local situation was to diminish it, that perhaps the poet today must be elsewhere to the dominant political culture, even to those in opposition. This led to discussion of the poet's relation to Chinese or Taiwanese culture today, and Wang thought that it was little different from the role it played in ancient Chinese culture. Tay reminded that poetry still plays a public role in newspapers and journals, and it was observed that poetry perhaps plays a more specialized role today in the United States, that although there is no presence of poetry in humanistic discourse in Europe there is a theoretical discourse that attempts to undermine the difference and that in Japan poetry and politics were traditionally not separate, though there was always tension, and that in the modern period there has been a separation with consequent loss of that valuable tension.

At this point the conference turned to matters pertaining principally to Japan. The two papers from Japanese scholars emphasized the problem of language, the problem of the structure of Japanese with respect to translation in Chiyuki Kumakura's "History and Narrative in Japan," the problem of the relation of language, particularly written language, to nation and empire in Kojin Karatani's "Nationalism and Ecriture."

Kumakura argued that Japanese differs from Western languages and even Chinese in such fundamental ways that Japanese culture has never been well understood in the West. Nor have the Japanese well understood the West. He pointed out that Japanese has only one point of view, the speaker's, and that this single point of view is interpersonal in a way foreign to Western thought. This means that all verbs, adjectives, and relationals record the speaker's perceptions and observations. The result is that, strictly speaking, there are no objective descriptions in Japanese, only the speaker's reactions. This is also true with respect to time, in that a Japanese sentence always proceeds from the speaker's present. The result is that there is no system of tenses to produce an objective historical discourse. Events are recollected in the present and not projected objectively into a past.

Arguing that for these reasons the novelist Murakami Haruku badly misread a story by Raymond Carver, Kumakura raised the question of whether the Japanese have "ever really learned Western languages" and the more general question of whether the Japanese language can handle abstract thought, whether it can transform the concrete, personal, and present constantly implicit in the language into the abstract.

These speculations led to Kumakura's description of Japanese narrative as governed by only one point in time, "the temporal focus being on the narrator's internal 'present' moment with no linguistic distinction between narrating time and story time."

These Kumakura regarded as limitations, but he observed that they have made possible an "interpersonal" consciousness that is not omniscient yet goes beyond the bounds of Western "individual" consciousness. This is reflected in the term "ningen" for human being in Japanese, which translated literally means "among men" or "interperson."

Kumakura's paper led to discussion of possible differences between Japanese and Western notions of subjectivity as well as objectivity with emphasis on problems of translation.

Kojin Karatani's paper first addressed questions related to written and spoken Japanese. Phonocentrism was already present in eighteenth-century Japanese scholarship, before the movement to consolidate written and spoken language. Nationalism was foremost in the movement to privilege phonetic writing within the cultural sphere of the Chinese written character. Observing that the modern nation takes shape with the creation of a vernacular *written* language (as was the case of Dante in Italy, where the resistance was to Latin), Karatani argued that Saussure excluded writing from his theory not because he was himself phonocentric but instead to reveal the way in which phonocentrism tacitly internalizes the written language and as a result the nation-state.

Eighteenth-century Japanese scholars sought a Japanese that was prior to Chinese characters, but they overlooked the fact that this effort was not really phonocentric but an attempt to translate written Chinese into Japanese. In this they were like Dante. Dante did not transpose spoken language into writing. Rather, he wrote in a vernacular as a form translating written Latin. Latin, in turn, was a translation of Greek written documents, thereby becoming the standard dialect. Japan was the only country to employ Chinese characters as phonetic signs and absorb it into their writing. With the introduction of Western-style historical linguistics in Japan came the identification of Japanese (as the language of the nation-state) with Saussurean "langue." The misinterpretation of Saussure caused Tokieda Motoko to criticize Saussure, for he regarded Saussure as the source of identification of "langue" with the Japanese nation-state.

This paper gave rise to a number of issues including the universalizing diffusion of Anglo-American throughout many Asian countries where the United States has no explicit imperial relations. It was observed that with Anglo-American it was not a question of a linguistic imperialism first but rather a cultural power and influence that the language followed upon. Further, the current resurrection of nationalism in new forms has been a defensive reaction against American capitalism, technology, especially teletechnology, and all those forces that exert the power of delocalization. It was cautioned, however, that there are degrees of difference in the reception of Anglo-American as the "lingua franca" in different areas and for different reasons including the very practical ones of "transliteration."

Clearly, language was a fundamental problem to which the conference constantly returned even when the overt topic was nationalism, colonialism, imperialism, or literature and its dissemination. What should be the appropriate language of a postcolonial culture with its uniques historical context? Professor Krieger remarked in his short paper responding to the two conferences up to that time that he had come to realize the "immense force of the postcolonial moment in cultures facing the revolutionary changes of the second half of the twentieth century," and he mused on the problem of the untranslatable and on the desire of the group to preserve differences ("the preservation of otherness") even as he worried about the threat of the banishment of the "same" in the urge to express identity. It seemed to be agreed, that somehow negotiation between same and other needed to be thought through anew.

Is (Was) There No Tradition of Defense of Poetry in Chinese Culture? Why Has There Had to Be One in the West? (1995)

[The following essay, hitherto unpublished, grew out of my participation in *Conference 2*, described in the previous essay, and conversations with my colleague Ching-hsien Wang. Although the essay did not address issues that concerned me in the following pages, the papers and discussions intensified my caution about using English words to describe ideas expressed in Chinese and Japanese or in any other language or culture. The experience directly affected this essay, along with helpful and challenging written comments on it offered to me by Professor Haun Saussy.

The conference also reminded me of an issue always present but sometimes foolishly ignored in literary scholarship and criticism devoted to writers in English—the historical context and changes in the meaning of words over time. One has to pay attention, for example, to just what Blake, around two hundred years ago, meant by "vision," "inspiration," "imagination," "intellect," and "contrariety."]

> My sons, my disciples, why do you not study the poets?
> —Confucius, *Analects* xvii, 9

> There is an ancient quarrel between philosophy and poetry.
> —Plato, *Republic*, x, 607b

Not long ago, learning I was working on a book about the defense of poetry (actually *The Offense of Poetry* [Seattle: University of Washington Press, 2007]), my colleague Ching-hsien Wang, himself a well-known poet (Yang Mu) and scholar of *The Book of Songs*, remarked to me that there was no tradition of defense of poetry in China. No one would have thought it necessary. This seemed to me as surprising as defense was a fact in the

Is (Was) There No Tradition of Defense of Poetry in Chinese Culture? (1995)

West. Why, if Professor Wang was correct, did the fact of defense seem virtually inevitable to me, a Westerner, whereas to my colleague it was close to unthinkable in Chinese culture? In the West poetry is to such a great extent definable in terms of tension and conflict inside and out that to imagine a source of tension removed seemed to me almost a question of whether there could be any cultural or intellectual role left for poetry. Clearly, however, there could or should be, because of the Chinese example. Or is there some fundamental difference between Chinese poetry and Western poetry that accounts for the former's long history of survival without the nearly constant life-giving (to my Western eyes) challenge to its right to exist? Or has there actually been a defense of sorts in Chinese literary thought, though perhaps of a different character not quite definable to me as "defense" because not responding to explicit attacks like those of Plato, Stephan Gosson, and Thomas Love Peacock? In his *Readings in Chinese Literary Thought*, Stephen Owen remarks that literary theory generally arises when "a need is felt to justify poetry."[1] He points out that in pre–Han and Han thought there was an "intensely theoretical current," and "classical exegesis became the means for traditionalists to justify the value of texts whose authority had once been simply taken for granted."[2] But although this may have been a defense in practice, it was not in itself a theoretical argument in poetry's behalf. Owen also notes elements of defense elsewhere: For example in Lui Hsieh's (c. 465–522) *Wen-hsin tiao-lung*, Liu, who anticipates the familiar modern Western complaint that literature is merely superfluous ornamentation, is not making a statement in response to a specific attack. It might, nevertheless, be noted that Liu was a lay scholar in a Buddhist temple, and Buddhist thought did not revere *The Songs*. Despite all this, Owen's detection of a concern for defense may arise from his own compelling Western awareness of the need for it.

In both East and West, of course, there has been a vigorous discourse of literary criticism in spite of important differences among traditions. One difference appears to be that there has been little tension between Chinese poets and Chinese critical discourse about poetry, except among some poets declaring what poetry is good and what is bad. Today in America, where criticism has become mainly the province of professors and has turned into "theory," poets often claim to dislike critics and theorists as much as playwrights and producers hate drama reviewers. Some of them claim that academic critics and theorists actually hate poetry, and they offer certain critical styles as evidence. And then, of course, there is the matter of the attack on poetry from Plato onwards.

I intend here to consider the nature of the attack and defense in the West, and offer some remarks about literary thought concerning poetry in China (to the extent that I know anything about it), with interspersed speculation on the questions in my title.[3] I feel confident enough to discuss the first matter, but with respect to the second I am dependent on translations, secondary material in English, and the advice of knowledgeable colleagues, none of whom is responsible for the errors that may appear here. This is at best a foray and makes no claim to be complete. Instead it seeks correction and amplification.

The attack on poetry, at least among the surviving ancient Western texts, begins, of course, with Plato's identification in *Republic* of the poets with rhetors and sophists. The charges are well-known: imitation twice removed from the Idea and irrationality, perhaps by virtue of divine possession, but also, more than likely, not. Besides, how could one tell? Behind the attack, the assumption about language is the one that has had the most repercussion in the history of the subject. The attack on imitation was turned in poetry's favor by Aristotle, and, with a few exceptions, imitation was appropriated by defenders of poetry. The attack on rhetors and sophists, however, stretched into distrust of tropes and modern philosophy. The classic example is John Locke in a section of *An Essay Concerning Human Understanding* (1690) called "Of the Abuse of Words":

> ... if we would speak of things as they are, we must allow that all the art of rhetoric, besides order and clearness, all the artificial and figurative application of words eloquence hath invented, are for nothing else but to insinuate wrong ideas, move the passions, and thereby mislead the judgment, and so indeed are perfect cheats [x, 34].

Without discussing here Locke's cheating indulgence in the trope of cheating, I observe that Locke prefaces his remark by allowing that such things are admissible in "discourses where we seek pleasure and delight" instead of "information and improvement," but this is a division that seems inapplicable in Chinese discourses on poetry.

The Lockean view persists in various forms in modern utilitarianism and logical positivism, and it is a quiet presence in analytical and ordinary language philosophy as well as in linguistically oriented theory where it is either implied or stated outright that poetry is a "deviation" from normal discourse.

Is (Was) There No Tradition of Defense of Poetry in Chinese Culture? (1995)

Before the attack became centered on language, it took the form of charges of irrationality (poetic madness) and the seduction of readers with useless and dangerous fantasies, misleading the susceptible into absurd or immoral beliefs and acts. Also, poetry came under attack because it was allegedly useless and anachronistic in a world dominated intellectually and defined by the natural sciences, both theoretical and practical.

But with Plato, and very often later, despite his clear distrust of rhetors and sophists, there is a profound ambivalence about poetry. As has often been pointed out, Plato casts his work into mimetic form, the very type of poetry he has Socrates complain about; Socrates concocts "myths" and asserts his respect for Homer and other poets. Yet Socrates proposes banishment of imitative poets:

> ... when any one of these pantomimic gentlemen, who are so clever that they can imitate anything, comes to us and makes a proposal to exhibit himself and his poetry, we will fall down and worship him as a sacred, marvelous, and delightful being ; but we must inform him that in our state such as he are not permitted to exist; the law will not allow them. And so when we have anointed him with myrrh and set a garland of wool upon his head, we shall send him away to another city [*Republic* iii, 3988ab, Jowett translation].

Allowed to remain is the more severe storyteller who "will imitate the style of the virtuous only," but even this admission is elsewhere cast in doubt. If the ambivalence is not already present in Socrates' ironic manner, it is surely made good later, where he invites poetry to "prove her title to exist in a well ordered state," admitting his consciousness of her charms. The proof of poetry's worth he will even allow to be made "in some lyrical or other meter" or, by those who are not poets, in prose. The proof, he declares, should show that poetry is not only delightful but also "useful to states and human life." (x, 607cde)

The ancient quarrel that Socrates declares to have persisted between philosophy and poetry goes on not only in Plato himself, but also in later writers. In his prison cell, deeply depressed by age, ill fortune, and impending execution, the Roman politician and philosopher Manlius Severinus Boetrhius, vainly trying to write the *Consolation of Philosophy* (c. 523) with the muses of poetry at his bedside, is startled by the appearance of the stern muse of philosophy. She speaks

> "Who," she demanded, her piercing eyes alight with fire, "has allowed these hysterical sluts to approach this sick man's bedside? They have no medicine to ease his pains, only sweetened poisons to make them worse. These are the

very women who kill the rich and fruitful harvest of Reason with the barren thorns of Passion. They habituate men to their sickness of mind instead of curing them .... be gone and leave him for my own Muses to heal and cure [i, 1, Watts translation].

But poetry does not disappear under the force of this Socratic attack. Philosophy herself, only a paragraph later, speaks in verse; and each chapter thereafter contains a poem by Boethius, who is by now, however, under Philosophy's guidance. She prescribes the "persuasive powers of sweet-tongued rhetoric," but she warns that these powers will "soon go astray" unless Boethius follows her instructions. Further, Boethius admits that rhetoric (and music) is effective, but only while one is listening. It is not a cure, only a temporary palliative. If the emphasis is on teaching rather than delighting, there yet remains an ambivalence toward the attack on poetry. Or, perhaps the poems in Boethius's text are not to be regarded as poems at all but instead as curious hybrids of verse and moral philosophy, pleasantly decorated philosophical discourse.

Ambivalence is less obvious and attack more overt in Stephan Gosson's notorious and witty *School of Abuse*. By now the sophists have dropped out of the list of criminals, to be replaced by a colorful crowd of poets, pipers, player, and jesters. This list is eventually expanded to include fencers, dicers, dancers, tumblers, carders, and bowlers; but it is actors and poets upon whom the attack is mainly leveled, and it is mummery and other dissolute behavior with which they are charged. The impulse for Gosson's attack, oddly dedicated to Sir Philip Sidney, seems to have been the Puritan movement against the theater, although apparently Gosson himself was not a Puritan. He was, in fact, a popular playwright, whose plays were being performed in London even as he was confessing his wrongdoing in having written them. Gosson's complaint is against pretense and deception. Although it seems to have had a contemporary religious purpose, it harks back to Plato's attack on imitation and its implied subterfuge, conscious or otherwise. Yet it is a good thing that Gosson does not include rhetoricians among his villains, for he is himself a master of rhetoric in the elaborate fashion then current. His writing is full of ornament and possesses no little wit. His is without question a *performance*, a one-man show.

The charges of unreason and deception had their long day, but they were finally replaced by an attack still with us: What possible use has poetry in modern life? In common usage this question is rhetorical and implies the answer "none." Any teacher of English has heard of a parent's having

Is (Was) There No Tradition of Defense of Poetry in Chinese Culture? (1995)

put this rhetorical question to a student. Beyond the many assertions made in the name of utility that Oscar Wilde ridiculed in his "Decay of Lying" (1889), the classic utterance here is Thomas Love Peacock's "The Four Ages of Poetry" (1820). It is a witty piece of invective, with tongue in cheek, irritating enough to having elicited almost at once a solemn reply by Percy Bysshe Shelley (though not published until 1840, after his death). Peacock was himself a literary man, mainly a satirist, so from Shelley's point of view his behavior was something of a treason of poets, though the two were friends.

Peacock's argument is that in the earliest, or what he calls the iron, age of poetry, the poet had status as a means by which a king or tribal chieftain made known "the fame of his achievements and the extent of his possessions." The age of iron was followed b y the golden and silver ages. In the golden age, poetry attained its perfection, but its perfection was at once its maturity and the beginning of its decline. The silver age, in which was produced the "poetry of civilized life," ended in fastidiousness and monotonous harmony of expression The age of brass, which followed, ushered in the state of obsolescence, in which poetry suffered a "second childhood" and sought to return to the "barbarism and crude traditions of the age of iron." To this point Peacock has been charting the history of ancient poetry; the modern world repeats the cycle, though with a difference. The difference is the nostalgia that characterizes all efforts to return. In his time, Peacock argues, poetry has come round again to an age of brass, which glorifies the primitive:

> A poet in our times is a semi-barbarian in a civilized community. He lives in the days that are past. His ideas, thoughts, feelings, associations, are all with barbarous manners, obsolete customs, and exploded superstitions.

The inspirations of poetry are "the rant of unregulated passion, the whining of exaggerated feeling, and the cant of factitious sentiment." Peacock goes on to declare that in modern life the best expression is that "into which the idea naturally falls." Since poetry must give way to the advance of reason and science, "poetry can no longer accompany them in their progress, but drops into the background, and leaves them to advance alone." For him, reason is best addressed "in the simplest and most unvarnished phrases." It is no wonder that Shelley rose to this bait, even though it is written with tongue in cheek.

In philosophy, the more recent treatments of language on the model of symbolic logic and the notion that poetry (and figurative language generally) is a "deviation" became common, even ascribable to some critics of an analytical bent. The instances of this are too numerous to collect here, but it is worthwhile to notice that they arise and go along with the epistemological privileging of the object over the subject, as in Locke, and the resultant relegation of poetry to the subjective, which becomes identified with the unreasoning emotions and passions. This is, of course, the very thing that Socrates worried about whenever the poet or rhetor appeared. Associated with this division is the utilitarianism, mentioned before, of the parent who tells his daughter that you can't do anything with a degree in literature.

So the modern attack has usually been attached to a rage for utility and a certain mathematical idea of language (also present in Plato's suggestion that youth is well advised to study mathematics, not poetry). There was an ancient quarrel between philosophers and poets, and there is a modern one as well. The modern attack also contains if not an ambivalence then an irony, sometimes unconscious. One may consider John Stuart Mill's recantation after an education in utilitarian philosophy from his father—a recantation brought about by the reading of Wordsworth. More recently, there was I. A. Richards' struggle to turn Coleridge's theory of imagination into a materialist one, presumably thereby saving poetry for modern life.

In Western literary thought the strategy of defense has been either to capture the enemy's key term by redefining it or to accept Socrates' challenge to prove that poetry both delights and teaches, sometimes by enlarging the scope of delight and/or the range of knowledge conveyed. Aristotle's response with respect to drama was to redefine imitation and to substitute the experience of purgation of pity and fear for the didactic and entertaining. The charges dramatized by Boethius and leveled against poetry by Gosson and others were answered by responding to Socrates' challenge. There was a seemingly endless series of efforts to rewrite and to justify the old Horatian saw of *dulce et utile*. Even many most recent efforts exhibit some variation based on this familiar formula. But the problem has too often, maybe always, been that a defense on these grounds turns poetry into decorated moral philosophy, as in Scaliger, Sidney, and a host of Renaissance Italian philosopher-critics. An occasional innovator like Giacomo Mazzoni attempted to infuse the popular neo–Platonism of the day with a respect for poetry's special identity. In Mazzoni's case, it was with a theory of the image or "idol," but didacticism and delight or something very close to the latter, crept in when Mazzoni considered poetry's civil value.

Is (Was) There No Tradition of Defense of Poetry in Chinese Culture? (1995)

It is not really until Kant that some break in this impasse occurs, and even in his *Critique of Judgment* (1790) we find him compelled to answer Plato's complaint that if poetry invades the state, pain and pleasure will be its rulers. Kant uses the same terms but enlarges the scope of pleasure and then divides it in order to establish the notion of disinterested pleasure or, as he sometimes calls it, satisfaction. But Kant manages to go further. In the *Critique of Judgment* we find the following passage, which I must quote at length:

> Of all the arts *poetry* (which owes its origin almost entirely to genius and will least be guided by precept or example[4]) maintains the first rank. It expands the mind by setting the imagination at liberty and by offering, within the limits of a given concept, amid the unbounded variety of possible forms accordant therewith, that which unites the presentment of this concept with a wealth of thought to which no verbal expression is completely adequate, and so rising aesthetically to ideas. It strengthens the mind by making it feel its faculty—free, spontaneous, and independent of natural determination—of considering and judging nature as a phenomenon in accordance with aspects which it does not present in experience either for sense or understanding, and therefore of using it on behalf of, and as a sort of schema for, the supersensible. It plays with illusion, which it produces at pleasure, but without deceiving by it, for it declares its exercise mere play, which however can be purposively used by the understanding ["Analytic of the Sublime" liii, Bernard translation].

Kant goes on to distinguish poetry from at least one type of rhetoric:

> Rhetoric, insofar as this means the art of persuasion, i. e. of deceiving by a beautiful show (*ars oratoria*), and not mere elegance of speech (eloquence and style), is a dialectic which borrows from poetry only so much as is needful to win minds to the side of the orator before they have formed a judgment and to deprive them of their freedom.

What Locke put together—poetry and rhetoric—Kant seems to have taken apart, or nearly. Poetry is accorded its own identity, function, and value. A line of neo-Kantian defense follows, which includes what might be regarded as a series of variations on these passages: Schiller on play, Coleridge (with the help of Schelling) and Baudelaire on imagination, Arnold on disinterest, Wilde and Bradley on poetry for poetry's sake, Ransom's appropriation of Kant for the New Crtiticism, and Frye's expansive notion of anagogy. This is, of course, a short list representing various forms of influence. At the end of it we see aesthetics ebb in favor of issues of interpretation. Frye declares no interest in aesthetics as such, and no interest in articulated value judgments as part of criticism. Yet his position can still be regarded as one of defense by virtue of his claim that literature is a universe of discourse symbolized by its anagogic containment of nature.

Here the Western defense rested for a while in what may now seem a complacence. It rested on the neo–Kantian view that there is a fundamental difference between the literary and other verbal forms. But Deconstruction tended to break down that distinction. It has been ironically observed many times that since the appearance of Deconstruction, which is supposedly a theory of difference, either all discourse is literary or all literature is discourse.

Deconstruction set in motion this double view with its declaration of the ubiquity of tropes. All texts, of whatever sort—philosophical, linguistic, anthropological, historical—came under the eye of deconstructive procedures. If all texts were susceptible to this approach, then the separate identity of the literary text, an identity laboriously constructed in the long history of the defense of poetry, was no longer of any importance as an interpretive category. Hardly anyone any longer, at least among the professors who had turned criticism into theory, spoke of beauty and aesthetic value judgments. But soon there were judgments explicitly or implicitly political or moralistic.

It seems to me that this brief history, if at all acceptable, endorses to some extent Peacock's story (though not necessarily all of its conclusions) that there has been in the West a decline in the status and role of poetry (a term that has been enlarged, as this essay has proceeded, to include "literature" generally). The poet in ancient Greece seems to have been important enough to generate Plato's attack. Plato's enormous influence, followed by the development of natural science since the Renaissance, put poetry in an embattled position. This seems not to have been quite the case in Celtic culture until it was absorbed by Graeco-Roman traditions. The poet there maintained an important role as keeper of the history of the tribe, glorifier of the king, and maker of curses against the king's enemies. Yet finally, as Thomas Gray's "The Bard" and W. B. Yeats's *The King's Threshold*" dramatized with modern nostalgia, the poets were banished from the seats of power, eventually into the hostile world of Grub Street and material commerce.

In summary, the attack on poetry follows on (1) the suspicion of irrationality, the identification of poets with rhetors and sophists, and later suspicion of tropes, (2) the rejection of false images, given sanction by the

Is (Was) There No Tradition of Defense of Poetry in Chinese Culture? (1995)

Platonic critique of imitation and the Puritan rejection of the graven image (especially in the theater), (3) the relegation of poetry to subjectivity and pure feeling as science advanced the claim of objectivity. And, it is important to add here (4) that poetry, having preceded Christianity in the West and having been identified with paganism, was put in an odd position *vis à vis* two of the most important documents shaping its history and conventions, the Homeric poems and the Bible. The identification with Homer raised Christian suspicions even beyond Plato's. The privileging of the Bible as holy scripture, despite its poetic qualities being recognized, cut it off from poetry in ways that made it difficult even today to identify without ambivalence the Bible with the poetic. Many teachers who have sought to treat the Bible as poetry know this only too well, some having ended up in court. All this has been in spite of such revered eighteenth-century works as Bishop Lowth's *Sacred Poetry of the Hebrews* and Herder's *Spirit of Hebrew Poetry*.

I hope this brief account is sufficient to begin to establish a comparison of the history of Western literary thought to that of Chinese literary thought, which appears to contain none of the needs for defense that were present in the West.

The history of Confucianism and its relation to and use of Chinese poetry stands in stark contrast to the Platonic ambivalence. There was from the outside, so to speak, no philosophic attack on poetry. (By "outside" here I mean those who were not poets or literati). Professor Haun Saussy has reminded me, however, that though there may have been no external enemy of poetry, there were many passionate debates among poets about what was true poetry and not, what was proper style and not, and what was genuine against what was superficial and excessively clever. So there was enmity among poets generated by intellectual infighting about what was poetry's authentic voice.

Moreover, Confucianism, not recognizably a religion to many Western eyes, claims no founding holy text calling for historical and dogmatic belief. There is, rather, a revered group of texts concerned with right behavior and *praxis*, but not based on received revelation. The poetic text prior to the texts allegedly authored by Confucius or his followers was *The Book of Songs*, by tradition edited and ordered by Confucius himself. To Western eyes, *The Songs* seem secular in subject matter, being interpreted without reference to a privileged historical ground of meaning or mystical revelation. Still, to say only that they were secular follows a Western distinction between the secular and the religious that doesn't seem applicable to *The Songs* or, for that matter to Confucian thought. In his time, poetry was closely connected to music and ritual. *The Songs* were a normative discourse, part of a moral and didactic scheme committed to the maintenance of social order.

Though there is still some disagreement over whether one can appropriately call the traditional interpretation of *The Songs* allegorical, it is clear that the Western fourfold method of exegesis invented for the Bible by Cassian, advocated by St. Thomas Aquinas, and semi-secularized by Dante to give his poem a certain acceptability is different in method from exegesis of *The Songs*.[5] The status of poetry in China gave it a decidedly different function and prestige. The closest thing to it in the West would seem to be the role of the Celtic poet in the court of a king, but the motives were different. The Confucian interpretation was oriented toward *praxis,* and as a result *The Songs* gained and maintained prestige as a model for the poetry to follow. The Confucian *Analects* is entirely respectful of *The Songs*, and in the *Analects* the voice of Confucius in a few words gives *The Songs* a functional importance that poetic defenses in the West struggle to assert:

> Poetry is able to stimulate the mind, it can train to observation, it can encourage social intercourse, it can modify the vexations of life; from it the student learns to fulfill his more immediate duty to his parents, and his remoter duty to his prince; and in it he may become widely acquainted with the names of birds and beasts, plants and trees [*Analects* xvii, 9, Soothill translation].

The seeds of modern resistance to Confucian traditionalism are present here, but the emphasis on poetry as leading to *praxis* and not as either revelation of "truth" or heretical assertion persists. Nor was the aim coercion by rules, but rather influence. The function and force of *The Book of Songs* was entirely different from that of Western scripture. "Let the character be formed by poets, established by the laws of right behavior, and perfected by music" (*Analects* viii, 8). This is also a far cry from Plato. Poetry and philosophy are not at war but identical.

Stephen Owen observes that no divine authority was granted to Chinese poetry. Its authority was its psychological and physiological naturalness, though one could argue that what is at any time declared natural is so defined by power. Owen argues that as time passed and an "intensely utilitarian current ran through pre–Han and Han thought," poetry was given these qualities by a certain mode of interpretation as justification for its existence. But it seems to me that because divine authority was never given to Chinese poetry and there was no other text with that kind of authority (at least in the Western sense) poetry did not require defense against the kind of charges often leveled against it in the West, including heresy. Furthermore, the traditional mode of interpretation, being practically oriented, was not burdened by the notion of a grounding event or supposedly original meaning. Joseph R. Allen points out that interpretation of *The Songs* in China mirrored the political landscape at any particular time.[6] This is probably true in any culture in some way, but the situation is intensified where a certain *praxis* is the aim and a grounding event lacking. *The Songs*, then, were useful and applicable in different ways to different situations. Thus, as opposed to Western utilitarianism, Chinese utilitarianism envisaged no break between poetry and use, though the use was most of the time contribution to the maintenance of order by the powerful.

In the same way, the distinction between delight and teaching, which so many critics sought to mend, does not seem to be meaningful in Chinese thought. It is not that utility (teaching) is emphasized at the expense of delight. It is rather that the equation of delight with irrational feeling and teaching with reason is simply not thought. One can go further and conclude that in Chinese tradition there is no division between conceptual thought and poetry. This distraction was bequeathed to the West by Platonic philosophy and entrenched by modern empiricism and the resultant subject-object division. Virtually all writers of Western defenses of poetry have felt compelled to respond, as Shelley did to Peacock.

There are other differences worth mention that contribute to the absence of attack or defense, at least in traditional China. The importance of the role of epic in ancient Western poetry contrasts to the importance of the lyric as exemplified by *The Songs* in China. The epic, identifies national character in the form of a story—often of origin—that encourages specific belief. A group of lyrics does not do this, at least not in the same way or with the same results. Instead, one has potential models for behavior. Scholars, nevertheless, debated historical accuracy and context. Individual lyrics were regarded as having been spoken by real people in real circumstances. One might note here the anxiety in the West about allegorical interpretation of the Bible and the insistence on a historically grounded typological reading as fundamental, truth lying in the event and its prophetic meaning rather than in the emergent principles of right action.

It does not seem so strange, in the light of all this, that *The Songs* were a major topic in the imperial examinations until early in the twentieth century, that for a long time literary works were important achievements in the business of state, and that poetry was intimately known and used by everyone in the courts. As Ts'ao P'i asserted, "... literary works are the supreme achievements in the business of state, a splendor that does not decay."[7] Rather than generated in reaction to attack and impelled to defense, Chinese traditional literary thought seems to be most concerned with how to be a good poet, make good poems, and avoid making bad ones. The gulf between criticism and theory on the one hand and poetry on the other does not seem substantial. In some critics the two seem almost to merge, and in others they do merge. Though he may underestimate the humor present in some Western *ars poeticae*, there is some truth to Tony Barnstone's remark, "In contrast to the normally austere and humorless Western tradition of *ars poetica*, Chinese writers, though sometimes equally pedantic, have through many dynasties made their pronouncements witty and aphoristic, magical and profound, spiritual or satiric."[8] Of course there were disagreements or concerns about the state of poetry. Stephen Owen points out that in the mid-thirteenth century, for example, in *Ts'lang's Remarks on Poetry* by Yeu Yu there is a "sense of crisis and loss," a belief that poetry had declined.[9] In Ts'ao P'I there is a timeless remark, the gist of which is familiar to Westerners: "Literary men disparage one another—it's always been that way."[10] In 1686, Yeh Hsieh's *Discourse on Poetry* sought to arrest what he observed as decline by a means that reminds us of Northrop Frye's desire, expressed in *Anatomy of Criticism* (1957), to systematize criticism. Yeh remarks,

> The reason poetry has been unable to rouse itself to some lasting vitality is that the criticism of poetry, for its entire history has been disorganized and lacking in unity.[11]

The argument sees nothing like Frye's system, but it is like Frye's in that it declares that poetry depends on a vigorous critical tradition. Such a criticism, however, would not be obsessed with defense.

Whether an attitude toward poetry that does not require its defense has persisted in China in the last eighty years or so is a different question and one that I am not competent to answer. Western modernism seems to have been introduced and assimilated virtually together with Western romanticism and realism. Leo Ou-fan Lee has shown effectively the importance of the appearance in translation of writers from Byron to Rolland to

Is (Was) There No Tradition of Defense of Poetry in Chinese Culture? (1995)

Chinese writers of the early twentieth century.[12] What the long-term results of these and later developments out of a chaotic century are remain to be seen. Can we expect attacks on and defenses of poetry to appear in China?

AFTERWORD: In recent times, according to Xudong Zhang, one of the important forces to consider is

> ... the gravitational effect of traditional culture, polarized by a pragmatic engage (as represented by Confucianism) and a pessimistic nihilistic resignation (as represented by Daoism and Buddhism) which undermined pressing concerns about and dealing with the modernist dilemma.[13]

This strikes me as too neat, but the extent to which Chinese culture has recently been more Westernized is illustrated by Zhang's book, which is laced almost to unreadability with the jargon of Western postmodernist politically oriented critical theory.

Yet the Confucianist tradition persists and has undergone a sort of rebirth known as New Confucianism. It is led in part by Chinese intellectuals educated and in some cases now teaching in the United States. In the West, new interest in Confucius even crept into the semi-popular press in 1999 and produced a rather superficial article in *The Atlantic Monthly*. The author's interest was devoted mainly to the inquiry of American scholars into the questions of whether Confucius's words are actually preserved in *The Analects* and other texts, whether Confucianism was ever really Chinese or created by Jesuit missionaries, and even whether there ever was such a person.[14] These questions have little bearing, if any, on those raised in this essay, and the answers, were they achievable, would not be likely to have much effect on the New Confucianism (or the old). They do suggest an incursion into Confucian studies of a Western-style empirical search (need I say obsession?) for origins that appears to be at odds with Confucianism, whether new or old, and the old's body of semi-legendary history.

Four Problems (Among Many) for Humanistic Thought (1995)

[This hitherto unpublished essay gathered some thoughts responding to the first three meetings of the Conference on Humanistic Discourse and was distributed to its members at the fourth. A few small changes have since been made, but none changing the sense.]

The four problems I intend to discuss overlap. They are technology, politics, belief, and translation. "Problems" is by no means the perfect word, but "obstacles" would be worse. My intention is to show that humanistic thought should be in a relation of intellectual strife with each. The ground of humanistic discourse is poetry, which at its best and by its very form engages in that strife. Perhaps "tension" is a better word than strife, which I steal from Heraclitus, for I do not want to suggest an adversarial opposition, but instead, as with Heraclitus, one of justice: "Jurisdiction is strife, and everything comes about by way of strife and necessity."[1] The humanities, if worthy of the name, must play critical roles, that is, the roles of critics of all cultural situations in which the possibility of oppression in any form and from any direction is a danger. It was Matthew Arnold, to my knowledge, who first identified what we now call the humanities with a criticism of life. He was implicitly criticized by W. B. Yeats in the poem "Ego Dominus Tuus" for expressing the weakness of the age, contrasting criticism with what he called search for the image. Many have attacked Arnold for his accompanying notion that we should study the best that has been thought and said as a formula for oppression, but one might save the idea by connecting the best with the critical in the sense I shall propose.

Some modern philosophers and most poets have recognized as problems the four I have mentioned—in expressions ranging from alarm to less

Four Problems (Among Many) for Humanistic Thought (1995)

strident or more oblique forms of assertion. With respect to technology, Heidegger comes first to mind, warning against the power of technology to separate us from life. Yeats playfully opposed the abstractness from life of scientific symbolism by insisting that he preferred a little duckweed in his water and had never met that naked creature H2O. Eliot asked, "Where is the knowledge we have lost in information," as if he were anticipating the rise of the computer and artificial intelligence. Yet few say that technology and its works should be suppressed, as if that were possible. Many imaginative writers have been wary of politics, as Yeats explicitly was in the last poem in his *Collected Poems*. This was despite a career involved in Irish political life, culminating in a senate seat, and the presence in his work of many poems with political comment. Politics involves the temptations of power, and power tends to suppression and censorship. The tradition of defenses of poetry in the West owes its necessity in part to political and moralist suppression. The defenses were often efforts to respond to attempts at suppression. It is worth noting [as I did in Essay Seven] that there seems to have been no tradition of defense of poetry in China, apparently because its value was not called in question, at least until recently. Is that because it was not perceived to play an explicitly antithetical role? Because of the hierarchical culture that located the writing of poetry near the top—knowledge of poetry being required for government service? Because poetry seemed appropriate for a cultured man to write? Because there was no Plato, no Locke, no Descartes in Chinese intellectual history? It appears that the history of what we call the humanities, to say nothing of humanism, in the West is so different that enormous pressure is put upon any effort at translation of these terms. Leo Ou-fan Lee's enlightening paper presented at our second meeting is helpful in showing the historical and linguistic complexities of this problem and indicating how Western nations have invaded and influenced the academic concept of the humanities in universities in Asia. Translation is always an issue. No one can eradicate politics.

 Belief has always been a problem, intensified as the result over time of religious inquisition and the collapse of the patronage of poets. It became a theoretical issue in the early twentieth-century with Eliot's essay on Dante, Yeats's *A Vision*, and subsequent academic discussions.[2] Like politics, belief generates censorship and worse. Yet no poet I know would suppress belief entirely.

 I return to translation but in a somewhat broader sense. How does technology translate? Often with difficulty, as anyone who has tried to read VCR instructions knows. Recently in London, I was innocently involved in but quickly emancipated myself from, a friend's attempt to tape a television program for later viewing. The set was newly acquired, the manual a translation, presumably for Britain, from the Japanese. This was truly a multicultural situation or, perhaps more accurately, an impasse. Two hours into this effort, my friend called the place from which he had purchased the set, appealing for instruction. Over the phone a competent, arrogant, nerdishly precise programmer (or someone of that ilk) proved unable to reveal in any simple language the one step that was apparently missing from the manual and might have solved the problem. It must have been so elementary that both the programmer and writer of the manual, who may well have been Japanese, had forgotten it or seen no reason to include it. Perhaps there was no jargon term for it or no acronym.[3] (It seems to me that this is often the case in a situation of translation, where there is a hidden cultural premise or assumption somehow unavailable.) My friend vowed he would return the VCR the very next day, but in the morning, renewed by a full English breakfast, he tried again, succeeded apparently by chance, only to discover a blank tape. It is worthwhile noting here that the VCR is, like the computer, absolutely literal-minded. One can communicate with it only on its excruciatingly apoetical level.

My friend was involved in a problem of translation in three senses: linguistic, cultural, and interpretative. The problems are enormous, leading many to speak of untranslatability with respect to all three senses. Translation can be like technology in its tendency toward abstraction, that is, selective extraction of a text of what seems useful or trendy at the time.

The humanities are properly in favor of transcultural communication and understanding, but in one sense they are against translation in that they warn against the inevitability of distortion of or selective abstraction from a text. Technology, politics, and belief are, of course, dominant cultural forces, and translation, with all its problems, has emerged as more and more important in the shrinking world.

In the third meeting of this group, which was devoted to papers by guests from Eastern Europe, we were surprised and perhaps at times appalled by the reactionary attitudes we heard voiced in some of the papers. These attitudes were sadly understandable as release of anger against the recent regime, but they seemed intellectually unproductive at best and at worst cynical and anachronistic. They exemplified a typical situation in which there is adopted merely the other side of the enemy's story. One paper called for a return to a philology generally discredited among humanists in the West. Another opposed virtually all forms of modernism and seemed to advocate a return to a religiosity that the author identified with Russian literature of the nineteenth century. It was not that any of us preferred a position on the left or one in the middle. Rather, we almost instinctively desired a third position critical of the opposition itself.

Our second meeting on East-West issues had been interesting in part because we ourselves mirrored the problem of cultural translation. Some of us thought the papers not theoretical enough. (Did this express a desire to produce a sort of technology of the humanities?) We were sometimes impatient with some of the mundane knowledge the papers imparted. One sensed a cultural difference that questioned the translation of "humanities" itself. Could we have been better translators of the word, just for a start? Would that have required the effort to achieve a third position, not between but other than?

Is there a third position possible where translation is at issue? What have translators of texts usually striven for? I suggest two extreme goals, both fictions. There is the drive for literality grounded on some principle of accuracy; fealty to the text is the piety connected with this view, which can be traced back through the Western tradition of *mimesis*, with a certain amount of literal-mindedness thrown in. At its best, this approach requires a lot of cultural and linguistic recovery.

There is the drive for adaptation, emphasizing fealty to, or perhaps pity for, the reader. Here one seeks a roughly equivalent contemporary or local diction, style, and tone. Motives here vary from desire to appeal to a large audience to serious efforts to attain a language familiar and somehow metaphorically related at the level of expressiveness to the original. This suggests a romantic motive, perhaps, though earlier translations of Homer into heroic couplets would have to go here as well.

In their extreme forms, these two modes would produce absurdities, the argument between their fictive supporters a mutual negation. Perhaps the most important thing to recognize, transcending these, is the temporal location of any work and any translation, requiring new ones from time to time.

Most humanists rightly agree that translation is desirable and necessary, but it is also in a sense impossible, as sameness is impossible except in a metaphor, and then it is always joined indivisibly and usually invisibly with difference. There is irony for interpretation in all of this. Translation can be done, but it cannot be done.

Among texts, poems are those that most fully challenge us to acts of translation. As a somewhat arbitrary collection of academic disciplines the humanities begin, or should begin, with the telling to children of poems and stories, just as Vico thought civil culture began with poetic wisdom. There is perhaps something instinctive in the tendency of children to like and remember almost word for word—often word for word—poems and stories, whether nonsense rimes or more stately lyrics. Adults are often surprised and even shocked by what children like. Children seem to have the capacity to liberate poem or story from belief as adults understand it. Adults often seem anxious about an unacceptable dogma in a poem or may severely insist on an acceptable dogma to abstract from it. Blake called such moral readings stings in the tail. Keats hated a poem that has a design upon us. We have heard recently of efforts to suppress Mother Goose and certain fairy tales to say nothing of *Huckleberry Finn*. The youngest children seem not to care about what bothers adults in these things. A little older, they can be irritated by moralistic or any censorship of texts.

Every culture has a body of ancient and folk literature. Teachers need not moralize on it. What I have come to call "antithetical" [see especially Essay Thirteen] is outside the oppositions between belief and disbelief, even outside good and evil, subject and object. These oppositions are often tools of power. In adult culture and education should point to the poetic ground and upwards to the more abstract social and natural sciences. There needs to be a periodic return to the ground as a guard against the inhumanity of abstractions that create the problematic sides of technology, politics, translation (including interpretation) and belief.

As cultural forms, poetry and the "languages" of the fine arts are the necessary friendly antitheses to these things and to the binary oppositions institutionalized by the tribe. It would be ridiculous to suppress these oppositions, but they require critique. Humanistic critique is best when it is not a frontal assault offering only the panacea of another belief, but rather an invitation to more thought. It should also have a certain irony about itself, so that it can provide support for the intellectual strife that Blake said goes on in heaven. It makes justice a possibility. It is both an international and intercultural form, or should be.

"Literature" and the Visionary Tradition (1995)

[The following two previously unpublished essay were delivered in somewhat different form on December 12, 1994, at a colloquium titled *Literature and Its Relation to the Humanities in the West*. The event took place at the Hong Kong University of Science and Technology. Murray Krieger and I shared the platform, and both of us delivered two papers designed to approach two matters in contrasting but not necessarily opposed way. The first one here briefly described a tradition of poetry and literary thought from Vico and others, including Blake, into the twentieth century. The second, "'Literature' into 'Ecriture,'" reviewed the movement from Phenomenology through Structuralism to Deconstruction. Our shared assumption was that it was important to discuss important historical currents perhaps not fully known to all the participants.]

The placing of "literature" in quotations marks in my title may require some explanation. It does not reflect our view that literature is some fictitious entity. Nor does the title of our four discourses as a whole "What Was Literature?" mean to indicate that we think literature has disappeared as such. The point is that in several quarters it is thought that the age of literature as an institution has come to an end. Just as it is assumed that the notion of literature was invented in Germany early in the nineteenth century, so it is assumed that literature died with the demise of Modernism and the accession of theory in Structuralism and poststructuralist Deconstruction, followed by the politically moralistic, with its external aims, into theory itself.

"Poetry," "drama," and even "novel" are all older than "literature," and all expressed differences of genre. "Literature" grouped them together and identified a tradition and a canon. A newcomer, like "novel," had to fight its way under the tent of this term, much as "American Literature" had to fight its way into the academic curriculum. I mention all of this for two reasons: our story is (1) in part about the movement to erase the important alleged differences between literature and other uses of language and is (2) a brief account of how the tradition of the defense of poetry became a defense of literature when the latter term began to be substituted for the former in some critical practices.

The tradition of the defense of poetry, which seems to have begun with Aristotle, assumes a difference between poetry and other forms of discourse. Aristotle was actually talking about drama in *Poetics* and defending *mimesis* against Plato. Further, this first surviving defense did what all subsequent defenses have done: point out a difference. Plato had been the first to do this. For him, poetry, to its disadvantage, was different from philosophy, indeed at war with it. Aristotle contrasted poetry to history. The modern New Criticism in America differentiated poetry from science and emphasized that poetry employed language differently. It is this last distinction that postmodernism calls in question. To some extent, it is the romantic poets and critics who early in the nineteenth century marked the turn to linguistic interests in criticism, just as philosophy turned to language. This unwittingly set the stage for the very difference on which members of the defense insisted.

In order to illustrate this point, it is useful to go back to a precursor, Giambattista Vico and his book *The New Science* (1725). Vico's treatment of poets was one of the first to be grounded in linguistics. For him, the most primitive people were naturally poets because they thought only in concretion, bing incapable of producing what he called "abstract universals." Thus, when they employed what passed with them for universals they expressed what Vico called poetic "allegories"—gods like Zeus and heroes like Achilles, who embodied a congeries of particulars in yet another particular. Vico regarded Homer as one of these figures, which he called "imaginative universals," there being in his view, no single individual who was author of *Iliad*. The logic of these primitive people Vico called "poetic logic," a logic of tropes, of which, to his mind, the most important were metaphor, metonymy, synecdoche, and later irony. As history moved from the age of gods to that of heroes and then that of men, there grew up the abstracting powers and the dulling of the poetic impulse, though it never fully subsided and indeed returned periodically as nations went through the cyclic *ricorsi* that constituted part of Vico's vision of history.

In his *Defense of Poetry* (1821, pub. 1840), Percy Bysshe Shelley argued without recourse to Vico that this cyclical process was the deadening and

"Literature" and the Visionary Tradition (1995)

then refurbishment of language, and the latter was in the hands of poets, but Shelley included many philosophers and historians among his poets. A little earlier William Blake, sounding rather like Vico, had observed the decline of language from poetic naming to the abstractions of priestly and monarchical control of culture.

A romantic visionary tradition was developing that saw poetry as the source of all language as we know it. Tropes were not, then, deviations from normal discourse but the soul of discourse itself and the ultimate source of all thought. There came to be an important connection between this line of poetic defense and Kantian philosophy, first in Wilhelm Von Humboldt's researches on language, and later in Ernst Cassirer's emphasis on the constitutive powers of symbolic forms, of which art, including literary art, was one, though Cassirer had some trouble identifying literature with both art and another of his symbolic forms, language, which seemed in his philosophy to have different aims. Cassirer called science an "abbreviation of reality," a necessary one, while art was an "intensification" of it. He described the two as processes of abstraction and concretion respectively.

Among modernist critics, the visionary line was continued in such works as Philip Wheelwright's *The Burning Fountain* (1954) and Herbert Read's *Icon and Idea* (1955). In these works, poetry was seen as having a visionary function and character. Especially in Read's book there is a tendency to claim that poetry is the ancestor of all language as we know it.

The suggestion in these works is that poetry has done what the invention of abstract universals has not, that the visionary is also the creative. This tradition would then not only create "far other worlds and other seas," as Andrew Marvell wrote, but also reconstitute the world of mundane experience, which might otherwise recede totally to the status of the purely quantified objects of mathematical symbolism. Poetry, it is claimed, does this by virtue of its linguistic difference, which Wheelwright characterized as that between "expressive" and "steno" language. However, there are not two languages, but rather two or more developments and uses of it.

The great modern poets clearly in this tradition are Blake, Wordsworth, Coleridge, Shelley, Keats, Emerson, Yeats, and Stevens. The tradition, of course, has several elements, and not all poets are characterized by all of them, but it can be said that two of them, present in all, are intensity of focus on the individuality of things and the interrelation of perceiver and perceived. Some poets, but not all, opt for something bordering on mystical transcendence, in which the relation is with the supposedly unperceivable by way of the symbol, but the main line is intense vision transformative of the mundane. Perhaps a remark by Blake in a letter Dr. Trusler, who had rejected one of his paintings, will stand for the tradition generally:

> ...This world is a World of Imagination & Vision [.] I see Every thing I paint in This World but Every body does not see alike. To the Eyes of a Miser a Guinea is more beautiful than the Sun & a bag worn with the use of Money has more beautiful proportions than a Vine filled with Grapes. The tree which moves some to tears of joy is in the Eyes of others only a Green thing that stands in the way [E702].

What we see in the visionary line is a gradual loss of confidence, not in the rightness of the poetic vocation but in its cultural power to make a difference.

Indeed, the difference itself has been eroded, for the notion of poetry as the ground of all language can be seen ironically as the beginning of the destruction of the difference between poetry and other uses of language. In postmodern theory, it seems that either everything has become or always has been poetry, or nothing is or ever was poetry. There has triumphed, momentarily perhaps, the notion of *ecriture*, that is, the reduction of all language to a certain model of writing. Essays have been written treating Kant, Hegel, and others as if their use of language is no different from a poet's use. Their tropes have been studied as if they behave just as tropes do in poems. Their works have been treated via theories of narrative. Poems have been read as parts of the universal discourse of power. But this takes us to the next paper.

"Literature" into "Ecriture"? (1995)

[See the bracketed preface to the previous essay "Literature" and the Visionary Tradition. It was deliberately written for those not well acquainted with the movements here briefly described.]

"Literature" threatened to disappear or to swallow everything linguistic because of three intellectual movements that followed one on another: Phenomenology, Structuralism, and Deconstruction. I'll take up these three briefly.

The phenomenological movement, as it appeared in literary theory, was an attack on epistemology, specifically on the division of subject and object. Or, rather, it was an attempt to bridge the gap presumed by epistemology since the times of Descartes and Locke. Operating on the slogan that consciousness is always consciousness of *something*, phenomenology emphasized the so-called "intentional" act. The attack on subject/object was immediately attractive to a literary criticism that remained in the debt of romantic thought. The tendency was to think of poetry as the best form of philosophy. But the phenomenologists had to face the question of the role of language in intentionality, and in this they faced difficulties. They treated language principally as a medium by which consciousness actively constituted intentional objects. In various forms of phenomenological criticism, the poem was a mediation joining the consciousness of the author to that of the reader (Georges Poulet), constituting the world and making contact with the reader by activating a reverie without the intervention of rational inquiry (Gaston Bachelard), etc. Phenomenology was opposed to the structuralist movement that so influenced subsequent theory, but it also contributed to the structuralist breakdown of the difference between literature and other forms of language.

Structuralism was based on the linguistic theories of Ferdinand de

Saussure, or perhaps the pseudo–Saussure of the influential text *Course in General Linguistics*. The book is actually a transcription and editing by students of their notes on Saussure's lectures. (Most professors would hate, I am sure, to be represented by their students' lecture notes!) There is controversy over whether some of the ideas in the text were really Saussure's. He developed the principle of linguistic difference, which emphasized the notion of language as a closed system or structure of signs, each of which assumes a signifier and a signified. The signified is always composed of another word or of other words in the system. The overriding principle of difference is that every sign is defined by its difference from every other sign in the system. Thus there is only difference with no positive terms. Further, every relation of signifier to signified, let alone the external, so-called referent is arbitrary. The result of this, Saussure seems to have hoped, was the possibility of a science of linguistics, the troublesome physical or ideal object or referent having been eliminated (or, as we say, "bracketed") from a science of linguistics.

The tendency of this departure from diachronic or historical linguistics into a purely synchronic one with the referent bracketed had a number of consequences in literary criticism and theory:

(1) An attack on mystical concepts of the symbol on the ground that there is an entirely arbitrary relation of sign to referent and with it the wholesale rejection of a symbolism that would posit a referent drawn into language from either a spiritual or natural world beyond. Metonymy triumphs over metaphor by implying only a juxtaposition rather than an identity and

(2) the valorization of allegory as an honest use of language, recognizing that language cannot jibe with or force itself on reality. (Paul de Man)

(3) Because of the Saussurean relation of signifier to signified the idea that difference creates an infinite chain of differences and deferral of meaning because there is no longer any ground outside the system, consequently no first or original word that has been, so to speak, given. Thus, Deconstruction. (Jacques Derrida)

(4) The resultant rejection of the concept of closure, unity, wholeness, etc. in the light of this endless deferral.

(5) The break-up of any hope that meaning can be captured in an interpretation. This had been the view at least approached by many predecessors (for example, Cleanth Brooks's attack on paraphrase of poems), but these predecessors had held to a notion of aesthetic or

formal closure and the partial capture of meaning, while Deconstruction, which found its strength in Derrida's carrying Structuralism to logical absurdity in its own terms, insisted that words like closure and unity were obsolete.

(6) "Wall to wall language" (a phrase invented, I think, by Edward W. Said). Saussure equivocated about the referent, but Derrida dismissed it as impossible in Saussure's system, in which, he showed, there was neither exit nor end. Like modern physics' curved space, we move along the chain of signifiers in a great arc but will return to the starting point only in an infinite length of time.

(7) Emphasis on the linguistically fundamental nature of tropes, which from the point of view of symbolic logic make language unstable and must be treated as deviation, excrescence, or mere beautification.

(8) The assumption that critical interpretation is an endless process, not just because of historical and linguistic change but because of textual openness. Deconstructive approaches spread rapidly to historical, philosophical, and even scientific texts (causing occasional satire and parody). Indeed, Derrida began his work discussing mainly philosophical, not literary texts.

(9) The assumption that everything is "ecriture," everything is a text. Instead of language mirroring the world, the world mirrors language. In the work of Roland Barthes, for instance, subjects we used to think of as having existence external to language, are treated as texts and are modeled on structures of language: fashions in clothing, wrestling, and other sports—practically anything. Jacques Lacan declared that the unconscious was "like a language."

The result: Literature became either nothing or everything. You could take your choice, probably made on the basis of what discipline you favored. The speed with which these consequences invaded Western literary study was astonishing, but there was quickly resistance, particularly from those with political and other agendas in which culture and the world was "material." No other trend at this writing has entirely avoided what has been described above or captured the field. Most changes in literary thought come as the result of eventual boredom or exhaustion, and this happens much more rapidly than in the fairly recent past. Exhaustion seems to be the state at present.

"An Antithetical Turn" (1996)

[Readers of the previous essays have seen this turn occurring in my work. The essay places my position in the context of literary thought toward the close of the twentieth century. It also attempts to clarify my language by contrast to those of my late colleagues at the University of California, Irvine, Murray Krieger and Wolfgang Iser. I have found their work congenial, but with some differences, mostly but not all, of emphasis and terminology. Someone else would have to clarify the differences and similarities. The concepts of antitheticality, derived from W. B. Yeats, and contrariety, from William Blake, form the basis of my argument in *The Offense of Poetry* (2007).

This essay originally appeared in *Why Literature Matters: Theories and Functions of Literature*, eds. Rudiger Ahrens and Laurenz Volkmann (Heidelberg: Univeritatsverlag C. Winter, 1996).]

William Blake declared that in 1798 it would cost a man his life to defend the Bible. He was taking the side of Thomas Paine against Bishop Watson's criticism, defending Paine's hatred of priesthood and criticizing what he regarded as egregious misreadings of the Bible by churchmen. To defend poetry (in the larger sense of the term) in 1995 is not to my knowledge life-threatening, though to write it may be, as Rushdie and Mahfouz have discovered. There is little doubt, however, that in the world of critical theory and the academy to defend poetry is likely to brand the defender as a reactionary or quaint outsider whose relevance to the main trends of intellectual labor is in considerable doubt.

Early in this waning century it did not seem so, even though critics generally thought that poetry and the world of human affairs were somehow at odds and had been for a century. The Aestheticists, the Expressionists, the Russian Formalists, the New Humanists, the New Critics, the Neo-Aristotelians, the Leavisites, the so-called "vision" critics—these all explicitly or implicitly remained in the tradition of the defense of poetry that began with the ancient interpreters of Homer and proceeded through writers as diverse as Aristotle, Boccaccio, Mazzoni, Sidney, and Shelley. English Renaissance criticism alone contained a whole range of apologists: Rainold, Lodge, Webbe, Puttenham, Harington, among others. All of these rose to defend against attackers: Plato's Socrates; medieval churchmen; Castravilla, Bulgarini, and other denigrators of Dante, the Puritan Stephen Gosson, and the satirist Thomas Love Peacock.

These defenses became part of the history—the canon, if you will—of literary criticism, or, as we now say, theory. Sometimes they were too narrowly conceived or too narrowly concerned with local issues to be entirely convincing. Sometimes they addressed issues that no longer seem important. But in criticism and theory old issues have a way of returning to us in modem dress. In every case, these apologists sought to contribute to poetry's health and that of the culture at large.

It was a sign of the times that in 1983 Murray Krieger felt the need to write "An Apology for Poetics," in which he recognized that it wasn't merely poetry that required defense but the whole enterprise of a mode of studying it—that enterprise initiated by Aristotle and called "poetics."[1]

In his "Apology," Krieger observed that in Sidney's day poetry required defense from a view that it could offer no truth and thus had no proper function, the assumption being that discourse had as its only proper aim truth. So poetry would have to be excluded from discourse as a dangerous deviant. Krieger observed also that in recent times the opposite had occurred and in virtually all recent fashionable theoretical work poetry had become no different from any other discourse. He suggested that either poetry had become everything in the realm of language or it had been reduced to nothing. His view and defense of poetics was grounded on the notion that poetics requires the "separate definition of the poem." Only with this can claims be made that poetics has a subject. One of the terms that functions importantly in his "Apology" and in the colloquium at Konstanz that followed it is "deviation," which implies that poetry deviates from a so-called normal discourse. Krieger was careful to claim that his distinction between normal discourse and its deviations was heuristic only. So I am not quarreling with him when I claim that if deviation is to be proposed as heuristic it should be entirely the other way around. The deviationist discourses are the special languages of the sciences, not poetry, which was and is "normal." The other term in Krieger's essay, even more important because not merely heuristic, or at least not quite so heuristic (because all theoretical terms are perhaps only heuristic) is "duplicity."

"Duplicity" is Krieger's term for what he regarded as the double claim that poetry makes: The poem's aesthetic closure and claim to unity are a sort of fiction made in opposition to the poem's own self-knowledge of closure's and unity's impossibility; or, rather, the closure is momentary only and the external world is acknowledged as *there* but also, by virtue of the acknowledgment, held in a closure that is now (and really always has been) open. The aesthetic moment of closure is an illusion that responds to anthropological need. This notion of duplicity, with which I have some sympathy, is nevertheless troubling because by its language it seems to privilege one side of the duplicitousness, the side acknowledging a truth deeper than the illusion momentarily held. (In this Krieger clung to at least a remnant of the existentialist position that had always attracted him and also to ontological and epistemological concerns.) This opposition I call a negation, stealing the term, as I have before, from William Blake, not Hegel.

In Blake's language, which I adopt for purposes of a poetics, a "negation" is a situation in which an opposition exists, but one side is privileged at the expense of the other. Thus, in historical Christianity soul is privileged over body, in Locke's epistemology object is privileged over subject, and so on. Negation is a situation of suppression and victory. A true "contrary" opposes negative opposition by offering a third term. This third term does not attempt to suppress or defeat the two mutually negating terms, but rather it offers an active equal opposition to and implicit critique of them on the ground that the negating pair is perhaps valuable if creatively and continually opposed and recognized as a fiction. A negating dyad, on the other hand, cannot tolerate the equal existence of a contrary third term. The contrary accommodates and welcomes the negative pair as part of itself in a Heraclitan tension.

Under Blake's influence, W.B. Yeats characterized this third term as "antithetical," implying its oppositional role in modem culture, and I shall do likewise. Blake's opposition to the Lockean object/subject negation recognizes negation's value when it operates according to what we may call the categories of scientific fiction-making, one criterion of which is a certain kind of use. But only when it is seen in contrariety with what Blake called "vision."

I pause here to remark that Krieger's argument gave privilege to the external world over the poem's world, whether that external world was seen as matter or words, though Krieger nearly recovered from his negation by knowing that externality was also illusion, that is to say, fictive. So my argument is friendly to Krieger's efforts in behalf of poetics, but I will attempt to shift the arena of discourse from the ontological and epistemological, where the notion of the external keeps cropping up, to the anthropological and ultimately the ethical. (I note in passing that Krieger has attempted to do the same in his most recent book.) As I do this, I claim for poetry (and the poetics of which it is the subject) the position of the contrary or "antithetical" third term in verbal culture, and I add that this triad produces a fourth which is the totality of the three and has traditionally been named "imagination," though Blake, in the mode of Vico's "poetic logic," where there are gods before there are abstract ideas, names this activity "Los" and calls him a "Zoa."

Since the term "imagination" has entered my discourse and "fiction" has also appeared, I pause to note as particularly stimulating the recent work of Wolfgang Iser in his book *The Fictive and the Imaginary*.[2] Here, as in Krieger's work, there appears to be a move towards the antithetical. For Iser, the fictive crosses a boundary like the old one between lies (poetry) and truth, but it "keeps in view what has been overstepped." In the fictive there is the coexistence of mutually exclusive worlds; the fictive requires a reality as other or it would not be comprehensible; yet the fiction/reality opposition (or what I call a negation with reality privileged) is inadequate and requires a third term, which Iser calls the "imaginary," neither transcendent nor synthetic in the Hegelian sense.

The coexistence of the mutually incompatible, when identified with the fictive, suggests that the fictive has something in common with metaphor. In the trope, a third term is implied as a contrary to the negation sameness/difference. A metaphor insists on sameness and difference at the same time. In this view of metaphor, it is not merely a pleasant decoration or a momentary deception that merely covers over a fundamental difference, nor is it a mystical assertion of the same, negating difference. Rather, it is an expression of an ethical state of identity. The term "identity" is for this purpose a double term in that it implies individual identity or difference while at the same time it can be said that this identity may be identical with something else. Clearly we are not speaking here ontologically but rather have moved to the level of the ethical, which is antithetical to the ontological view. That is, we would be crazy to claim that two things in nature clearly separate and distinct are also the same. But ethically it might make a good deal of sense to claim they are both same and different, as does a metaphor. This is the deeper, fully "experienced" reading of Blake's poem "The Lamb." That poem is finally not merely a vision of the same but of identity. On the other hand, "The Tyger" is a vision of natural alienation until one reads more deeply or "innocently" into it and discovers a contrary vision lurking in its language.

We have moved from consideration of the fictive to the trope. Particular attention needs to be given here to the central role of synecdoche in the poetic. This trope is, like metaphor, not merely a device, but is fundamental to the extent that the poetic, as Vico argued at length, begins with the concrete particular, submerging the mind in the senses, and producing not abstract universals but what he called "imaginative universals," that is, images that *embody* all that are their parts. The imaginative universal, being "concrete," requires enactment, that is, dramatic presentation in a story that is not just an allegorical representation of an argument.

Of course, antitheticality, because it harbors opposites, also harbors the seeds of drama. The discourse at the other pole from the poetic effects a purgation of tropes and also of drama, for the direction of abstract argument is linear and straightforward, moving toward the closure of truth achieved either by deductive or inductive means. Or it moves toward ever greater, more comprehensive hypotheses, remaining open, but with the fiction of a final truth ultimately to be achieved by the process. One may note that Plato's dialogues are variously locatable somewhere between the two poles depending on how genuinely dramatic they are, that is, how much Plato allows two sides to enact their dramatic relationship. True drama is always open to further interpretation, which does not end, though it may close formally, joining its beginning to its end.

Yet one senses also behind or surrounding or infusing all of its parts the larger gesture of the work itself, as one senses it in, say, a play of Wilde or of Shaw. This gesture, a term I pick up from R. P. Blackmur but use somewhat differently, escapes capture by the poem's words or its characters or even its narrator. It is purely presentation, in Suzanne Langer's sense. It is the poem's resistance to theory, in Krieger's. In mine it is pure antitheticality and is elusive to description or definition.

After these few remarks about fiction, trope, drama, and gesture under the title of the antithetical, let me now return to some more general observations. In the recent times that Krieger has studied, clearly a turn or move to a new level of abstraction in theory has taken place. The enormous intensification of literary study generated by modern and modernist defenses helped to generate the theoretical discourses that have tended more and more to alienate themselves from poetics, to say nothing of poetry itself. How many young professors and students in academic departments that in the past were centered on the study of literary texts now read almost no poetry, drama, or prose fiction, caught up in what passes for interdisciplinary scholarship or purely theoretical discourse? A defense of poetry today has to be one that asserts its cultural role in the face of the stupendous growth of the power of the visual media of film and television. It must also act in the teeth of academic trends that do not attack poetry so much as ignore it in favor of a soft form of social science.

One need not rehearse here the history of what I have characterized as a movement of abstraction. It includes the reduction, growing out of the structuralist principle of difference, of virtually everything to the model of textuality. It has more than once been ironically observed that a principle of difference has monolithically allowed no difference to poetry. This history has also included the triumph of "critical theory" or social thought, in the sense developed by the Frankfurt School, over "literary theory," poet or "poetics" in Krieger's sense. A direct outgrowth has been the relatively new academic fashion of culture studies or cultural critique (in England "cultural materialism," in America the "new historicism"). The argument here, of course, is that literary texts (though these movements question whether "literature" any longer exists as such) are never anything if not political by definition. Some go as far as to claim that it is immoral not to treat literary texts as their allegedly extractable political content. Thus the lecture hall and seminar room become the scene of moral instruction and in its worst forms self-congratulation and subtle harassment.

I am tempted, from my own experience and perhaps my Yeatsian inclination to see cyclicity or spiraling where others see only straight-line progress or regression, to think that "poetics" and "politics" move in alternate waves across the ocean of poetry. After fifty years in academic life, back to my time as a college freshman, I now witness a return (with, of course, a difference). I began study in a department where the literary historians, born of the philological tradition, the Parringtonians, and the Marxists were beginning to be challenged by the New Criticism. I witnessed also an attempt in the state legislature (partly successful) to purge Marxist-leaning faculty from the university. (It was, incidentally a New Critic who as chairman found himself morally obligated to defend those whom he opposed intellectually.) Those days were by turns exciting and depressing.

I have now participated in another turn of the spiral. The New Critics and the Deconstructionists, who supplanted them, are now replaced by the most recent modes of historical and cultural studies. Perhaps, as I suggested a few years ago, a great rough beast of new aestheticism is lurking somewhere in the desert.

It is clear to me that, *no matter who is in power* or appears to be in power performing acts of negation on an enemy, the tradition of the defense of poetry needs renewal. I am attempting to negate neither the political nor the aesthetic, but I am quarreling with both as they have been traditionally conceived in criticism. Both have produced valuable, and I should even say indispensable, insights, one-sided as they may have been. I quarrel antithetically with their opposition because I think it is an endlessly cyclical process going nowhere. They are two sides of the same coin, or, as Blake remarked about negations, both sides have adopted the same story and thrive parasitically on the deficiencies of each other.

Poetry, I think, has no enemies sophisticated enough or interested enough today to mount an attack. The problem is, rather, indifference among those who abstract toward political interests or reduce literature to undifferentiated textuality. Past defenses inevitably addressed the role of poetry in connection with the issues current in their times. At this point, some brief historical sketch may be of use.

Aristotle, to whom Plato bequeathed the language of mimesis, redefined that term to what he thought was the advantage rather than the denigration of poetry. This was an example of what Kenneth Burke called the "stealing back and forth of symbols," and it is typical of the long history of literary theory, the problem being that a trace of the former definition and its metaphysical or epistemological baggage remained in the stolen term. Aristotle's rhetoric was such that he never explicitly apologized for poetry, but rather for mimesis itself as a natural form of human behavior that carried a certain delight with it. He tried to strip the term of its derogatory aura. For him it was not a slavish copy of mere phenomena as it had been for Socrates in the *Republic,* and it had a certain benefit for the audience.

The problem of mimesis in the centuries during which the *Poetics* was lost to Europe remained. It became associated with the problem of the image, regarded as a lie or even a sacrilege. The classic medieval utterance is perhaps Boethius' in the *Consolatione Philosophiae* (c. 532), in which the muses of poetry are "seducing mummers" who offer "poisonous sweets" and "barren briars of passion" to unsuspecting readers. They accustom men to a disease. Stephen Gosson attacked piping and playing (the theater) as well as poetry and employed a similar rhetoric, which we shall see crops up again recently in a quite different context. The Socratic suspicion of mimesis was, of course, by Gosson's time leagued with religious distaste for graven images. The latter concern remained persistent. Joyce Cary's narrator Chester Nimmo, dwelling on his Victorian childhood in the remarkable novel *Except the Lord,* records his sense of pleasurable sinfulness when as a child he attended a play at a country fair.

But defense-minded Platonists tried to rehabilitate the image against the Platonic attack, which labeled it a dangerous second-hand copy. Plotinus is the best example: "... they give no bare reproduction of the thing seen but go back to the Reason-Principle from which Nature itself derives, and, furthermore, ... much of their work is all their own; they are holders of beauty where Nature is lacking."[3] Beauty, which is light, persists even in the darkness of matter.

We see this anti–Platonic Platonism in Giacomo Mazzoni's *Della Difesa della Comedia di Dante* (1587), where Mazzoni defends the image, or what he calls the "idol," though on different grounds. For Plotinus, as he says, "... each manifestation of knowledge and wisdom is a distinct image, an object in itself, an immediate unity, not an aggregate of discursive reasonings and detailed willing. Later from this wisdom in unity there appears, in another form of being, an image already less compact, which announces the original in terms of discourse..."[4] For Mazzoni, the purpose of the so-called mimetic arts (and both Plotinus and Mazzoni hold on to the term "mimesis") is to create idols, and yet at the same time Mazzoni sets aside the question of truth and substitutes "credibility," or what his commentator Robert L. Montgomery calls "the impression of authenticity or reality."[5] At the same time, Mazzoni connects poetry with the "civil faculty" and the interests of society. For him, poetry is the other side of active social life, the necessary other side, which he refers to as "cessation," by means of which there is both delight and profit.

One side of the coin implies, indeed demands, the presence of the other. Mazzoni struggles inside the vocabulary of mimesis to establish or acknowledge a doubleness. It is a difficult task, given the Platonic baggage, not to privilege one side. Both Krieger and Iser later discover that even without that impediment the task is difficult.

Sir Philip Sidney's defense, along the lines of his predecessor Julius Caesar Scaliger, retains mimesis, but he idealizes it, for it goes beyond nature. The language, though still tied to mimesis, anticipates Iser's notion of the fictive "overstepping" a boundary line, yet carrying along what it has paradoxically left behind. The famous passage is:

> Only the poet, disdaining to be tied to any such subjection, lifted up with the vigor of his own invention, doth grow in effect another nature, in making things either better than nature bringeth forth, or, quite anew, forms such as never were in nature, as the Heroes, Demigods, Cyclopes, Chimeras, Furies, and such like: so as he goeth hand in hand with nature, not enclosed within the narrow warrant of her gifts, but freely ranging within the zodiac of his own wit.[6]

The two sides of this coin produce a third somewhere between what Sidney calls the historical example and the philosophical precept, yielding an image: "A perfect picture, I say, for he yieldeth to the power of the mind an image of that where of the philosopher bestoweth but a wordish description."[7] The danger for this third term is that it threatens to collapse back into a mere representation of an abstract idea or what romantic theorists disparagingly called "allegory." It also appears to be not a contrary or antithetical third, but a sort of mediation or compromise. The opposition and resistance necessary to the antithetical is weakened or perhaps even destroyed.

Despite the turn away from a criticism that emphasized mimesis (Wordsworth's 1800 preface never mentions it), the issues surrounding it kept turning up as long as theoretical concerns were principally ontological or epistemological. In some modern cases a profound ambivalence toward poetry was the result. The structuralist movement would seem to have bracketed the problem of reference and thus that of mimesis, at least as it was traditionally conceived. Later there is not bracketing so much as the absolute declaration of the impossibility of mimesis or direct reference to the world in language generally. In a critic like Paul de Man both mimesis and the incarnate or miraculous symbol traceable back to Plotinus' image are rejected in favor of an "allegorical" or entirely arbitrary relation of word to thing or to another word. In fact, it is a complete disrelation of word to thing or word to word. In his accusatory rhetoric (language is seductive, duplicitous, rigorously unreliable), de Man seems to offer an attack on poetry (and all language) as illusion while at the same time arguing that poetry at least deconstructs the illusion it seductively presents. There is *here,* perhaps, a saving grace that Boethius, who used a similar rhetoric, did not allow to the muses. No doubt de Man thought that he had defended poetry because in his existential universe there was at least honesty in the admission of its momentary duplicity. There is nothing left of Sidney's better, golden world here, or of a world at all, only the existential condition. The question arises, oddly enough, of how, if we are epistemologically trapped in the semiotic prison, we can have any criticism by which to test language for duplicity. De Man presumed a knowledge of reality, a severe knowledge of nothingness, but also a total skepticism.

In an essay answering de Man's attack on symbolism, "'A Waking Dream': The Symbolic Alternative to Allegory," Krieger largely accepted the de Manian world or condition but held for the value of the momentary aesthetic illusion of the poem even as, in part because, it demystifies the very symbol it creates as it fulfills our anthropological aesthetic desire.[8] This aesthetic desire plays a role in Krieger similar to the role of mimesis in Aristotle, for Aristotle remarked of human pleasure in mimesis.

Both de Man and Krieger tell the same story, and the trace of the epistemological situation that required a theory of mimesis is still present in them. A certain reality, even if it is a reality of nothingness, is presumed that the poem is forbidden to reach except by negation of its own illusion. Their difference from each other is that de Man values the demystification and not the aesthetic moment, while Krieger would value both, though perhaps not with reasons sufficient to make us fully content with the aesthetic side. The concluding chapter of Krieger's latest work *The Institution of Theory* takes a more anthropologically oriented stance that strikes me as nearer to my own conception of antitheticality, while yet trying to maintain the existential commitment. He writes of the literary text's "resistance against ideology's repression" even as it may be contained by or contain an ideological component.[9] This is, of course, the trace of Deconstruction in Krieger's work. He further observes that a theory adequate to such a text would have to be able to resist its own institutional ideology, and this goes beyond Deconstruction as we know it today in the form of a method. I would call the resistance of which Krieger writes its antithetical nature, the undercutting of negation, which is always the form of ideology as straight-line discourse. Antitheticality is positively defined by the interrelationship of fiction, trope, drama, and gesture. But development of this definition must be postponed for lack of space here.

Percy Bysshe Shelley's "Defense of Poetry" (1821, pub. 1840) marked a turning away from mimesis partly because of Shelley's cultural and social, that is to say, anthropological interests and the changing notions of language current at the time. His eloquent passage about poets as the creative preservers of the power and life of language well expressed the turn he represents. His defense might be characterized as one of the texts marking the turning inside out of mimesis:

> [The poet's] language is vitally metaphorical; that is, it marks the before unapprehended relations of things and perpetuates their apprehension, until the words which represent them become, through time, signs for portions or classes of thoughts instead of pictures of integral thoughts; and then if no new poets should arise to create afresh the associations which have been thus disorganized, language will be dead to all the nobler purposes of human discourse.[10]

This passage bears the stamp of its time in its implication of an associationist psychology and seems at first to presume a mimetic representation of things by words, but it also emphasizes relations (Saussure would have said differences) and treats language as constitutive rather than imitative. Shelley historicizes the opposition of antitheticality to negation by arguing that poetic language cyclically subverts the fixities of the prevailing negations that have come to constitute a surrounding ideology. The subversive element for Shelley is metaphor and its reestablishment of associations or what I would call identities.

Shelley was answering Peacock's satiric essay "The Four Ages of Poetry" (1820), and it is worthwhile to pause with it for a moment. Peacock identified poetry, at least in its origins, with the primitive world and then described poetry's decline and obsolescence as reason triumphed over it. So for Peacock the modem poet was now "semibarbarian" in a civilized community. Almost a century before, Giambattista Vico had identified what he called "poetic logic" with the primitive human being's inability to create abstract universals and the consequent creation of a sublime "poetic metaphysics." Peacock's tongue was perhaps in his cheek, but Vico's was not, except possibly when he limited his theory to the gentile tribes, thus conveniently acknowledging Old Testament history as a divinely inspired exception.

These treatments of poets as primitive and anachronistic were, of course, turned by defenders like Shelley to poetry's advantage as philosophy turned from principally ontological to epistemological and thence to linguistic interests, which inevitably included consideration of metaphor and the other major tropes, particularly the ones Vico emphasized: metaphor, metonymy, synecdoche, and irony. We can trace the line, which became a line of defense, from Vico through Wilhelm von Humboldt to Ernst Cassirer on language, myth, and art, and Owen Barfield on metaphor. This line came under the influence of Kant, and generally it distinguished poetry from other things.

We can also see a phenomenological line of defense in which Heidegger enlisted Holderlin and other German poets as poetic defenders of poetry, so to speak; but this line blurred the distinction between poetry and philosophy, sometimes holding that poetry was the best philosophy. Here the ancient war between philosophy and poetry that Plato's Socrates spoke of became a struggle between the phenomenological tradition, which attempted in some versions to incorporate poetry into it, and Anglo-American analytical philosophy, in which poetry was likely to be regarded, in I. A. Richards' phrase, as "pseudo-statement." Deconstruction arose by fruitful contrariety out of phenomenology (as well as structuralism), and it was opposed as sophistry by the analytical school, which saw the dangers in it that Plato took pains to attack.

Within Deconstruction, de Man's severe suspicion of all language as seductive deceit was countered by Jacques Derrida's spirited identification of language with play. But if in de Man *all* poetry was complicit in that deceit (even as it knew itself to be so and tacitly admitted as much in its tropological structure), in Derrida all language was text, and the old distinctions between philosophy and rhetoric or philosophy and history were obliterated. The result was that in Derrida's tracks it was no longer certain what needed to be defended against what, if anything.

I hold that the difference between poetry and other forms of discourse is a valuable notion, though as in my *Philosophy of the Literary Symbolic* (1983) I admit that a dividing line cannot be drawn anywhere. A preferable figure (and I have no problem with figurative language to treat such matters, since all literary theory is merely heuristic) is a sliding scale between two never reachable extremes. In that book, I called these with some trepidation the poles of myth and anti-myth. While the terms were workable, they can be misleading out of a carefully made context, and I have not employed them here. The main cause, relative to my argument, is that they may too easily seem to be bipolar opposites, while the poetic, or what I then called "myth," is properly a third term antithetical to any simple bipolarity. This shift in terminology occurred in my collection entitled *Antithetical Essays in Literary Criticism and Liberal Education* (1990).

Thinking Through Blake

Let me now summarize what has admittedly been a summary statement and merely a brief prolegomenon to an extended new defense of poetry (and poetics). I have proposed a theoretical stance committed to viewing the poetic (or literary) as a third term rather than part of a dyad as in poetry/philosophy (Plato); poetry/religion (Arnold); poetry/science (the New Criticism); or as having no difference from discourse in general. In each conceivable dyadic situation (and all of these dyads are historically situated), one side of the dyad becomes privileged over the other. The poetry/science opposition remains with us in the tendency since romanticism for poetry to be identified with epistemological subjectivity and science with the privileged objectivity, unless one is to hold for a privileged solipsistic subjectivity, as in Pater. But the dyad is an invention of science that denigrated or, in the language of Blake, "negated" the subjective, identified the literary with it, and thus relegated the literary to the lesser side. A third term is always necessary to locate the literary properly, but not a transcendent term, which would in turn recommit the crime of negation against the negation it opposes.

This third term I have called "antithetical," appropriating it from W.B. Yeats. The notion is for me also somewhat reminiscent of Cassirer's idea of "symbolic forms" and the dialectical relation between the form of art and other forms that he hints at in the conclusion of his *An Essay on Man* (1946). But this dialectic is not Hegelian, teleological, or progressive toward an apotheosis of reason or of anything else. Rather, it would retain the opposition in a Heraclitan sense.

The argument I propose is that the literary is, or has been since the Renaissance, savingly antithetical to those forms of symbolization (not de Man's symbol) or fiction-making that seek to dominate the culture by dyadic means. The literary brings in the opposite to any culturally established dyad, often in spite of apparent authorial intention and the apparent ideological cast of the literary work. A pertinent historical example is Yeats's *A Vision* (1937). The whole movement of that complicated gesture is toward a statement about its own content that disengages our reading of the work from the issue of whether to believe the events it seems to recount and the doctrine it seems to present. It performs the antithetical to the negation belief/disbelief.

Antitheticality is characterized by the interrelations of fiction, trope, drama, and gesture. The literary expresses itself through these elements as a necessary contrary to and implicit critique of other cultural forms, providing what they lack or are capable of exploiting only to dyadic, negating, and thus suppressive ends. In this sense, the ethical is antithetical to onotology and epistemology. In so far as mimesis is the product of ontological and epistemological concerns, the ethical (and the poetic) is antithetical to it, though containing what it opposes.

Ekphrasis Revisited, or Antitheticality Reconstructed (2000)

[This essay was published in a book honoring the career of Murray Krieger. It begins by contrasting his position with that of Paul de Man, pointing out a certain existentialist similarity and very important differences. It proceeds by way of Giambattista Vico, Ernst Cassirer, and Giacomo Mazzoni to shift the argument from one based on epistemology to one grounded in ethics. The essay's original publication was in *Revenge of the Aesthetic: The Place of Literature in Theory Today*, ed. Michael P. Clark. © 2000 by the Regents of the University of California (Berkeley: University of California Press, 2000).]

Murray Krieger's *Ekphrasis* is a history, a self-consciously polemical history, of Western culture's shifting and ambivalent commitment to the concept of the natural sign. By the concept of the natural sign Krieger means the idea that a word has a fixed, unambiguous relation to a denoted object and, grounded on a "visual epistemology," is in a sense transparent; or it is a mimesis, a simulacrum; or it is, in the most radical version of *symbolisme*, a miraculous presence. By "visual epistemology," a term Krieger adopts from Forrest G. Robinson's book on Sidney, is meant a knowledge grounded in visual and spatial terms.[1] The history of this notion can be traced back to Simonides's alleged remark that poetry is a speaking picture, but complications set in with Plato's concept of imitation, the competing one in Aristotle, and the spatializing language of early literary theory that lends itself to Simonides's analogy of poetry and painting.

Krieger studies the various moments that arise from these beginnings. He remarks:

> There are those moments in which [criticism] is molded by the pictorial in language and those moments in which it is molded by the purely verbal as

Ekphrasis Revisited, or Antitheticality Reconstructed (2000)

non-pictorial; moments in which it is dedicated to words as capturing a stillness and moments in which it is dedicated to words in movement; or even moments dedicated to the more difficult assignment of words as capturing a *still movement*.[2]

The historical argument groups together, in a sort of metaphorical chain, space, the intelligible, logic, mimesis, and painting. Opposed to these are respectively time, the sensible, experience, free-ranging expression, and music. Krieger charts a movement in criticism from the former to the latter and thence to efforts to overcome the opposition. In general, he believes that modern theoretical criticism has sought—"through the two-sidedness of language as a medium of the verbal arts—to comprehend the simultaneity in the verbal figure, of fixity and flow, of an image at once grasped and yet slipping away through the crevices of language" (11). Ekphrasis is one time alluded to as a "temptation" (12), another time as an "ambition" (14). It is both of these because of its implication of the vain possibility that signs can miraculously become or contain the objects they denote. The historical movement is from the naiveté of the sign as pure sensuous mimesis of nature to the sign as intelligible yet still sensuous, making it possible to represent the unrepresentable (26). At this point there begins to develop, gradually, the hegemony of language *over* nature: "As we approach our own time, not only is primacy bestowed upon the arts of the word and of time (instead of upon the arts of picture and of space) but the spreading semiotic interest in texts absorbs all the arts, subjects them all to temporality and makes them all ripe for reading" (26).

The object of Krieger's polemic, we begin to see, is that aspect of poststructuralism which Krieger represents by Paul de Man's deconstructions of romantic symbolism and the notion of presence in the word, de Man favoring, in opposition to these things, absence and what he calls allegory. In a move characteristic of Krieger's tendency throughout his career to swallow and absorb theories opposed to his own, and in a manner not contrary to his own past existentialist tendencies, he accepts absence. But at the same time he argues for the valuable *illusion* of presence—as long as we and the poem know it ultimately *as* illusion. (This makes at least common sense, since no one really wants a painting or a poem actually to be the object it allegedly copies.) But for Krieger none of this obliterates the ekphrastic, which keeps reappearing in new, more sophisticated guises. In his view, postmodernism has not acknowledged its latest version: "the slippery version of the ekphrastic poetic which presses for a verbal play that acknowledges the incompatibility of time and space, while collapsing them into the illusion of an object marked by its own sensible absence" (28). This is really Krieger's own version of postmodernism, explicit in the work I am considering, but also implicit in the essays collected in his *Words about Words about Words* and subsequent books.[3] Krieger would have other oppositions, too, collapsed: the intelligible and the sensible, logic and experience, mimesis and expression, painting and music as analogues of poetry.

This collapsing of oppositions is always situated in the poem, along with the oppositions' persistence, so that Krieger can refer to an "undoing" that art performs on itself. This undoing makes possible one of art's cultural functions, which is to "stimulate the alienation that warns us away from a culture's delusions [principally the presumption that its governing signs are natural] that would legitimize its authority by an appeal to nature" (260).

De Man characterized language as "duplicitous" and "seductive," as if there were something devilish and evil in it. Krieger adopts the term "duplicitous" for poetic language without, I think, the intention of swaying us to mistrust it, but the suspicion necessarily lingers on, particularly when "duplicity" is coupled with "illusion" and it is implied that existential nothingness or absence is the only reality. The Oxford English Dictionary offers two meanings of "duplicity," the second of which expresses Krieger's intent:
1. The quality of being "double" in action or conduct (see Double); the character or practice of acting in two ways at different times, or, openly and secretly; deceitfulness, double-dealing (the earliest and still the most usual sense).
2. The state or quality of being numerically or physically double or twofold; doubleness.

Whereas de Man's usage emphasized the unreliability of all language, Krieger's points to the potential unreliability of any language presuming a one-to-one relation of sign to object, and he reserves "duplicity" for that peculiar doubleness in poetic art that knows itself as such and so declares itself. The ethical side here is the lesson that the poetic, by its implicit confession, warns us not to trust in the naturalness of any language—or the illusion. But there is a risk of denigrating human culture generally as illusion and therefore self-deceiving.

Krieger has come a long way to return, with a difference, to a word made popular and familiar by the New Criticism: irony. (I shall come back to this.) In Krieger's return—with, of course, the important difference that he explicitly gives a cultural or social role to poetic irony—he clarifies his longstanding allegiance to the New Critics, while also addressing contemporary cultural critics and maintaining a vestige of his existentialism. Thus de Man is swallowed whole and poetry apparently saved.

Yet Krieger is also Kantian. For him, things in themselves cannot be known (or uttered), but the terms of not knowing carry a negative suggestion not present in Kant—duplicity, illusion, and even paradox *(Ekphrasis* (22) . These terms render him closer to de Man than I think he would really like to be.[4] They are terms that cannot help privileging, and are spoken from the point of view of, the very same spatialized logic of the natural sign of which he is suspicious. It is difficult to see how language can be duplicitous (at least in the first sense) if things in themselves cannot be known, since there is no criterion to determine duplicity except within a strictly empirical system such as Kant constructs for the understanding. But an existential stance does not allow us this luxury as a way to truth.

Of course, if things cannot be known in themselves, language would be duplicitous if it claimed to know, though duplicity usually refers to a conscious lie, a pretense rather than an error. There is always the possibility, of course, that if things can't be known, language might be right by chance; but we could never know that it is. The existential negative and the Kantian constitutive cohabit uneasily, and the problem may be that the defense of poetry cannot finally be made in fundamentally epistemological terms. But let me follow the Kantian line a little farther before I suggest that the whole issue must be shifted from the epistemological to the ethical arena. (This, I think, is what Krieger has actually done, without explicit acknowledgment, in offering poetic art as a self-confessing illusion.) I shall eventually approach this sort of stance by way of Vico and Cassirer, discarding (to the extent that it can be discarded) the epistemological approach and the language of duplicity and illusion for a theory of ethical and empirical fictions.

The neo–Kantian line that proceeds through von Humboldt and Cassirer and does not leave untouched twentieth-century critics as diverse as Ransom, Wheelwright, and Frye shifts the epistemological question from perception to language. In Cassirer, the problem of language as illusion is given a positive twist in an argument drawn out of von Humboldt, but with a deeper source in Vico (about whom more later).[5] The negative, so to speak, is accepted:

> Instead of dealing with the things themselves man is in a sense constantly conversing with himself. He has so enveloped himself in linguistic forms, in artistic images, in mythical symbols or religious rites that he cannot see or know anything except by the interposition of this artificial medium.[6]

But this very envelopment produces both culture, with its positive as well as negative potentialities, and the set of interrelated human creations that Cassirer calls symbolic forms—myth, religion, language, art, history, and science (though Cassirer seems not to see that language is not separable from the others but rather fundamental to them). The positive turn is that Cassirer views human culture, which is structured by these forms, as a process of liberation. At the end of An *Essay on Man,* recognizing the "tensions and frictions," the "strong contrasts and deep conflicts between the various powers [these symbolic forms] of man," he hints at a possible Heraclitan "harmony in contrariety, as in the case of the bow and the lyre" (228). The issue is not whether any of these forms are simply wrong epistemological paths, leading inevitably to delusion, but rather that in each there can be a constitution of the real. Nevertheless, Cassirer still puts the issue in strictly epistemological terms, whereas it might better be put in terms of ends (as I believe Krieger very nearly or perhaps actually does). This would mean that we need not merely a theory of symbolic forms but one of fictions that have different (not exclusively epistemological) cultural purposes.

For this, it is helpful to return to Giambattista Vico.[7] Krieger points out that one of modernism's tenets (and one he would defend) is that poetry is a special and thus privileged form of discourse (though it is never quite clear why to be special is to be privileged). Terms like "defamiliarization" and "deviation" are employed in some versions of modernism to characterize what Krieger describes as a "structured resistance that obstructs and complicates, thus leading [language] to serve an other-than-normal form of discourse" *(Ekphrasis* 186). If we take a Vichean historical view, we are obliged to reverse the idea of deviation and declare that modernism's normality is really the special, deviating form and, in the early stages of human culture at any rate, the poetic is the normal. This view was to influence Cassirer's conjunction of language and myth, which he regarded as "near of kin" *(Essay on Man* 109). Recourse to a story of origins is unfashionable and from one point of view futile, but it may be worth some thought nevertheless.

Vico's story tells us that language began in fear of nature, that the first men were poets (by which he meant that they thought in a certain way), and that they were so because of their incapacity to create abstract universals. The first human fable for each people was that of a Jove, generated out of terror of the sky. Mythologies were the proper language of fable, and metaphors were fables in brief. This does not seem to be an auspicious beginning for any privileging of the poetic. Vico is ambivalent about these primitive men, whom he calls giants and thinks of as severely limited in intellect. But he also attributes a vast sublimity to their imaginative acts. Incapable of abstraction, the first men created what Vico calls "imaginative universals." Their wisdom was a "vulgar wisdom," a "crude metaphysics," the result of a wholly corporeal imagination, in which the particular had to serve as a universal. Unable to form "intelligible class concepts of things," these first men created particular poetic characters. They endowed physical substances with life by extending their own bodies into them: "In all languages the greater part of the expressions relating to inanimate things are formed by metaphor from the human body and its parts and from the human senses and passions."[8] (Cassirer makes the same point.)

The ancient gods and goddesses were human fables. In an important passage, which I shall quote at length, Vico gives Cybele, Berecynthia, and Neptune as evidence:

> By means of these three divinities ... they explained everything appertaining to the sky, the earth, and the sea. And similarly by means of the other divinities they signified the other kinds of things appertaining to each, denoting all flowers, for instance, by Flora, and all fruits by Pomona. We nowadays reverse this practice in respect of spiritual things, such as the faculties of the human mind, the passions, virtues, vices, sciences, and arts; for the most part the ideas we form of them are so many feminine personifications, to which we refer all the causes, properties, and effects that severally appertain to them. For when we wish to give utterance to our understanding of spiritual things, we must seek aid from our imagination to explain them and, like painters, form human images of them. But these theological poets [Vico posits a primitive poetic theology], unable to make use of the understanding, did the opposite and more sublime thing: they attributed senses and passions ... to bodies, and to bodies as vast as sky, sea, and earth. Later, as these vast imaginations shrank and the power of abstraction grew, the personifications were reduced to diminutive signs [128].

The poetry of these giants, which is really a mode or form of symbolization in Cassirer's terms, was wholly lacking in the important quality that Krieger attributes to poetic art, the self-consciousness that it is fictional.

But Vico's theory is a theory of fictions, and he makes a hard and fast distinction between the "certainty" that such fictions provide and "truth": "Philosophy contemplates reason, whence comes knowledge of the true; philology observes that of which human choice is author, whence comes consciousness of the certain" (63). The world of civil society comes from human minds, is made by men, and is grounded on the making of fables according to poetic logic. Because the giants could not *understand* nature, they made their fiction of it, creating culture.

Poetic logic thinks *in* tropes, the four principal ones being metaphor, metonymy, synecdoche, and irony. But irony came later and introduced the possibility of poetry in the sense in which Krieger uses the term. Vico remarks: "Irony certainly could not have begun until the period of reflection, because it is fashioned of falsehood by dint of a reflection which wears the mask of truth" (131). This marked a great change, since the earliest men were not able to feign anything false; their narrations were true to the extent that one can think of anything as true in a logic that does not include the false. But Vico does not pursue the study of irony and work out the developing interrelation of trope and reflection that his description of irony implies. Instead, he goes on to consider the four tropes together:

> From all this it follows that all the tropes (and they are all reducible to the four types above discussed), which have hitherto been considered ingenious inventions of writers, were necessary modes of expression of all the first poetic nations, and had originally their full native propriety. But these expressions of the first nations later became figurative when, with the further development of the human mind, words were invented which signified abstract forms or genera comprising their species or relating parts with their wholes. And here begins the overthrow of two common errors of the grammarians: that prose speech is proper speech, and poetic speech improper, and that prose speech came first and afterward speech in verse [131].

Important in all of this is the notion that, from a poetic point of view, poetry (in Vico's sense of tropological thinking) is the ground of all language and thus its normal form. The supreme deviation would not be poetry as we know it today but the special language devoid of tropes, mathematics. The fourth Vichian trope of irony marks the development of a reflective capacity that assumed the power to discover truth and falsity according to reason and science, relegating poetry not even to the province of a suspect certainty, but to the level of sheer opinion. However, irony is not what Vico refers to as a mere "figure," that is, an artificiality to be read *through* to whatever rational truth lies behind its veil. In romantic parlance such figures came to be called allegory, and denigrated, but Vico uses the term "allegory" to mean an imaginative universal rather than a figure for an abstract universal:

> The mythologies . . . . must have been the proper languages of the fables; the fables [like Jove] being imaginative class concepts, as we have shown, the mythologies must have been the allegories corresponding to them. Allegory is defined as *Diversiloquium* insofar as, by identity not of proportion [which would be like a simile] but (to speak scholastically) of predicability, allegories signify the diverse species or the diverse individuals comprised under these genera. So that they must have a univocal signification connoting a quality common to all their species and individuals [128].

Vico's distinction between truth and certainty was one between rationality (including the rational theology of his own time) and the poetic thought that constructs what Northrop Frye calls "myths of concern," fundamental to the structure of culture.[9] For Vico these would have been fictions, in the sense of human makings neither empirically true nor false, not the lies Plato accused the sophists and poets of perpetrating. A little extension of Vico through Kant leads to a general theory of fictions which unsettles the notion that the discourse of reason or science is normal. A theory of fictions or, in Cassirer's version, symbolic forms requires each fiction or form to function by its own laws, what Kant called categories.[10] All of these fictive forms are "languages" or employ language (in different ways and to different ends), although these can never quite be dissociated one from another, even if a culture may have attempted such a dissociation by suppressing one form or another.[11]

The Vichean moment of irony marks the very consciousness of fictionality that Krieger makes the cornerstone of his defense of poetics and of poetry. Without that consciousness, irony would be impossible. Consciousness of the fictive spread into all but the most naive forms of modern life, though it was not much theoretically developed until Bentham, and then it was applied principally to science and the law.[12] The theory of fiction as it applies to science as a form has its own special kind of irony. Science knows its projections are fictions but nevertheless posits a nonfictive external nature as an objective otherness beyond itself, declaring it to be the thing itself and knowable by empirical means. Yet this thing is a fictive constitution framed in the special language of number, a language that for other purposes was the dream of Plato, entirely free of the troublesome tropes that Vico makes the basis of poetic logic. Forms other than the poetic tend to mistrust the trope, and John Locke's view is tacitly behind this mistrust:

> If we would speak of things as they are, we must allow that all the art of rhetoric, besides order and clearness, all the artificial and figurative application of words eloquence hath invented, are for nothing else but to insinuate wrong ideas, move the passions, and thereby mislead the judgment, and so indeed are perfect cheats.[13]

Locke admits that what he calls wit and fancy are nice for entertainment, but trivial and unrelated to serious pursuit of truth. In them men find "pleasure to be deceived."[14] For Locke, tropes may at best be illustratively heuristic. In fundamentalist forms of religion, tropes are taken as literal truth (or, in more sophisticated forms, as having a literal *level*), and read as what Krieger calls in one place "straight-line discourse."

Vichean irony and Krieger's poetics offer fictions in which there is no deceit because deceit requires an objectivity by means of which a criterion of truth can be determined. We are dealing in Vico with what he calls "certainty," and until there was irony there could be nothing opposed to the certainty of fable. But with the object as the emerging criterion, certainty and the parvenu truth came into an opposition in which one sought to negate the other and control the intellectual realm.[15] The certain became subject to the criteria of empiricism and rationalism. Irony can be seen as poetic logic's answer to this effort to subdue certainty, but poetic logic cannot be sustained on epistemological grounds alone and, indeed, could never in Vico's terms have been fully epistemologically motivated. Arising, according to Vico, out of fear, poetic logic expressed communal concern amid eventually constituted tribal orders. To consider irony only from an epistemological point of view would be to play by the rules of the alleged enemy and would have to end in some form of fundamentalist faith or in existential negation, as it does in de Man and in many other cases. A vestige of this fate remains in Krieger's accommodation of de Man. The existential Krieger must give up all truth except absence, but the Kantian Krieger would recover a constituted form, though only as a maker of illusion. Then, at the critical moment, Krieger reinvigorates the aesthetic illusion as that which insists that all constitutive forms, particularly the forms we want to call natural—natural law, natural science, naturalistic writing—are equally the makers of illusion. The aesthetic illusion, in its elegance, in its irony, is the only honest illusion, a beacon illuminating the naturalistic and hegemonic pretensions of all others. So what was thoroughly negative in de Man is turned half way toward the positive in Krieger.

I should like to place alongside this view—a sameness with a difference—a concept of the poetic as "antithetical," a term I appropriate from Yeats. (Krieger employs the term once in *Ekphrasis* [188], but in an entirely different sense: to characterize postmodern critics opposed to the aesthetic.) Modern poets, by whom I mean here those who have come since the invention of irony, cannot inevitably fail to lie, as Vico claimed the earliest poets could. But critics at least since Sidney have taken pains to argue that the question of truth and falsity is irrelevant to what the poet is about. Yet the tendency of criticism and theory to revert to epistemological terms has remained compelling. Antitheticality is a rising up neither of a countertruth nor of a falsehood: it is the poetic tendency to propose ethical oppositions to the fixities of what I, following Blake, call negations, that is, binary oppositions in which one side would suppress the other.[16]

One could say, of course, that Aristotle already shifted the ground of literary apologetics away from epistemology, in his remark about it being better to paint the hind with horns than to paint it inartistically. But the shift did not hold, since Aristotelians generally reverted in later dramatic criticism to rigorous insistence on the unities of time and space, returning to canons of imitative accuracy. Most turns toward ethics since Aristotle defend poetry with the notion that it presents an allegory of moral teaching, as is the case (with a certain amount of backing and filling) in Sidney's *Apology*.

In Renaissance criticism, the closest thing to an ethical defense based neither on canons of accuracy nor on recourse to moral allegory is Giacomo Mazzoni's argument in behalf of the credible idol and that aspect of poetry he identified with the "civil faculty." Mazzoni opposes "credible things," which may include the marvelous, to the true and the false, the possible and the impossible. In other words, he establishes an antithetical contrary to these binary oppositions (negations). For Mazzoni, the civil faculty "not only professes to understand the justness of human actions but also the justness of the cessation of human actions," that is, play, amusement, game, pleasure.[17] Mazzoni identifies imitation with the delight that Aristotle attributed to it, more than with accuracy as such. The idol should be "correct," but its correctness is grounded on accurate representation of the credible marvelous, not of natural objects. Pleasure is directed toward the socially useful: "Perfect poetry is game and is modified by the civil faculty;

insofar as it is recreation it has delight as its end [cessation], but insofar as it is modified or, so to speak, characterized by moral philosophy, it puts delight first in order to provide a later benefit" (101). The benefit is to the "civil community," so Mazzoni is doing more than reuttering the old Horatian maxim of delightful teaching: heroic poetry spurs soldiers to glory; tragedy instructs the great about the downfall of great persons; comedy consoles those with but modest fortunes (103). These values are perhaps not ours, but we can read them as part of an attempt to avoid the subjugation of poetry to the expression of abstract moral code expressed in allegorical particulars.

The concept of imitation—except when hedged around by someone like Mazzoni, who opposes the denigration of the false by the true in literary criticism—is part of a Platonic negation, since imitation is always false. Mazzoni offers the credible marvelous as a contrary antithetical to the Platonic negation of phenomena on the one hand and imitations twice removed from truth on the other: "Since the poet has the credible as his subject, he ought therefore to oppose credible things to the true and the false, the possible and the impossible, by which I mean that he ought to give more importance to the credible than to any of the others I have enumerated" (78). In Vichian modern times, after the development of irony, one discovers the growth of negating dyads—the true and the false, the good and the evil, the soul and the body, the object and the subject—in which the first in each dyad is favored and would negate the second. In short, ideology is negation. In Krieger's *Ekphrasis,* space and time are a negation; after the domination of space, time takes over the negating role. What rises up in the apologetics for modernist art is, I think, a contrary antithetical to this negation, as, using another terminology, Krieger indicates. Literary criticism began by favoring space, lurched all the way to favoring time, but Krieger himself favors a third situation: "The special and two-sided role assigned the language medium in poetry allows it to supervise the paradoxical coexistence of time and space, of the sensible and the intelligible, of mimesis and free-ranging expression" (*Ekphrasis* 206).[18]

The ethical role of poetry does not lie in its presentation of moral codes, whether these codes are cunningly held behind a "natural" veil or allegorically abstracted from a poetic surface. To so assume would be to accept the negation we characterize as the split of content and form, with form negated. Nor is poetry's ethical role to raise up the suppressed half of every dyad and overthrow the previous hegemony. An example of this is the overcoming of spatial form (painting) by temporal form (music) as the principal analogy for poetry only to reestablish negation and threaten a cyclical changing of places from space to time and back. Nor is poetry's role to compromise between the two terms of the dyad in an effort to obliterate their difference or to transcend them. Such obliterations would be the obliteration of history, the devaluation of all that, for example, we can learn from past negations and past discourse about poetry. Negations are necessary to our thought and, in fact, a category of certain symbolic forms—if they were not present we would invent them. They are expressions of difference which tend to suppress sameness. Hence they are pernicious only if they are not vigorously opposed. To suppress the negation is to repeat the crime. Poetry can provide a sustaining active contrary to the negations, however useful, that began to be developed, in Vico's story, when human beings invented irony along with self-consciousness.

Prior to that critical moment, poetic logic ruled life. The model here is metaphorical thought, in which it was possible to think and live the identity of metaphor. But identity was not sameness. In Bronislaw Malinowski's story, the savage mind could declare its identity with animals, yet it did not mistake this as sameness by attempting to cohabit with lions and crocodiles.[19] Identity, if we must define it by recourse to our negating vocabulary, is sameness and difference at the same time and in the same place. It is expressed in the logic of metaphor. Poetry became antithetical in opposition to the dominating differences of our culture and the suppression of sameness, much as modern science had to struggle against the stifling sameness of established myths of concern.

Poetry, then, and criticism are not properly grounded on epistemology, but can offer the ethical stance of positive antitheticality characterized by the trope, and contrary to the negation of difference and sameness. The poem knows both sameness and difference in the trope. Criticism, which would be of the progeny of irony in Vico's story, may proceed from a commitment to absence (difference), as in Krieger's existentialist tendency, but it ought to take poetry's point of view to the extent that it can. Therefore, I would hold that the poetic illusion as offered by Krieger is still a little too much like delusion, because he drags an epistemological bias out of his argument with de Man, whereas poetry's arena is the ethical realm, in which existential truth-illusion is the negation to be antithetically opposed. Sidney, and particularly Mazzoni, were struggling in this direction; Krieger has succeeded in getting farther. What he poses for poetry is ultimately an ethical function.

Even with the accommodation of the postmodern that Krieger is prepared to make in his swallowing of de Man, his argument will not be satisfactory to those who represent postmodernism's postdeconstructive phase. The reason is that postdeconstruction, in which must be included the new historicism, varieties of feminism, and the new pragmatism, has generally attacked, from one fixed political ideology or another, all that Krieger represents by the natural sign, even the fictively natural sign. Having begun as antagonists of some ideological fixity, postdeconstructive critics end up asserting a new one in the pay of their own desires, which would be declared natural if the word were in fashion.

So I salute Murray Krieger. He has traveled his own route through the history of aesthetics. He has maintained, but not blindly, his loyalties. My own route and my language have been somewhat different—his focus has been principally on theory, mine on poetry—but we end with similar ethical roles for both. I maintain my language, he his: as Blake said, opposition is true friendship.

Quest and Cycle
(2005)

[This unpublished essay was written for a lecture and subsequently revised. It was intended as a defense both of poetry and of a literary criticism that knows its own limitations. Criticism is here described as "ironic reading." Emphasis is on inquiry and recognition that any criticism is provisional.]

I propose a fiction that presents the history of thinking about literature as a conflict of cyclical and linear movements. The cycle is a repeated movement from invention or innovation to decadence and back, or from inquiry to dogma and back. To trace the movement, one could imagine a long cycle from Plato and Aristotle to the dogmatists of the Church, from Renaissance critics to neo-classical rules and explicit moralism, from the rise of aesthetics to postromantic impressionism, from early twentieth-century objectivists to the political dogmatists of today. It can be seen that these cycles have become progressively shorter and at this rate may well eventually equal in duration the cycle of fashion in Paris.

The recent cycle would be from some commitment to the nature of the literary, connected to implicit or explicit defenses of poetry, to the hardening and distortion of the gains of such moments, abstraction from and reduction of the literary, even the declared obliteration of it. Then would come the return.

The quest proposed is a continued effort, never completed, to express the essence of the poetic, which in periods of decadence it devolves on poets themselves to sustain, sometimes in an underground state. At moments of invention, poets and theorists seem to be in league, though not always. We had an example of league early in the twentieth century, when those who were formative agents of the New Criticism leagued with or were poets. It was no coincidence that creative writing programs were mainly developed in American universities at about the time the New Criticism came into being. They leagued together against the dullness that they perceived philology and literary history to have become. It is interesting that creative writers in the academy have tended to become estranged from the main lines of what is now called simply theory, ideologically oriented.

One can detect moments when quest and cycle have struggled in a single person, indeed many moments. At the beginning of my fictive history, Plato is on both sides. When he puts politics first, as in *Republic*, or subsumes poetry under rhetoric, as in *Ion*, he banishes the poets. When poetry has the power to move him, he bows to it. It has often been observed that when he writes he is frequently a poet. Plato, as we know, recognized "an ancient war between poetry an philosophy," and his work embodies and dramatizes the struggle between his political desire for concord and what he perceived as poetry's insistence on discord, or what William Blake called "intellectual warfare."

For the New Critics the struggle seemed to be between poetry and science, and that struggle was embodied in one of the major figures of the period, I. A. Richards. Today the struggle is between poetry and theory itself. One can detect in the writings of some major scientists the realization that the poetic in, say, Vico's sense of a way of thinking or Coleridge's sense of imagination lies at the beginning of or perpetually underneath their thought. But in our decadence it is theory itself that has become the enemy of poetry, even as some on the poetic side have attempted to embody the conflict in their work.

I think the question is once again raised, in stark terms, whether there can be a theoretical discourse that does not eventually negate poetry by pretending to contain or explain it fully in its own categories. Even if there might be such a theory, and I don't think there can be, we would still have to respond to a statement like Plato's: Is there inevitably a war between theory and poetry?

As literary scholars, we used to say, or tacitly assumed, that theory ought to be *literary* theory, that is, study of the nature of poetry and poems—from the inside out rather than from a pre-established position outside. Then we said that it should be a study of the underlying assumptions of a critical practice, chiding predecessors that they did not have enough self-consciousness or even, perhaps, awareness of the implications of what they were doing. Then we deconstructed (almost) all assumptions. Then there was the battleground of warring political or moralistic (usually in combination) factions.

Quest and Cycle (2005)

There is always a choice to be made. We have to accept the difference between poetry and philosophy, poetry and science, but not the war, unless it is Blake's "war and hunting in heaven," a progressive dialectical contrariety. Some things should be in the position of mediation, that is to say, something must occupy a position of self-irony, looking both ways. Philosophy and poetry have, most of the time, acted on opposed assumptions about language and its uses, and in our time theory, as it becomes more committed to an ideological position, works from philosophy's linguistic assumptions. This leads to acts of interpretation that are efforts of translation across a difference, subduing poetry to another form of thought and expression. The cyclical movement I have imagined may seem inevitable. It is, after all, a source of intellectual growth as well as decay, and the growth always leaves a mark. Can there be a mediating third form, that is workable enough to keep in mind its own tendency to the desire for power and containment. Its quest should be for a reading that tries to avoid capture of the poem for its own particular uses, a quest that is strong and assertive enough to resist efforts to reduce poetry to some kind of illustration or whipping boy for whatever dogma is in power or striving for power. This quest is impossible to achieve, impossible to end. The terms it must work with are those of contrary forms, but it is worth it, this talking to others in their own language.

I cannot supply a totally uncorrupted name for this mediating activity. I could simply call it criticism, but the word has been so variously applied that I will give it a rest. I'll call it ironic reading, which ought to keep in mind its own tendency toward desire for power and containment and recognize that its quest for *the* reading must not capture poetry for its own uses, but rather open up reading to the use poetry always wants to be.

Ironic reading should begin with and sustain respect for the poem as such, beginning with an empirical study of its drama and internal relations, moving outward to its cultural significance, its place in the world, and ending with recognition in the face of time and change of such reading's provisional nature and its endless quest.

Theory as it is frequently practiced today may have put in jeopardy the role of the humanities in the public eye as well as in the academy where, for a number of reasons [see Essay Fifteen], they are embattled already. It is questionable whether a public is prepared to support a supposedly humanistic discourse that is perceived as having little respect for its objects of study and as a battleground of politicized factions striving for power.

Some may say that the public is always culturally reactionary, but I think the public will always, given half a chance, respect poetry and the places where it is vigorously defended.

Today's decadence happens to occur at a time when humanists find the academy seeming to sell out to corporate interests and to narrow-minded ignorant vocationalism. If poetry is allowed to speak and be heard, it will prove antithetical to such things. But for it to be heard, we must allow it to speak, as it inevitably does, *to* our theoretical dogmas, not *through* them by selective interpretation.

Origin(ality) (2007)

[There have been many speculations on the origin of poetry and more, of course, on the sources of specific works; but origins, if they can be determined, explain very little. At some point toward the end of the eighteenth century, originality became a value term, connected with the idea that a poem was the self-expression of the poet. But many things affect the poet's expression, and for this reason the poet has sometimes been seen as a medium, though exactly what has been mediated has never been clear. These thoughts lead to questioning the value of origin and originality as ideas useful to literary thought. The following essay has hitherto been unpublished.]

There was a time, not too long ago, when it was thought that if we could discover the origin of a thing, we would come to understand it. Thus, scholars speculated on the origin of language and myth, searching back to some place, time, and sometimes people, where, when, or by whom language and myth were invented. The history of these efforts, flowering in Europe in the late seventeenth century and abundant in the eighteenth, is, though often depressing, occasionally comical or tragi-comical.[1] It tells us stories about futile ingenuity, the search for language and myth itself ending in myth-making. Early in the twentieth century, the search for origins was largely abandoned in favor of the search for structure, but that activity was short-lived compared to its predecessor, Deconstruction attacking not only the whole notion of origin but also that of structure itself, spatialized structure being decentered just as time and history had been deprived of an originating moment.

Yet we seem to need myths, which now and then are the odd and rarely acknowledged sources of our knowledge-making. They are fictive origins, not origins in the sense in which I have been using the word. At least they are not as long as we do not regard them as treatable in terms of the opposition of truth and falsehood. Myths are inevitably dangerous when taken as truth or false.

"Stories" is a better word for what I am talking about. We all have our favorite stories. One of mine is Giambattista Vico's principal one, which happens to be about an origin—the origin of language. Vico says that language began in and as poetry, poetry in his mind being a way of thought and expression that in its earliest times acted according to its own form, belonging to which he included metaphor, metonymy, synecdoche, and (historically later) irony. The movement that Vico does not incorporate into his story is the eventual emancipation of poetry from belief and the opposition of truth and falsehood. This emancipation, however, seems to be implicit in his notion of irony, but he does not develop it. So, in his story with the rise of reason and science, poetry seemed to have no place to go except to allegory in its crudest sense as prettified or coded discourse. There it was once again swallowed by the categories of belief and disbelief. One might describe the introduction of irony as the moment when poetry came to know itself. It should be no surprise that irony and the question of belief came to be two of the major subjects of discussion in the period of the New Criticism, to which with respect to these matters we can again refer without embarrassed apologies. What would be the knowledge that poetry came to have about itself? It must have been the recognition of itself as fictive and antithetical to the opposition between truth and falsehood. The most eloquent utterance on this point, well in advance of Vico, was, of course, Sir Philip Sidney's in his *Apology for Poetry* (1595):

> Now, for the poet, he nothing affirms, and therefore never lieth. For, as I take it, to lie is to affirm that to be true which is false ... the poet ... never affirmeth. The poet never maketh any circles about your imagination, to conjure you to believe for true what he writes.

Sidney had recourse to allegory to defend poetry. Poetry's self-recognition is antithetical to allegory defined as code, which is surrogate to the use of language that poetry, as irony, opposes.

That language can perhaps be described either as Platonic or as empirical. These forms presume either an idea or a realm of matter that words seek to approximate or copy. Sir Joshua Reynolds blended the two in his *Discourses on Art* (1797), and William Blake vehemently attacked him for it in his annotations to the first five of Reynolds's discourses. (For a discussion of these, see my *Blake's Margins: An Interpretive Study of the Annotations*, chapter six, 2009.) The realms of idea and matter are offered by Plato and John Locke respectively as unchanging originals.

Origin(ality) (2007)

Later in the eighteenth century a cult of originality began to flourish among poets and critics. The document most famous for expressing its tenets is, of course, Wordsworth's preface to the second edition of *Lyrical Ballads* (1800), which identified poetry as something dwelling in the poet, whose poem is an expression of that original power. The poet, according to Wordsworth is a unique being, "endowed with more lively sensibility, more enthusiasm and tenderness, who has a greater knowledge of human nature, and a more comprehensive soul than are supposed to be common among mankind." Putting aside any comment on the self-satisfaction of Wordsworth's statement, we can see that this view generated a later opposition. T. S. Eliot seems to have been answering Wordsworth on the question of originality:

> ... we pretend to find what is individual, what is the peculiar essence of the man. We dwell with satisfaction upon the poet's difference from his predecessors.... Whereas if we approach a poet without this prejudice we shall often find that not only the best, but the most individual parts of his work may be those in which the dead poets, his ancestors, assert their immortality most vigorously.[2]

Twenty-five years later, this idea was echoed, but in a different key, by Northrop Frye:

> [Whitman] was right, being the kind of poet he was, in making the content of his own "When Lilacs Last in the Dooryard Bloomed" an elegy on Lincoln and not a conventional Adonis lament. Yet his elegy is, in its *form*, as conventional as "Lycidas," complete with purple flowers thrown on coffins, a great star drooping in the west, imagery of "ever-returning spring" and all the rest of it.[3]

Eliot moved originality from the poet as unique sensibility to the poem as a unique object with an ancestry. He was never explicit about poetic structure. Frye implied that the poem was a formal container and the form was derived from conventions of poetry. Eliot's displacement of the poem from the poet came before Deconstruction of the self as origin would, in any case, have forced it. Frye seemed to be wise enough to see that deconstructions of poems would be played out on the field of content. He risked momentarily splitting form and content, even as he tried to keep them together.

Historically, what we seem to have had in the production of criticism is a cyclicity of the valorization of convention to that of originality, while the better poets went on being both at the same time. Originality can be emphasized by a critic whether the critic is interested principally in form or in content. Criticism, or as it is named today theory, now tends toward content, inevitably (as in any age) a selection of contents: for example, race, class, and gender, to repeat the dominating critical interests of the last few decades. It is no surprise that today criticism of prose fiction dominates, for in it form is more easily reduced in importance or even ignored in favor of content, which appears to be more easily extracted. (There are other reasons as well).

You may have noticed that I have employed "unique" instead of "original" in my mention of Eliot. The choice was deliberate, for I intend to offer the notion of "unique identity" as an antithetical opposition to both originality and convention, difference and sameness, and, for that matter, form and content. But before I do that, I recall the curious case of Pierre Menard, the author of *Don Quixote*. In Borges's fiction, Menard is described as the writer of certain chapters of *Don Quixote*, word for word as Cervantes wrote them, but with subtle differences of significance, mainly but not entirely because he is writing in the twentieth, not the sixteenth, century. It is the same *Don Quixote*, but different. Sameness submitted to time generates a difference in itself. Borges's story is a fable about reading. It raises in his reader a number of speculations. What, for example, would Menard's text be if he had changed, say, one phrase of Cervantes? Would this textual rather than temporal difference have the interest for us that Borges has caused Menard's textually same *Don Quixote* to have? Would not Borges's story then rouse in us a deep distrust of Menard, and perhaps charges of plagiarism? And that in spite of Frye's wonderful remark that copying within fifty years is plagiarism, but after that it is influence?

My Menard speculation will not hold. What if, say, Robert Benchley had in 1930 published "The Raven" as his own, with one phrase of the refrain "never more" changed to "never mind?" Plagiarism or parody? Isn't there something we could appropriately call original there?

But to be more serious, it is common knowledge that Shakespeare stole as much as he could find of use from Geoffrey of Monmouth and various plays not out of copyright (had there been copyright in those days). Yet his work is regarded as presenting so distinct a voice as to make it extremely difficult to conjecture anything about him from his texts.

Can anything really be described as original? Probably not. Maybe "unique identity" might be used, as I shall try to show by recourse to the only Chinese writing known to me (through Stephen Owen's translation and commentary). It is that of Yeh Hsieh (1686).

Origin(ality) (2007)

> Rules are an empty name and thus not to be considered as if existing actually. On the other hand, rules are determinate positions and thus not to be considered as nonexistent.[4]

Rules, he argued, should not be allowed to regulate what a poem can be, yet one can see the rules implicit in the poem once one has read it.

Yeh's two charming figures connected with this are the growth of a tree, unpredictable in its details, but in every part a tree, nevertheless.[5] The tree metaphor and the question of the tree's identity is familiar to Western readers from W. B. Yeats's "Among School Children":

> O chestnut-tree, great-rooted blossomer,
> Are you the leaf, the blossom, or the bole?

where the figure is temporalized.

The second figure is that of clouds and is worth quoting at length in Owen's translation:

> But let us suppose that the pattern of Heaven and Earth were to be regulated by rules. Then when Mount T'ai was going to send out its clouds, it would first muster the tribes of clouds and give them their orders: "I am now going to send you clouds out to make "the pattern of Heaven and Earth." You, go first; you follow; you, go up; and you, you there, lie low. You, cloud, shine; you, make ripples like waves; you, double back in; you spread out in the sky; you, open up wide; and you, lock your gates fast. And you over there, you shake your tail." If Mount T'ai sent them out like this and brought them back like this, then there wouldn't be the least vitality in any of them. And this would be the formation of the pattern of Heaven and Earth!? The result of such a situation would be that Heaven and Earth would feel that the presence of Mount T'ai was a burden; and Mount T'ai in turn would feel that having clouds was a burden. And those clouds would still have to be sent out every single day![6]

Beneath this is Yeh's fundamental analogy between poem and nature, and here Yeh preceded the popular Western notion of organicism and Wallace Stevens's remark in his *Adagia*: "The poem is a nature created by the poet."[7]

As far as we know, nature is unique and has its own inviolable rules. It is fair to say that it would be impossible to imagine them prior to nature's existence except in the form of some myth. By the same token, a poem has a unique identity, even Menard's *Don Quixote*, which is identical to Cervantes.' Someone once complained to Picasso that Gertrude Stein did not resemble his portrait of her. "She will," he replied. Many works have been thought on first appearance not to be poems at all, only to be accepted in time as an unpredictable branch of poetry after all.

Criticism should always strive to perform antithetically to the discernable cyclicity of formal and material concerns, and to the opposed emphases on originality and convention. Every work is necessarily unique. Uniqueness is not a term of evaluation, as originality was made to be at one time. Unique identity absorbs (in opposing) both originality and convention. We think easily of one's identity as unique, but unique things can be identical, as in the case of twins, same yet different All of Vico's tropes harbor sameness and difference at the same time, antithetical to their being only same or different.

Postscript on the originality of what I have written here:

I confess that I have plagiarized from myself in that in a previous essay I have used the Picasso-Stein example, borrowed from somewhere that I forget. I have also previously quoted and/or referred to Frye on Whitman and Frye on plagiarism. I have certainly quoted those very words of Sidney, Wordsworth, Yeats, and Stevens before. This is all plagiarism twice removed, I suppose, and morally classifiable with or below Plato's imitators and certainly without the saving grace of divine madness. Also I have elsewhere (more fully and better) set forth my concept of antitheticality, shamefully mixed and concocted, a little distorted perhaps, from remarks made by Blake and Yeats. I have before said the same thing that I have said here about Vico in addition to making use of him whenever it suited me. Little that's original here! But my essay inevitably has its unique identity. If some Pierre Menard should some three hundred years from now write it verbatim (that this is a crazy fiction I need not assure you) it will be same and different.

The Marriage of Imagination and Intellect (2013)

[This essay, intended to be a true conclusion, draws in part from a previously published one and from four paragraphs from an earlier book. The essay, here revised and amended, was "William Blake: Imagination, Vision, Inspiration, Intellect," *Inventions of the Imagination: Romanticism and Beyond*, eds. Richard D. Gray et al., Seattle: University of Washington Press, 2011, pp. 68–76. The four paragraphs are those having to do with Wordsworth and appeared in my *Blake's Margins: An Interpretive Study of the Annotations*, McFarland, 2009.

The essay's aim is to consider what has taken place in the past few decades following the rise of Deconstruction and the problems that have since arisen. I have gone beyond intellectual questions into matters external to literary study that have and will have an effect on the teaching of literature in the university. There follows a discussion of Blake's use of two words, "imagination" and "intellect" in an attempt to show how a superficial popular separation of them, not uncommon in thinking about education, could threaten literary study.]

I

In 2001, I published a fairly long essay in which I concerned myself with changes that were occurring in the profession of English studies.[1] I discussed external and internal matters causing change in the profession. The most important ones were as follows: English, or rather, literature written in English, had participated in what is popularly called globalization. It was now written in places far from England and expressed broader cultural concerns. The teaching of the literature of Britain had become more challenging under these conditions. Of course, English and American literature had always been influenced by the literature of other languages.

The most important basis for understanding literary tradition has always been the classical literature and the Bible. Unfortunately most students have known little about either, and, indeed, they know less and less about literature written prior to the twentieth century. Globalization and the feminist movement have had their effect on what has been called the "canon," that is, the list of presumed great works. Can a canon exist if there are fewer and fewer readers of what it allegedly has contained? Can it exist if competing interests insist on many new works being introduced as properly belonging to it?[2]

II

These have been issues with reasonably simple pedagogical answers internal to the discipline. They have been or could have been managed by curricular reform. Of course, everything is difficult, but the ones that are particularly vexing and maybe by now impossible to deal with intelligently are produced by external forces. They are the changing relation of business to higher education, the tendency of universities to utilitarianism in the face of social forces, mainly economic, and, either driving or responding to all of this, the burgeoning digital technology as it invades teaching. My 2001 essay did not foresee the rapidity with which this technology, along with the phenomenon of for-profit institutions, took hold, and we have seen comparatively nothing yet. The phenomenon known by the acronym MOOCS (Massive Open Online Courses) has, as I write, become a symbol of this development, the principal example having been a philosophy course taught at Harvard with the potential to reach thousands of students on line. Debates over courses like this have generated many purely educational questions and raise the perhaps more important and far-reaching ones about the fate of the profession itself. Will there be jobs for young faculty? Will faculty research and scholarship be limited to a few "elite" universities? If so, will this affect the quality of teaching over time? Who will be in charge? These issues outweigh the internal ones, and they affect the internal ones, every teacher, and every student. It would be foolish, as I write, to predict whether good or ill or, more likely, a mixture will result or even that we will soon understand what has happened.

It seems to me that the humanistic disciplines have the most to fear from these developments. Who are the people leading these developments?

Do they take seriously the teaching role of the humanistic scholars? I am afraid that in recent decades within universities forces having little to do with the new technology have been at work. Many universities have for years been shifting faculty positions from the humanities as those positions have become available through retirement, death, or failure to reach tenure. (Will the concept of tenure survive much longer?) Some universities have reached monstrous size, outgrowing, as many think, their present structures. English departments now have more students to teach and fewer professors to teach them. To fill the gap, many departments have had to hire large numbers of so-called teaching assistants from the ranks of graduate students plus lecturers without security of employment—all cheap labor without representation or appropriate benefits. (It has been a long time since most teaching assistants actually *assisted* professors.) Partly as a result, departments, needing teachers, have admitted a relatively large number of graduate students during a period when the number of jobs they aspire to has for years been in sharp decline. The number of graduate students has also been held up by the desire of faculty to teach graduate seminars.

In the university from which I am now retired, virtually all of the so-called freshman and sophomore courses in English are now taught by teaching assistants or lecturers. In some cases, graduate students have deliberately prolonged their movement toward the degree in order to hold on to their supposedly temporary jobs, the scarcity of positions being no better or perhaps worse than in the recent past. Low-level administrators seem to accept this state of affairs, some having known nothing else in their careers. Upper-level administrators apparently have no quarrel with this.

It is no secret that English departments have been complicit in their fate. Some of them have been scenes of internal strife of an unparalleled nature. Some of this, one might say, has been inevitable in a period of significant change. It has always been true that battles over who teaches and who is taught have occurred, leaving sometimes a disgruntled group, of what is called deadwood on one side and sometimes victorious ideologues on the other. The latter group generally provides the deadwood for the succeeding cycle, including people left behind for other reasons. Some people, of course, ride out change, either for or against it, pursuing an independent course.

It may be no surprise that recently there has been no clearly defined intellectual movement or even new "ism," given the lack of jobs, the contraction of budgets, and the decline of overhead money from government. Perhaps the many politically and intellectually motivated movements affecting literary study and cultural thought in the twentieth century and their waning, along with the attendant infighting, have rendered young scholars of the twenty-first more cautious or attracted to less fixed, more eclectic positions.

It has been cyclical in the past for there to be cries declaring a crude practicality the proper aim of higher education. This has tended to be followed by lament from business interest over the "illiteracy" of newly graduated college students. I have lived long enough to experience three turns of this wheel: the depression thirties, the fifties, when veterans of World War II graduated, and the present recession. The first two of these ended mercifully with the recognition by most involved, including business, that graduates needed better verbal skills. This time, I think the utilitarian drive, stronger than ever in an increasingly technological society, in which universities have embraced business, may have a much longer life and may even come to seem permanent. It is fueled not only by economic recession but also by the curious situation in which more books are published (both print and electronic), but attention span among students seems to have shortened. Teachers, I am told, have far greater trouble getting students to read anything even of moderate length (including assigned reading) or to write what used to be regarded as a paper of standard length.

The MOOCS phenomenon, previously mentioned, reflects a temptation to discover through technology a way to economize. Intellectual arguments both for and against MOOCS have recently become spirited. Small liberal arts college faculties seem generally skeptical, holding out for the value of small classes. But in the larger institutions small classes are almost things of the past. There are important educational and intellectual questions here that will take time to work out. However, the question of available resources or lack of the same is likely to prove decisive, leaving almost everything changed.

With respect to all of the external forces I have mentioned, the humanities, and perhaps primarily literary study, have already experienced and will further experience the greatest dangers. The drive for practicality, which has in the past been devoted to short-term ends, tends to create a bifurcation between the humanistic disciplines and those regarded by business and the public as of principal educational value. With the increasing influence of business on universities along with other economic forces, it is not difficult to recognize that the so-called practical subjects tend to be regarded as truly intellectual and the others as having to do only with the imagination, often popularly confused with the unreal.

III

William Blake took pains to reject this sort of proposition. He would have regarded it as what he called a negation. I close this book with a discussion of Blake's views on this matter and the four words he would have regarded as particularly relevant: imagination, vision, inspiration, and intellect, particularly the first and fourth.

I begin with a remark by W. B. Yeats. In 1897, Yeats published two essays on Blake. One was titled "William Blake and the Imagination" and the other "William Blake and his Illustrations to *The Divine Comedy*."[3] In juxtaposition, though Yeats did not emphasize the point, the two titles indicate something important about Blake's notion of imagination that separates him from the so-called English Romantics who used the word: rigorous insistence on the relation of imagination to sight, to visual art, to inspiration, and to intellect.

I mention now three things connected with this: First, Blake belonged in many of his tastes and attitudes to an intellectual and artistic generation prior to that of the English romantic poets. Some have called that generation, at the end of which came Blake, the "Pre-Romantics," but as Northrop Frye wryly remarked a half-century ago, he knew no groups of poets who thought of themselves as merely precursors of a later, more important movement.[4] Born 1n 1757, Blake was thirteen years Wordsworth's senior, fifteen years older than Coleridge, thirty-one older than Byron, thirty-five than Shelley, thirty-eight than Keats. Among the poets whose work he illustrated and knew well were Young (born 1683), Blair (born 1699), and Gray (born 1716). He spoke well of Macpherson, Cowper, and Smart. These were all poets of styles appealing to a taste different from that of the Romantics. In Blake's extant writings, only Wordsworth and Byron, among the Romantics, are mentioned. Blake's annotations to Wordsworth's *Poems* and *The Excursion* could not have been written before 1814, and his dedication of *The Ghost of Abel* to "Lord Byron in the wilderness" is of about 1820, when Blake was 63.

Second, Blake was a professional engraver and visual artist, and most of his mentions of imagination have to do with visual art, especially painting and engraving. Blake's was a painter's and engraver's imagination, and for him imagination was connected literally to sight. But "sight" was not an adequate word for what he had in mind. His word was "vision," which for him was an act of mind, intellectual, not merely the passive reception of sense data. He said that we see "through the eye," with the mind.

Third, in his long poems, Blake was a maker of chains of metaphor that, if followed out, imply the identification of all things with each other, while individuality remains. This characteristic of his poetry has a parallel in his critical writings, where imagination implies vision, vision implies inspiration, inspiration implies intellect, and intellect implies imagination. These are all words that Blake frequently employed.

The tendency today is more commonly to identify the intellectual with the theoretical and even with the applied sciences and imagination with the arts. This tends toward what Blake called "negation," the very thing that seems to propel universities today. He would have none of that. He writes of the "labours of Art & Science" (E232). He urges the religious to "discountenance every one among you who shall pretend to despise Art & Science" (E231–232), and he asks the rhetorical question "What is the Life of Man but Art & Science?" (E232). For Blake, the Holy Ghost, which dwells in man, is an "intellectual fountain" (E231). In the great apocalypse of *Jerusalem*, intellectuals are identified with and as artists:

> ... at the clangor of the Arrows of Intellect
> The innumerable Chariots of the Almighty appeard in Heaven
> And Bacon & Newton & Locke, & Milton & Shakspear & Chaucer
> [E257].

Blake was severely critical of Bacon, Newton, and Locke, whom he identified with a false philosophy of subject and object, but in his apocalypse these negations become contraries "equally true" and part of the conversation in eternity. "Go! put off Holiness/And put on Intellect," Los, Blake's heroic blacksmith, shouts (E252). So intellect does not negate imagination but joins with it in the productive contrariety of Art and Science.

To say that Blake's notion of imagination was grounded in sight requires that we understand just what he meant by vision. It is well to remind ourselves that his generation and the poets he read had more spatially oriented imaginations than did the Romantics. The notions of imitation and *ut pictura poeisis* still had life in literary criticism. The first thing to observe is just how literally connected with seeing Blake's notion of vision was. And how important for him "image" was in the word "imagination."

In a letter of August 23, 1799, Blake wrote to the reverend Dr. Trusler,

> This World is a World of Imagination & Vision I see Every thing I paint in This World, but Every body does not see alike.... Some See Nature all Ridicule & Deformity & by these I shall not regulate my proportions, & Some Scarce see Nature at all But to the Eyes of the Man of Imagination Nature is Imagination itself. As a man is So he Sees.... To Me This world is One continued Vision of Fancy or Imagination [E702].

Over the next decade or more, Blake seems to have refined slightly the language of his statement; nevertheless, it presents, when clearly understood, a view that Blake held all of his life.

The fundamental way to consider Blake's statement is epistemologically. In his poem *Milton*, Blake has Milton say that he has come "to cast off Bacon, Locke & Newton from Albions covering/To take off his filthy garments, & clothe him with Imagination" (E142). This is to reject the epistemology of subject and object and introduce a way of seeing that frees the mind from the abstract fiction of an object lacking the so-called secondary qualities of perception. It isolates these qualities from the real. Blake identifies nature with this dull objectivity. Nature is the deluding product of a faith solely in what Blake calls "general knowledge," and it is rare when Blake uses "nature" in any other way. In his late years, Blake annotated Wordsworth's *Poems* and remarked, "natural objects always did & now do weaken deaden & obliterate Imagination in Me" (E665], and he saw in Wordsworth "the Natural Man rising up against the Spiritual Man Continually" (E665). "Spiritual" meant for Blake the appropriate way of seeing, literally vision. It had little, if anything to do with mysticism as we usually think of it. Nature was for him the external world, unreal when regarded as apart from man; it was constructed by the dominant philosophy of the time and projected as an other. This is the nature that is the "Ridicule & Deformity" of Blake's letter.

It is also the product of a mistaken view of what it is to see. For Blake, the material eye as a source of vision is a delusion. We do not see passively with it. Our minds see *through* it in two senses: see through it if one is still to speak *as if* there were a material body separate from mind; see through it if one can recognize it as a delusion of matter. The truth is that when the so-called outer world is seen, it is the projection of an active intellect.

Imagination is intellectual. That act is an act of imaging. In the same letter to Trusler, Blake refers to what he calls "Spiritual Sensation" (E703), a phrase I think he would not have used later because of sensation's connections to the notion of the passive reception of sense data. Spirit is intellectual.

But all people do not imagine the world in the same way. Some people have weak imaginations. The "greatest of all blessings," Blake remarks, is a "strong imagination, a clear idea, and a determinate vision" (E693). Some minds see more intensely and therefore more clearly than others, but even equally strong imaginations will see things differently. In a description of his "Last Judgment," Blake writes, "its vision is seen by the [Imaginative Eye] of Every one according to the situation he holds." (E554; Blake later deleted "Imaginative Eye," because for him it is the mind that sees.) Great artists see alike, that is, intellectually and actively rather than copying or recording a passive response of sense; yet their visions will be individual, different, though metaphorically related. Art does not improve; situations vary and change; genius can be equaled but not surpassed.

Seeing, or vision, as I shall call it from now on, is grounded for Blake on clarity, which is achieved by intense concentration. There should be nothing mysterious about it. Blake rarely uses "mystery" in an honorific sense. He usually thought of mystery as something imposed by a priesthood or an elite in order to maintain power, and religion should be devoid of it. For him, the most important thing in art is outline and "attention to minute particulars."

> A Spirit and a Vision are not, as the modern philosophy supposes, a cloudy vapour or a nothing; they are organized and minutely articulated beyond all that the mortal and perishing nature can produce. He who does not imagine in stronger and better lineaments, and in stronger and better light than his perishing mortal eye can see does not imagine at all [E541].

The passage implies remarkable intensity of vision that seems to have been characteristic of Blake's activity when he drew what are called his "visionary heads." Allan Cunningham, one of Blake's earliest biographers, tells a story, perhaps somewhat embellished, about Blake that informs us about his practice:

> He was requested to draw the likeness of William Wallace—the eye of Blake sparkled, for he admired heroes. "William Wallace!" he exclaimed, "I see him now, there, how noble he looks. Hand me my things!" Having drawn for some time, with the same care of hand and steadiness of eyes, as if a living

sitter had been before him, Blake suddenly stopped and said, "I cannot finish him—Edward the First has stepped between him and me."[5]

This passage suggests a discipline of creative vision that required projection of an image (as on a blank wall) and then the drawing of it. When Blake said he copied imagination he meant something like this. If another visual idea gets in the way, the vision is suspended or changed. (Blake was having some fun here, in that Wallace was the frustrating Scottish foe of Edward I.)

All of Blake's likes and dislikes in painting, and they are vigorously expressed, arise from his emphasis on intensity and clarity of vision. (We can notice that a professional engraver might very well emphasize the importance of outline.) "Nature has no Outline: but Imagination has" (E270); and if there is no "determinate and bounding form" (E550) there is no "idea in the artist's mind" (E550). Copying nature ends up with only what the material eye can see. Rubens as an influence is "a most outrageous demon" (E547) who leads followers to "blotting and blurring" (E546). Chiaroscuro is an "infernal machine" (E547). The mortal eye, with which these styles work, is caught up in the flux of time and cannot seize intellectually on anything and fix it clearly in vision. Over and over, Blake's long poems emphasize proper vision. In *Jerusalem*, for example, Blake views time as a huge visual pattern, and elsewhere he chastises historians for reasoning on events. They should present acts for all to visualize, not theories about acts (E544). Acts alone are real, and anything that "is not an action is not worth reading" (E544).

Blake presents his own version of what Sir Philip Sidney treated as a poetic improvement on nature. One difference is that Sidney thinks of beautification, while Blake thinks of clarification. The latter is a different sort of improvement in that it is composed of inventions of "intellectual vision" (E757) that go beyond what the mortal eye can see. Thus Blake complains that what he also calls the corporeal eye, separated from imagination, sees not only passively but also dully:

> What it will be Questioned When the Sun rises do you not see a round disk of fire somewhat like a Guinea O no no I see an Innumerable company of the Heavenly host crying Holy Holy Holy is the Lord God Almighty I question not my Corporeal or Vegetative Eye any more than I would Question a Window concerning a Sight [E565–566].

In a description of an illustration he made to Milton's "L'Allegro," Blake speaks of "The youthful Poet sleeping on a bank by the Haunted Stream by Sun Set [who] sees in his Dream the more bright Sun of Imagination" (E684). But one does not have to dream to imagine; one can do it consciously looking through the eyes. Indeed, the imagination is not a state of mind that one turns on and off; Blake remarks, "it is the Human Existence itself" (E132); and he holds in his annotations to Berkeley's *Siris,* "Jesus considerd Imagination to be the Real Man" (E663). The sun of the passage I have offered is not an allegorical image standing for an abstract idea. It is a visionary idea, not a substitute for a Platonic one. It is what it is and refers only to itself. As such, it communicates vision to the reader who makes identification with it, something impossible with an object. About his "Last Judgment," Blake remarks,

> If the Spectator could Enter into these Images in his Imagination approaching them on the Fiery Chariot of his Contemplative Thought if he could Enter into Noahs Rainbow or into his bosom or could make a Friend & Companion of one of these Images of wonder which always entreats him to leave mortal things as he must know then would he arise from his Grave then would he meet the Lord in the Air & and then he would be happy [.] General Knowledge is Remote Knowledge it is in Particulars that Wisdom consists & Happiness too [E560].

Blake makes an important distinction between what he calls the daughters of imagination and the daughters of memory. They are the true and false muses respectively. Inspired by the daughters of memory, a painter is "confined to the sordid drudgery of facsimile representations of merely mortal and perishing substances" (E541). "Walking in another man's style, or speaking or looking in another man's style and manner" (E547) is the same. An art based on memory cannot create, only copy and mirror the false knowledge of the passive subject, but in the apocalypse a redeemed memory is married to imagination.

More than an improvement on nature, indeed a denial of it, vision at its greatest intensity sees potentially into the infinite in a thing. But Blake's infinite is not a Platonic realm without image; it is the "regions of my Imagination" (E705). Every moment is a window into it. The fundamental principle of imagination is the synecdoche:

> To see a World in a Grain of Sand
> And a Heaven in a Wild Flower
> Hold Infinity in the palm of your hand
> And Eternity in an hour [E493]

These are by no means casual lines. Infinity is the largest and the infinitesimal is the smallest of things, and they are identical. Synecdoche supports

The Marriage of Imagination and Intellect (2013)

Blake's notion of the individuality and yet communality (by that trope) of what imagination creates. "This world of Imagination [of minute particulars] is the World of Eternity" (E555). In the religion of imagination or the proper imagining of religion, the Savior *is* the human imagination; and the human imagination is the Savior. It is what saves us from a living death in the world of vegetable nature. Jesus is the spirit of imagination in man, no more, no less. There is "no other Gospel than the liberty both of body & mind to exercise the Divine Arts of Imagination" (E231).

Every artistic imagination produces according to its own individuality what "Eternally Exists" (E554). A string of metaphorical identities relates all things. In *Jerusalem* there is described a receptacle of all that can be imagined and can occur:

> All things acted on Earth are seen in the bright Sculptures of
> Los's Halls & every Age renews its powers from these Works
> With every pathetic story possible to happen from Hate or
> Wayward Love & every sorrow & distress is carved here
> Every Affinity of Parents Marriages & Friendships are here
> In all their various combinations wrought with wondrous Art
> All that can happen to Man in his pilgrimage of seventy years [E161].

This is the collective imagination of all art, a synecdoche to which belongs every visionary act in all of time. The apocalyptic act in *Jerusalem* is a vision: "All Human Forms identified even Tree Metal Earth & Stone" (E258).

Blake held Chaucer in high regard, and he describes Chaucer's pilgrims as "Visions of ... eternal principles or characters of human life" that "appear to poets in all ages" (E536). Blake remarks that Gray's vision of eternal characters can be seen "in the person of his bard on Snowden" (E543). Every great artist enters in vision into a place that is seen according to his or her situation. To enter it does not require servile allegiance to prior models, but to one's own individuality. (This is not to say that an artist need not learn the techniques of his craft.) Beyond these images, metaphorically unique but also identical (just as two sides of a metaphor include both sameness and difference), art does not, need not, and cannot go.

But there is always danger if these humanly made images are erected into gods, or even one God, and given divine names. As such they become destructive to humanity, for properly "All deities reside in the human breast" (E38). Objectified, they are no better and probably worse than kings. Thus, for Blake Jesus is and must remain an imaginative creation, supremely human. It is a misfortune that, as Blake says,

> The Nature of Visionary Fancy or Imagination is very little Known & the Eternal nature & permanence of its ever Existent Images is considerd as less permanent than the things of Vegetative & Generative Nature [E555].

The imaginative expression of vision is for Blake a continuum that cannot be divided into invention that is then executed in some external form. The execution *is* the invention, a process of creation and discovery. At the beginning of *Milton*, Blake connects the brain to the hand in poetic and artistic creation when he asks his muses to

> ... Come into my hand
> By your mild power; descending down the Nerves of my right arm
> From out the Portals of my Brain [E96].

The idea comes into being in the execution, just as a reality comes into being in imagination. The two, which are one, cannot be divided by an "idiot Reasoner" who "laughs at the Man of Imagination" (E131) and might say, if he were trying to be an artist, "I have wonderful ideas, but somehow I can't express them." This is a true dissociation, both of sensibility and imagination.

Yeats made some mistakes about Blake in his essays. He called Blake a mystic, neglecting to declare just what he meant by that word, the vagueness of which in common usage goes against all that Blake required of art. Yeats said that Blake was unfortunate in being an artist who had to invent his own symbols. But for Blake, all artists had to do that. If they had borrowed or stolen, they had to make the symbols their own in the contexts they had created. For a chapter title in his *Fearful Symmetry: A Study of William Blake*, Northrop Frye shortened Yeats's phrase "too literal realist of the imagination," leaving out the "too."[6] He was right to do so. Frye was writing a book of literary criticism, and he was right to have argued elsewhere that "literal" ought to have something to do with the literary rather than with its opposite.[7] If that is the case, a poet cannot be too literal, and the real is what the imagination literally envisions, imaginatively and intellectually.

Chapter Notes

Introduction

1. Ithaca: Cornell University Press, 1995. Second edition: New York: Russell & Russell, 1968.
2. Tallahassee: Florida State University Press, 1983; Seattle: University of Washington Press, 2007.
3. "Blake and the Postmodern," *William Blake: Essays for S. Foster Damon*. Providence: Brown University Press, ed. Alvin H. Rosenfeld, 1969, pp. 3–17.
4. "Structure, Sign and Play in the Discourse of the Human Sciences," *The Languages of Criticism and the Sciences of Man: The Structuralist Controversy* eds. Richard Macksey and Eugenio Donato, Baltimore: The Johns Hopkins Press, 1970, pp. 247–265, followed by discussion.
5. In *Criticism* VIII, 4 (Fall 1966) pp. 1214–1249, reprinted in *Critical Theory Since Plato*, New York: Harcourt Brace Jovanovich, 1971, pp. 1223–1230.
6. "Blurred Genres," *The American Scholar* 49:2 (Spring 1980), pp. 165–179, reprinted in *Critical Theory Since 1965*, eds. Hazard Adams and Leroy Searle, Tallahassee: Florida State University Press, 1986, pp. 514–523.
7. *An Essay on Man*, New Haven: Yale University Press, 1944; *Substance and Function and Einstein's Theory of Relativity*, tr. William Curtis Swabey and Marie Collins Swabey, Chicago-London: The Open Court Publishing Co., 1923.
8. *An Essay on Man*, p. 25.
9. *The New Science of Giambattista Vico*, revised translation of the third edition (1744), trs. Thomas Goddard Bergin and Max Harold Fisch, Ithaca: Cornell University Press, 1968. On the example of Pomona see p.128. For my discussion of Vico, see *Philosophy of the Literary Symbolic*, pp. 7–12.
10. On Blake and science, see Harry White, "Blake's Resolution to the War Between Science and Philosophy," *Blake: An Illustrated Quarterly* 39, 3 (Winter 2005–06) pp. 108–125. Also of interest is White's "Blake and the Mills of Induction," *Blake Newsletter* 10, 4 (Spring 1977), p. 110.

Blake, *Jerusalem,* and Symbolic Form (1975)

1. The one purely Jungian study, W. P. Witcutt's *Blake: A Psychological Study* (London: Hollis & Carter, 1946), is quite unreliable. Other critics have here and there used Jungian insights. The archetypal, non–Jungian approach was originated by Northrop Frye in *Fearful Symmetry* (Princeton: Princeton Univ. Press, 1947).
2. "William Blake and His Illustrations to the *Divine Comedy*" (1897), *Essays and Introductions* (London: Macmillan, 1961), p. 119.
3. Symons' *The Symbolist Movement in Literature* (London: W. Heinemann, Ltd., 1899), dedicated to Yeats, studies Nerval, de L'Isle Adam, Rimbaud, Verlaine, Laforgue, Mallarmé, Huysmans, and Maeterlinck.

Chapter Notes

4. Ernst Cassirer, *Die Philosophie der symbolischen Formen,* Berlin, 1923–1929; *An Essay on Man* (New Haven: Yale Univ. Press, 1944).

5. See especially Frye's remarks about Blake's influence on him in *The Critical Path* (Bloomington: Indiana Univ. Press, 1971), pp. 13–14.

6. See Giambattista Vico, *The New Science* [1744], rev. trans. Thomas Goddard Bergen and Max Harold Fisch (Ithaca: Cornell Univ. Press, 1968), pp. 116–20.

7. *Romantic Image* (New York: Macmillan, 1957), pp. 138–61.

8. Among useful general commentaries are Harold Bloom, *Blake's Apocalypse* (Garden City, N.Y.: Doubleday, 1983), pp. 365–433, and Northrop Frye, *Fearful Symmetry,* pp. 356–403. There have been several recent essays of considerable ingenuity, two of them in S. Curran and J. A. Wittreich, Jr. (eds.), *Blake's Sublime Allegory* (Madison: Univ. of Wisconsin Press, 1973). The first, Roger Easson's "William Blake and His Reader in *Jerusalem,*" pp. 309–327, argues that *Jerusalem* is a "poem about itself." The character-city Jerusalem in the poem is an allegorical representation of the poem. Easson sees four elements in the poem which represent different aspects of its narrator—"authorial intrusion, dramatic narration, visionary narration, and visionary definition." This view touches on matters that lead to my conception of the poem as an act. However, the most valuable aspect of Easson's essay is his treatment of the relation of the poem to its reader. The second essay, by Stuart Curran, "The Structures of *Jerusalem,*" studies the ways *Jerusalem* can be examined and finds seven structures of various sorts. Curran also briefly reviews other recent essays on the subject of *Jerusalem's* structure. These two essays each offer numerous insights, but they do run dangers. Easson may press his allegory beyond what the text actually insists on. Curran finds so many structures that either one's skepticism is aroused as to their real presences or one begins to imagine that anyone might play at the structure-finding game. A third essay in this book, Karl Kroeber's "Delivering *Jerusalem*" is marred by a combative rhetoric and the erection of straw men. Kroeber points out some obvious differences between *Jerusalem* and *Finnegans* Wake but goes to the opposite extreme from those he claims *see* only similarities. It would be useful to have an essay like Easson's about *Finnegans Wake* and its reader, in which similarities to and differences from Blake are systematically set forth. The essays in this book appeared after my own was written.

Contemporary Ideas of Literature: Terrible Beauty or Rough Beast? (1977)

1. *In Search of Literary Theory* contains essays by M. H. Abrams, E. D. Hirsch, Jr., Northrop Frye, Geoffrey Hartman, Paul de Man, and the editor, Morton W. Bloomfield. For bibliographical details on the anthologies cited in this essay, see Murray Krieger's introduction. Further references will cite the editor's name and the anthology page numbers only.

2. *The New Apologists for Poetry* (Minneapolis: Univ. of Minnesota Press, 1956).

3. *Structuralist Poetics: Structuralism, Linguistics and the Study of Literature* (Ithaca: Cornell Univ. Press, 1975).

4. It appears in Gras, pp. 157–63; Polletta, pp. 123–28. The latter also includes Barthes's essay on *Phèdre,* and the former another section of his work on Racine.

5. Roman Jakobson, "Two Aspects of Language: Metaphor and Metonymy," in Gras, pp. 119–29; Georges Poulet, "Phenomenology of Reading," in Polletta, pp. 103–18; Martin Heidegger, "Holderlin and the Essence of Poetry," in Gras, pp. 27–41; Jacques Derrida, "Structure, Sign, and Play in the Discourse of the Human Sciences," in Macksey and Donato, pp. 247–72; Jacques Lacan, "Of Structure as an Inmixing of an Otherness Prerequisite to Any Subject Whatever," in Macksey and Donato, pp. 186–200.

6. See, for example, Alan Bass, "'Literature'/Literature," in Macksey, pp. 341–53; and Jacques Derrida's remark, quoted by Bass, that "literature annihilates itself through its own

Chapter Notes

illimitability" *(La Dissemination,* [Paris: Seuil, 1972], p. 253). On this point also note Tzvetan Todorov, "The Notion of Literature," *NLH,* 5, No. 1 (Autumn 1973), 5–16.

7. In Macksey, pp. 66–71.
8. *Ibid.,* p. 70.
9. See my *Critical Theory Since Plato* (New York: Harcourt Brace Jovanovich, 1971), pp. 892–904 for Blackmur, and pp. 928–41 for Tate's "Literature as Knowledge."
10. The New Critics would, however, never have employed a word like "reconstitutes," for it would have seemed to them to indicate the dominance or superiority of the critical act over the work.
11. See *"Abecedarium Culturae:* Structuralism, Absence, Writing," in Simon, pp. 372–73.
12. *Ibid.,* p. 369.
13. Gerald R. Bruns, *Modern Poetry and the Idea of Language* (New Haven: Yale Univ. Press, 1974).
14. "What's the Use of Theorizing about the Arts," in Bloomfield, pp. 1–54.
15. *The New Science of Giambattista Vico,* rev. trans. of the 3rd ed. of 1744, trans. T. G. Bergin and M. Fisch (Ithaca: Cornell Univ. Press, 1968), p. 100.
16. Ernst Cassirer, *An Essay on Man* (New Haven: Yale Univ. Press, 1944), p. 76.
17. Wilhelm von Humboldt, *Humanist Without Portfolio: An Anthology of the Writings of Wilhelm von Humboldt,* trans. Marianne Cowan (Detroit: Wayne State Univ. Press, 1963), p. 246.
18. *Ibid.,* p. 293.
19. See the previous essay in this book.
20. Von Humboldt, p. 249.
21. *Ibid.,* p. 218.
22. Ernst Cassirer, *Language and Myth,* trans. Susanne K. Langer (New York: Harper and Brothers, 1946), p. 98.
23. *The Burning Fountain: A Study in the Language of Symbolism,* rev. ed. (Bloomington: Indiana Univ. Press, 1968). See esp. chapter 5, "Traits of Expressive Language."
24. *Anatomy of Criticism* (Princeton: Princeton Univ. Press, 1957), pp. 350–52.
25. "How Ordinary is Ordinary Language?" *NLH,* 5, No. 1 (Autumn 1973), 41–54.
26. Michel Foucault, *The Order of Things (Les mots et les choses)* (New York: Random House, 1973), esp. pp. 17–44.
27. *Guide to Aesthetics,* trans. Patrick Romonell (Indianapolis: Bobbs Merrill Co., 1965), p. 23.
28. Cassirer, *An Essay on Man,* p. 228.
29. In my "Yeats, Dialectic and Criticism," *Criticism,* 10, No. 3 (Summer 1968), 185–99.
30. *A Window to Criticism: Shakespeare's Sonnets and Modern Poetics* (Princeton: Princeton Univ. Press, 1964), pp. 57–58.
31. As I am trying to do in a work in progress. It came out as *Philosophy of the Literary Symbolic* (1983).
32. In Bloomfield, p. 250.
33. Paul de Man, "The Rhetoric of Temporality," in *Interpretation: Theory and Practice,* ed. Charles S. Singleton (Baltimore: Johns Hopkins Press, 1969).
34. Paul de Man, *Blindness and Insight* (New York: Oxford Univ. Press, 1971), p. 9.
35. *Ibid.,* p. 11.
36. *Ibid.,* p. 17.
37. *The Fate of Reading* (Chicago: Univ. of Chicago Press, 1974), p. 97 and pp. 308–12.
38. De Man, "The Rhetoric of Temporality," p. 174.
39. Interestingly enough, de Man's position on this point has something in common with the critique of the American New Critics made by the Chicago neo–Aristotelians some years ago. They complained that the New Critics made one characteristic of a poem (possession of

the trope irony) into a sign of the poetic quality of the poem—an essence. What really happens in Cleanth Brooks's "Irony as a Principle of Structure" is a wrenching of the term "irony" out of the classical rhetorical vocabulary to be used as a term describing the nature of the poem as a whole. In other words, Brooks does with "irony" what the romantics began to do with "symbolism," but both terms tend to slip back to their tropological meanings when critical discourses lose rigor.

40. *Speculations,* ed. Herbert Read (1924; rpt. New York: Harcourt, Brace and Co., 1936), p. 120.

41. This concept of linguistic theft is nicely expressed in Burke's *Attitudes Toward History,* The New Republic Series, 2 (New York: New Republic, 1937), 229.

42. De Man, "The Rhetoric of Temporality," pp. 175–76.

43. *The Romantic Ventriloquists* (Seattle: Univ. of Washington Press, 1963), p. 5.

44. De Man, "The Rhetoric of Temporality," p. 190.

45. *An Introduction to Metaphysics,* trans. Ralph Manheim (New Haven: Yale Univ. Press, 1959), p. 105.

46. *Ibid.,* p. 172.

47. *Art and Reality: Ways of the Creative Process* (New York: Harper and Brothers, 1958), p. 16.

48. T. S. Eliot, "The Metaphysical Poets," *Selected Essays 1917–1932* (New York: Harcourt, Brace and Co., 1932), p. 247; William Blake, in "The Marriage of Heaven and Hell"; Michel Foucault, *The Order of Things,* p. 44.

49. The phrase is from the C. F. MacIntyre translation (New York: New Directions, 1949), p. 8.

50. *"The Renaissance* (New York: Boni and Liveright, 1919), p. 196.

51. Friedrich von Schiller, "Conversations with Eckermann," in *Critical Theory Since Plato,* p. 516.

52. *Ibid.,* p. 515.

53. Percy Bysshe Shelley, "A Defense of Poetry," in *Critical Theory Since Plato,* p. 500.

54. Bruns, *Modern Poetry and the Idea of Language,* p. 262.

The World-View of William Blake in Relation to Cultural Policy (1993)

1. All quotations from Blake's work are from *The Complete Poetry and Prose of William Blake,* ed. David V. Erdman, rev. ed. (Garden City: Anchor Press/Doubleday, 1982), referred to in parentheses after quotations as "E."

2. *Times Literary Supplement,* June 17–23, 1988, p. 684.

3. *The Autobiography of William Butler Yeats* (New York: Macmillan, 1953), p. 196.

4. This matter I discuss at some length in *Philosophy of the Literary Symbolic* (Tallahassee: Florida State University Press, 1983), especially pp. 99–116.

5. *Fearful Symmetry: A Study of William Blake* (Princeton: Princeton University Press, 1947); "Notes for a Study of *Milton,*" *The Divine Vision,* ed. Vivian De Sola Pinto (London: Victor Gollancz, 1957); "The Road of Excess" and "The Keys to the Gates," *The Stubborn Structure* (Ithaca: Cornell University Press, 1970).

6. I discuss this matter of what I call the "open synecdoche" at some length in "Synecdoche and Method," *Critical Paths, Blake and the Argument of Method,* ed. D. Miller, M. Bracher, and D. Ault (Durham: Duke University Press, 1988), pp. 41–52. Reprinted in my *Antithetical Essays in Literary Criticism and Liberal Education* (Tallahassee: Florida State University Press, 1990, pp. 21–51.

7. In "The Marriage of Heaven and Hell" Blake describes reading the Bible "in its infer-

nal or diabolical sense," that is, giving free rein to its imaginative rather than theological or legalistic implications.

Is (Was) There No Tradition of Defense of Poetry in Chinese Culture? Why Has There Had to Be One in the West? (1995)

1. *Readings in Chinese Literary Thought* (Cambridge, Mass. And London: Harvard University Press,1992), 42. Or, as it is put by Steven Van Zoeren, "By the Han, if not before, the idea that the Odes could serve as persuasions was given a new twist: the promulgation of the Odes was claimed to be one of the privileged means by which the moral transformation of the empire could be achieved. Moreover, the Odes could be used not only to persuade others but to persuade oneself. Their close study, especially their memorization, recitation, and internalization, became a central element in the Confucian program for personal mortal transformation." *Poetry and Personality: Reading, Exegesis, and Hermeneutics in Traditional China* (Stanford: Stanford University Press, 1991), 14. One might add that *The Songs* became one of the Confucian classics that required study if one wished to advance in government service.

2. Owen, 43.

3. I expand on these matters in the chapter "Attack" in *The Offense of Poetry* (Seattle: University of Washington Press, 2007), 29–63, and discuss the history of defense in the next chapter, 64–91.

4. It is interesting that Sidney locates the poem *between* the precept of philosophy and the example of history, but one must note that the very term "example" causes the precept and thus moral philosophy to be privileged, since the example has to be of *something* that it illustrates or copies. Kant is talking here not about the content of the poem but instead about the external rules (or relative lack of rules) that can be established for poetic composition. But there is an interesting contrast here, nevertheless, in that Kant (almost) seems to recognize the need to evade the notion of pre-established or external rules, while Sidney, by locating the poem between precept and example, seems destined to have to be content with an extractable or pre-established verbal content. I say Kant *almost* evades the problem of rules because of the phrase "least guided," but his argument elsewhere does evade the problem as it is expressed here. On the other hand, here he may merely mean by precept and example to refer to learned literary conventions.

5. With respect t to the discussion of the question of Chinese allegory, see Pauline Yu, *The Reading of Imagery in the Chinese Poetic Tradition* (Princeton: Princeton University Press, 1987), But see Haun Saussy, *The Problem of a Chinese Aesthetic* (Stanford: Stanford University Press, 19983), esp. 13–73.

6. "Postface: A Literary History of the *Shi jing*," *The Book of Songs*, ed. Joseph R. Allen (New York: Grove Press, 1996), 351.

7. T'sao P'I (187–226), "Discourse on Literature," in Owen, 68.

8. *The Art of Writing: Teachings of the Chinese Masters* (Boston and London: Shambhala Publications, 1996), ix.

9. Owen, 393.

10. Owen, 58.

11. Owen, 493.

12. *The Romantic Generation of Modern Chinese Writers* (Cambridge, MA, 1973).

13. *Chinese Modernism in the Era of Reforms* (Durham NC: Duke University Press, 1997), 104.

14. Charlotte Allen, "Confucius and the Scholars," *Atlantic* 283:4 (April 1999), 78–83.

Incidentally the West's own search for origins persists. That old dead horse, the question of Shakespeare's identity was exhumed in the very same cruel month in a group of articles written by various hands in *Harper's* (April 1999), 35–62.

Four Problems (Among Many) for Humanistic Thought (1995)

1. *Ancilla to the Pre-Socratic Philosophers,* tr. and ed. Kathleen Freeman (Cambridge, MA: Harvard University Press, 1956), 30, No. 80.
2. For example, *Literature and Belief: English Institute Essays 1957,* ed. M. H. Abrams (New York: Columbia University Press, 1958).
3. The rise of the acronym to hitherto unknown heights is perhaps a suppression of metaphor and therefore poetry by technology or at least an offshoot of it. What does AIDS have to do with aid? What do CINCPAC, COMSAT, NATO, and SEATO have to do with anything? There are, of course, the irritating acronyms that deliberately offer meaning by way of a trope, for example MADD.

"An Antithetical Turn" (1996)

1. Murray Krieger, *Words about Words about Words* (Baltimore: The Johns Hopkins University Press, 1988), 107–19.
2. Wolfgang Iser, *The Fictive and the Imaginary* (Baltimore: The Johns Hopkins University Press, 1993).
3. Plotinus, *The Enneads,* Stephen McKenna, trans!. (London: Faber and Faber, 1954), 422–3.
4. Plotinus, *Enneads,* 427.
5. Robert L. Montgomery, "Translator's Preface," Giacomo Mazzoni, *On the Defense of the Comedy of Dante* (Tallahassee: Florida State University Press, 1983), 21.
6. "An Apology for Poetry," *Critical Theory Since Plato,* Hazard Adams, ed., rev. ed. (Forth Worth: Harcourt Brace Jovanovich, 1992), 145.
7. "Apology," 148.
8. Krieger, *Words,* 271–88.
9. Murray Krieger, *The Institution of Theory* (Baltimore: The Johns Hopkins University Press, 1994), 87.
10. "A Defense of Poetry," *Critical Theory Since Plato,* 517.

Ekphrasis Revisited, or Antitheticality Reconstructed (2000)

1. Forrest G. Robinson, *The Shape of Things Known: Sidney's* Apology *and Its Philosophical Tradition* (Cambridge, Mass.: Harvard University Press, 1972).
2. Murray Krieger, *Ekphrasis: The Illusion of the Natural Sign* (Baltimore: Johns Hopkins University Press, 1992).
3. *Words about Words about Words* (Baltimore: Johns Hopkins University Press, 1988); *A Reopening of Closure: Organicism Against Itself* (New York: Columbia University Press, 1989).
4. An earlier Krieger's use of the term "miracle," following Ransom, put him closer than he wanted to be to the *symboliste* tendencies in New Critical theory. His essay "'A Waking Dream': The Symbolic Alternative to Allegory" *(Words about Words about Words,* 271–88),

Chapter Notes

directed toward de Man, expressed his liberation from, and historicization of, a purely miraculous symbol. On the notion of the romantic version of the miraculous symbol, see my *Philosophy of the Literary Symbolic* (Tallahassee: Florida State University Press, 1983), especially chapter 1.

5. It is puzzling that Cassirer does not make much mention of Vico, even though there are echoes of him in Cassirer's work.

6. Ernst Cassirer, An *Essay on Man: An Introduction to a Philosophy of Human Culture* (New Haven: Yale University Press, 1944), 25.

7. I shall dwell on Vico because I believe that Krieger's theory, like Vico's, is best seen as a theory of fictions. In *Philosophy of the Literary Symbolic* and later work I have followed a Vichian direction, while Krieger's has been through the history of aesthetics generally and the New Critics. The line of fiction theory I have followed is not mentioned by Krieger. Vico and Blake are mentioned once and in the same sentence in *Ekphrasis*, but (if I understand the sentence) they are misread, being assigned to "a Neo-Platonic mythic anthropology ... in which all differences are dissolved, or rather have not yet come to exist" (166). Cassirer appears nowhere, nor do Frye (with the exception of a footnote in the appendix) or Wheelwright.

8. Giambattista Vico, *The New Science of Giambattista Vico*, trans. Thomas Goddard Bergin and Max Harold Fisch from the third edition (1744) (Ithaca: Cornell University Press, 1968), 129.

9. Northrop Frye, *The Critical Path: An Essay on the Social Context of Literary Criticism* (Bloomington: Indiana University Press, 1971).

10. One might think of Vico's tropes as "categories" of a poetic logic. A somewhat different effort to offer the characteristics of a poetic logic is present in Philip Wheelwright's *The Burning Fountain: A Study in the Language of Symbolism* (Bloomington: Indiana University Press, 1954).

11. I use the word "dissociation" deliberately to recall T. S. Eliot's famous phrase "dissociation of sensibility," which can be read as a suppression of poetic logic (including the trope of irony).

12. See C. K. Ogden, *Bentham's Theory of Fictions* (New York: Harcourt, Brace & Co., 1932). The next major effort after Bentham's, neo–Kantian in character, was Hans Vaihinger's *The Philosophy of "As If,"* trans. C. K. Ogden (New York: Harcourt, Brace & Co., 1925). Neither Bentham nor Vaihinger had the slightest notion of what to do with poetic fictions. In the one place where he mentions them, a footnote, Vaihinger relegates them to "figments."

13. John Locke, *An Essay Concerning Human Understanding* (1690), chapter 10, section 34, excerpted in *Critical Theory Since Plato*, rev. ed., ed. Hazard Adams (Fort Worth: Harcourt Brace Jovanovich, 1992), 268. Here we have duplicity again, which further suggests that Krieger's usage is ironically offered from the point of view of the enemy. There is less irony, perhaps none, in de Man's usage.

14. Ibid.

15. This situation is what prompted Frye to speak of the "myth of freedom" (Vico's "truth") growing up to oppose the "myth of concern" (Vico's "certainty"). Later these myths changed places, and concern expressed the worry that the myth of freedom, which came with the development of modern science, is no longer free but itself oppressive. Frye takes the Blakean view that the oppressor is not free but a prisoner of his own epistemological certainty.

16. On antitheticality in Yeats, see my *The Book of Yeats's Vision* (Ann Arbor: University of Michigan Press, 1995).

17. Giacopo Mazzoni, *On the Defense of the Comedy of Dante: Introduction and Summary*, trans. Robert L. Montgomery (Tallahassee: Florida State University Press, 1983), 89.

18. There is an amusing parody of the spatialist-temporalist disagreement in Joyce's *Finnegans Wake,* a modernist work that is deliberately antithetical to this negation: Professor Jones attacks the temporal emphasis of Bitchson (Henri Bergson), which, he argues, should be dealt with *"ill tempor"* (James Joyce, *Finnegans Wake* [New York: Penguin, 1976], 164).

19. Bronislaw Malinowski, *Magic, Science, and Religion and Other Essays* (Boston: Beacon Press, 1948), 8ff.

Origin(ality) (2007)

1. An interesting anthology of such materials is *The Rise of Modern Mythology, 1680–1860*, eds Burton Feldman and Robert D. Richardson (Bloomington: Indiana University Press, 1972). For the tragi-comedy see Edward B. Hungerford, *Shores of Darkness* (Cleveland: World Publishing Co., 1963), esp. 29–34.
2. "Tradition and the Individual Talent," *Selected Essays* (New York; Harcourt, Brace, 1932), 4.
3. *Anatomy of Criticism: Four Essays* (Princeton: Princeton University Press, 1957), 102.
4. "The Origins of Poetry, *Readings in Chinese Literary Thought*, translator and commentator Stephen Owen (Cambridge, MA: Harvard University Press, 1992), 496.
5. In mentioning the tree here, I omit the notion of *ch'i* that Yeh is illustrating. Briefly the *ch'i* of the tree is its energy, force, or life, which would be destroyed if, for example, the roots were cut. Nothing external (like rules) drives this *ch'i*. See Owen, 506.
6. Owen, 509.
7. *Opus Posthumous* (New York: Alfred A. Knopf, 1957), 166.

The Marriage of Imagination and Intellect (2013)

1. "What Rough Beast?" *Innovation and Continuity in English Studies*, Frankfurt am Main: Peter Lang, 2001, pp. 1–24. The essay was written for the fiftieth anniversary of the International Association of University Professors of English. It is reprinted in the last chapter of my *Academic Child: A Memoir*, McFarland 2008.
2. I discussed this matter in "Canons: Literary Criteria/Power Criteria," *Critical Inquiry* 14:4 (Summer 1988), pp. 748–764, reprinted in my *Antithetical Essays in Literary Criticism and Liberal Education*, Tallahassee: Florida State University Press, 1990, pp. 166–183.
3. William Butler Yeats, "Ideas of Good and Evil," *Essays and Introductions*, London: Macmillan & Co., 1961, pp. 111–145.
4. "Towards Defining an Age of Sensibility," *Fables of Identity: Studies in Poetic Mythology*, New York: Harcourt, Brace & World, 1963, p. 130.
5. Allan Cunningham, *Lives of the Most Eminent British Painters* (rev. ed. 1830), as quoted by Mona Wilson in *The Life of William Blake*, London: Rupert Hart-Davis, 1948, p. 271.
6. Princeton, 1947, pp. 85–107.
7. *Fables of Identity*, p. 130.

Index

Abrams, M.H. 43; *In Search of Literary Theory* 40, 41
"Adagia" 169
Adams, Hazard 2; *Antithetical Essays* 145; "Blake and the Postmodern" 2; *Blake and Yeats* 2; *Blake's Margins* 166, 171; *The Book of Yeats's Vision* 65; *The Offense of Poetry* 2, 108; *Philosophy of the Literary Symbolic* 2, 15, 65, 145; "Synecdoche and Method" 70
Adorno, Theodor 5
Aeneid 93
Aesthetics 7
"All Religions Are One" 8
"L'Allegro" 179
Allen, Joseph R. 119
"Among School Children" 169
Analects 118, 121
Anatomy of Criticism 5, 46, 54, 65, 66, 68, 69, 120
Annotations to Berkeley's Siris 180
Annotations to Wordsworth 175
Antithetical Essays 145
"An Apology for Poetics" 135–139, 141
"An Apology for Poetry" 157, 166
Aquinas, St. Thomas 60, 118
Aristotle 60, 110, 114, 128, 135, 143, 148, 157
Arnold, Matthew 115, 122, 146

Babbitt, Irving 102
Bachelard, Gaston 41, 131
Bacon, Francis 27, 90, 176, 177
"The Bard" 116
Barfield, Owen 145
Barnstone, Tony 120
Barthes, Roland 2, 133; "The Structuralist Activity" 41
Baudelaire, Charles 17, 45, 115; "Correspondences" 17
Baumgarten, Alexander: *Aesthetics* 7

Being and Time 3
Benchley, Robert 168
Bentham, Jeremy 155
Berkeley, George: *Siris* 180
Blackmur, R.P. 14, 138; "The Critic's Job of Work" 14
Blackwell, Thomas 70, 71, 72, 76, 78–84; *Enquiry into the Life and Writings of Homer* 76; *Letters Concerning Mythology* 76
Blake, William 1, 3–5, 8, 9, 13, 17, 28, 48, 50, 51, 53, 61, 67, 69–71, 83, 84, 86–94, 108, 126, 127, 129, 134, 136, 137, 146, 157, 166, 170, 171, 175–182; "All Religions Are One" 8; Annotations to Berkeley's Siris 180; Annotations to Wordsworth 175; *Europe* 27; *The Four Zoas* 4, 9, 26, 27, 90; "The Ghost of Abel" 175; *Jerusalem* 8–10, 11, 18–19, 21, 22, 24, 25, 27, 38, 65, 72, 83, 92, 181; "The Lamb" 138; "The Laocoön" 22, 93, 95–97; "The Last Judgment" 89, 178; Letter to Butts 20; Letter to Trusler 130, 177, 178; "London" 13; *The Marriage of Heaven and Hell* 8, 11, 18, 19, 21, 22, 24, 25, 27, 38, 65, 72, 83, 92; *Milton* 8, 9, 13, 23, 26, 27, 177, 182; "On Virgil" 93; "There Is No Natural Religion" 13; "The Tyger" 138; "A Vision of the Last Judgment" 33, 70
"Blake and the Postmodern" 2
Blake and Yeats 2
Blake's Margins 166, 171
"Blake's Treatment of the Archetype" 90
Blindness and Insight 57
Boccaccio, Giovanni 135
Boethius Manlius Severinus 111–112; *The Consolation of Philosophy* 140, 114, 143
The Book of Yeats's Vision 65
Borges, Jorge Luis 168
Bostetter, E.E. 59, 61, 62

Index

Bradley, A.C. 115
Brooks, Cleanth 11, 12, 132
Bruns, Gerald R. 43, 63–64
Bryant, Jacob: *A New System of Mythology* 70
Bulgarini, Belisario 135
Burke, Kenneth 47, 54, 58, 140
The Burning Fountain 129
Byron, George Gordon Lord 120, 175

Carver, Raymond 105
Cary, Joyce 33, 61; *Except the Lord* 140; *A Fearful Joy* 61
Cassian, John 118
Cassirer, Ernst 3, 4, 12, 13, 14, 17, 28, 44, 45, 47, 48, 49, 50, 76, 95, 129, 145, 148, 151, 153; *Einstein's Theory* 3; *An Essay on Man* 3, 14, 52, 146, 152; *The Philosophy of Symbolic Forms* 12
Castravilla, Ridalpho 135
Celtic Researches 70
Cervantes, Miguel de: *Don Quixote* 168, 169
Chaucer, Geoffrey 181
Cheng, Hsuan 103
Coleridge, Samuel Taylor 51, 59, 62, 88, 114, 115, 175
Collected Poems 123
Confucius 103, 104, 117; *Analects* 118, 121
The Consolation of Philosophy 140, 114, 143
"Correspondences" 17
Course in General Linguistics 132
Cowper, William 175
The Critical Path 69
"The Critic's Job of Work" 14
Critique of Judgment 11, 115
Croce, Benedetto 51, 76
Culler, Jonathan: *Structuralist Poetics* 41
Cunningham, Allen 178

Dante 49, 106, 118, 123, 135; *The Divine Comedy* 92
Davies, Edward: *Celtic Researches* 70
The Decay of Lying 113
Defense of Poetry 63, 128, 129, 143
Defense of the Comedy of Dante 141
De Man, Paul 2, 56–60, 132, 142, 143, 145, 146, 148–151, 156, 159, 160; *Blindness and Insight* 57; "Literary History and Literary Modernity" 55; "The Rhetoric of Temporality" 55; "The Two Criticisms" 42

Dembo, L.S. 40
Derrida, Jacques 2, 12, 41, 47, 98, 132, 133, 145
Descartes, René 45, 54, 62, 123, 131
Discourse on Poetry 120, 168, 169
Discourses on Art 166
The Divine Comedy 92
Don Quixote 168, 169

Edward I 179
"Ego Dominus Tuus" 122
Einstein's Theory 3
Eliot, T.S. 61, 123, 167, 168
Emerson, Ralph Waldo 129
Enquiry into the Life and Writings of Homer 76
"Epipsychidion" 63
Erdman, David 96
"An Essay Concerning Human Understanding" 110
Essay on Criticism 5, 14
An Essay on Man 3, 14, 52, 146, 152
Europe 27
European Theory and Practice 40
Except the Lord 140
"The Existential Basis of Contextual Criticism" 2

The Faerie Queene 71
Faust 62–63
A Fearful Joy 61
Fearful Symmetry 1, 17, 65, 90, 182
The Fictive and the Imaginary 137
Fish, Stanley 49
Foucault, Michel 3, 49, 61
"The Four Ages of Poetry" 113, 116, 144
The Four Zoas 4, 9, 26, 27, 90
Freedman, Ralph 40
Freud, Sigmund 53, 67
Frye, Northrop 1, 5, 11, 12, 17, 65–69, 115, 155, 167, 170, 175; *Anatomy of Criticism* 5, 46, 54, 65, 66, 68, 69, 120; "Blake's Treatment of the Archetype" 90; *The Critical Path* 69; *Fearful Symmetry* 1, 17, 65, 90, 182; "Keys to the Gates" 90; "Notes for a Commentary on *Milton*" 90; "The Road of Excess" 90

Gadamer Hans-Georg 57
Geertz, Clifford 3
Geoffrey of Monmouth 168

Index

Gesprache uber Poesie 59
"The Ghost of Abel" 175
Girard, René 40
Goethe, Johann Wolfgang von 63, 83; *Faust* 62–63
Gosson, Stephan 109, 142; "The School of Abuse" 112
Gras, Vernon 42
Gray, Thomas 175, 181; "The Bard" 116

Harington, John 135
Hartman, Geoffrey 2, 57
Haruku, Murakami 105
Hegel, Georg Wilhelm Friedrich 130, 136
Heidegger, Martin 3, 4, 41, 43, 61, 122, 145; *Being and Time* 3; *Introduction to Metaphysics* 6
Heraclitus 60, 122
Herder, Johann Gottfried 45; *The Spirit of Hebrew Poetry* 117
Holderlin, Friedrich 41, 145
Homer 6, 73, 75, 76, 78, 111, 117, 128
Horkheimer, Max 5
Huckleberry Finn 126
Hulme, T.E. 58
Humboldt, Wilhelm von 4, 45–47, 129, 145, 151
"Hymn to Intellectual Beauty" 63

Icon and Idea 129
In Search of Literary Theory 40, 41
The Institution of Theory 143
Introduction to Metaphysics 6
Iser, Wolfgang 98, 134, 141; *The Fictive and the Imaginary* 137

Jakobson, Roman 41
Jerusalem 8–10, 11, 18–19, 21, 22, 24, 25, 27, 38, 65, 72, 83, 92, 181
Jesus 180, 181, 182
Joyce, James 12

Kamakura, Chiyuki 98, 105
Kant, Immanuel 3, 7, 11, 12, 21, 27, 41, 50, 53, 54, 59, 61, 62, 136, 145, 155; *Critique of Judgment* 11, 115
Karatani, Kojin 98, 105, 106
Keats, John 43, 126, 129, 175
Kermode, Frank 18, 69
"Keys to the Gates" 90
The King's Threshold 116

Krieger, Murray 1, 2, 40, 41, 53, 98, 106, 127, 134, 148–160; "An Apology for Poetics" 135–139, 141; "The Existential Basis of Contextual Criticism" 2; *The Institution of Theory* 143; "A Waking Dream" 143

Lacan, Jacques 41, 133
"The Lamb" 138
Langer, Suzanne K. 138
The Languages of Criticism and the Sciences of Man 40
"The Laocoon" 22, 93, 95–97
"The Last Judgment" 89, 178
Lee, Leo Ou-fan 98, 102, 103, 120, 128
Letter to Butts 20
Letter to Trusler 130, 177, 178
Letters Concerning Mythology 76
Lévi-Strauss, Claude 2
"Literary History and Literary Modernity" 55
Locke, John 6, 27, 89, 90, 114, 115, 123, 131, 136, 156, 166, 176, 177; "An Essay Concerning Human Understanding" 110
Lodge, Thomas 135
"London" 13
Lowth, Robert: *The Sacred Poetry* of the *Hebrews* 117
Lui, Hsieh 109
Lyrical Ballads 85, 142, 167

Macpherson, James 175
Mahfouz, Naquib 134
Malinowski, Bronislaw 159
Mallarmé, Stéphan 17, 43, 45, 61, 62
Mao, Zedong 102
The Marriage of Heaven and Hell 8, 11, 18, 19, 21, 22, 24, 25, 27, 38, 65, 72, 83, 92
Marvell, Andrew 129
Mazzoni, Giacopo 114, 135, 149, 157–159; *Defense of the Comedy of Dante* 141
Mill, J.S. 114
Miller, J. Hillis 2
Milton 8, 9, 13, 23, 26, 27, 177, 182
Milton, John: "L'Allegro" 179; *Paradise Lost* 31
Modern French Criticism 40
Montgomery, Robert L. 141
Mother Goose 126
Motoko, Tokieda 106
"Mythomystes" 72–74, 76, 77, 81

Index

The New Science 4, 12, 44, 47, 50, 70, 71–78, 80, 82–84, 127–129, 148, 151–157, 159
A New System of Mythology 70
Newton, Isaac 27, 38, 90, 176, 177
"Notes for a Commentary on *Milton*" 90
The Offense of Poetry 2, 108

"On Virgil" 93
Owen, Stephen: *Readings in Chinese Literary Thought* 5, 109, 118, 120, 168, 169

Paine, Thomas 134
Paradise Lost 31
Parmenides 60
Pater, Walter 62, 63, 146
Peacock, Alexander 109, 119, 135; "The Four Ages of Poetry" 113, 116, 144
Phenomenology of Reading 41
The Philosophy of Symbolic Forms 12
Philosophy of the Literary Symbolic 2, 15, 65, 145
Picasso, Pablo 169
Picus, Josephus 72
Plato 3, 6, 7, 11, 60, 93, 109–111, 114–117, 123, 128, 135, 138, 140, 145, 146, 148, 155, 166; *Republic* 110
Plotinus 140, 142
Poems 177
Pope, Alexander: *Essay on Criticism* 5, 14
Poulet, Georges 2, 43, 131; *Phenomenology of Reading* 41
Puttenham, George 135

Rainolds, John 135
Ransom, John Crowe 54, 115, 151
Raphael 88
Read, Herbert: *Icon and Idea* 129
Readings in Chinese Literary Thought 5, 109, 118, 120, 168, 169
Republic 110
Reynolds, Henry 71; "Mythomystes" 72–74, 76, 77, 81
Reynolds, Joshua 86; *Discourses on Art* 166
"The Rhetoric of Temporality" 55
Richards, I.A. 114, 145
"The Road of Excess" 90
Robinson, Forrest G. 148
Rolland, Romain 120
Rushdie, Salman 134

The Sacred Poetry of the Hebrews 117
Said, Edward W. 3, 40, 42, 13
Saussure, Ferdinand de 45, 106, 132, 133, 144; *Course in General Linguistics* 132
Saussy, Haun 108, 117
Scaliger, Julius Caesar 114, 142
Schelling, Friedrich Wilhelm Joseph 59
Schiller, Johann Christoph Friedrich 63, 82, 115
Schlegel, Friedrich: *Gesprache uber Poesie* 59
"The School of Abuse" 112
Shakespeare, William 168
Shaw, George Bernard 138
Shelley, Percy Bysshe 113, 119, 129, 135, 144, 175; *Defense of Poetry* 63, 128, 129, 143; "Epipsychidion" 63; "Hymn to Intellectual Beauty" 63
Sidney, Philip 114, 135, 142, 148, 157, 159, 179; "An Apology for Poetry" 157, 166
Simonides 148
Siris 180
Smart, Christopher 175
Socrates 6, 111, 114, 135, 145
Spenser, Edmund: *The Faerie Queene* 71
The Spirit of Hebrew Poetry 117
Stein, Gertrude 169
Stevens, Wallace 129, 170; "Adagia" 169
"The Structuralist Activity" 41
The Structuralist Controversy 40
Structuralist Poetics 41
Symons, Arthur 17
"Synecdoche and Method" 70

Tate, Allen 42
Tay, William 98–100, 104
"There Is No Natural Religion" 13
Todorov, Tzvetan 88, 89, 95
Ts'ao Pi 120
Twain, Mark: *Huckleberry Finn* 126
"The Two Criticisms" 42
"The Tyger" 138

Valéry, Paul 45, 49
Velocities of Change 40
Vico, Giambattista 4, 12, 13, 15, 18, 49; 137, 138, 144, 145, 166, 170; *The New Science* 4, 12, 44, 47, 50, 70, 71–78, 82–84, 127–129, 148, 151–157, 159
Virgil 76; *Aeneid* 93
A Vision 65, 69, 86–88, 123, 146
"A Vision of the Last Judgment" 33, 70

Index

"A Waking Dream" 143
Wallace, William 178–179
Wang, Ching-Hsien (Yang Mu) 103, 104, 108, 109
Wang, Hui 101
Watson, Bishop Richard 134
Webbe, William 135
Wheelwright, Philip 48, 151; *The Burning Fountain* 129
White, Hayden 40
Whitman, Walt 170
Wilde, Oscar 94, 115, 138; *The Decay of Lying* 113
"William Blake and His Illustrations to the *Divine Comedy*" 175
"William Blake and the Imagination" 175
Wittgenstein, Ludwig 43
Wordsworth, William 59, 88, 114, 129, 170, 171, 175, 181; *Poems* 177; "Preface to the Second Edition of *Lyrical Ballads* 85, 142, 167

Yeats, W.B. 4, 17, 61, 65, 83, 96, 129, 134, 136, 146, 157, 170, 182; "Among School Children" 169; *Collected Poems* 123; "Ego Dominus Tuus" 122; *The King's Threshold* 116; *A Vision* 65, 69, 86–88, 123, 146; "William Blake and His Illustrations to the *Divine Comedy* 175; "William Blake and the Imagination" 175
Yeh, Hsieh: *Discourse on Poetry* 120, 168, 169
Yeu, Yu: *Ts'lang's Remarks on Poetry* 120
Yu, Pauline 98, 99

Zhou, Zouren 102
Zudong, Zhang 121

www.ingramcontent.com/pod-product-compliance
Ingram Content Group UK Ltd.
Pitfield, Milton Keynes, MK11 3LW, UK
UKHW042010140426
5217IPUK00015B/1089